THE MEASUREMENT OF ATTITUDES TOWARD PEOPLE WITH DISABILITIES

THE MEASUREMENT OF ATTITUDES TOWARD PEOPLE WITH DISABILITIES

Methods, Psychometrics and Scales

By

RICHARD F. ANTONAK, ED.D.

Professor of Education
Developmental Disabilities Program
University of New Hampshire
Durham, New Hampshire

HANOCH LIVNEH, PH.D.

Associate Professor
Department of Counseling and
Educational Psychology
Rhode Island College
Providence, Rhode Island

With a Foreword by

Harold E. Yuker, Ph.D.

Mervyn Schloss Distinguished Professor of Psychology
Director of the Center for the Study of
Attitudes Toward Persons with Disabilities
Hofstra University
Hempstead, New York

CHARLES C THOMAS • PUBLISHER
Springfield • Illinois • U.S.A.

Published and Distributed Throughout the World by

CHARLES C THOMAS • PUBLISHER
2600 South First Street
Springfield, Illinois 62794-9265

ISBN 0-398-05404-5

Library of Congress Catalog Card Number: 87-23590

With THOMAS BOOKS *careful attention is given to all details of manufacturing and design. It is the Publisher's desire to present books that are satisfactory as to their physical qualities and artistic possibilities and appropriate for their particular use.* THOMAS BOOKS *will be true to those laws of quality that assure a good name and good will.*

Printed in the United States of America
Q-R-3

Library of Congress Cataloging in Publication Data

Antonak, Richard F.
The measurement of attitudes toward people with disabilities: methods, psychometrics, and scales/ Richard F. Antonak, Hanoch Livneh.
p. cm.
Bibliography: p.
Includes indexes.
ISBN 0-398-05404-5
1. Handicapped—United States—Public opinion. 2. Attitude (Psychology)—Testing. 3. Psychometrics. 4. Public opinion—United States. I. Livneh, Hanoch. II. Title.
HV1553.A62 1988 87-23590
305'.90816—dc19 CIP

FOREWORD

ATTITUDES toward disabled persons are complex and multifaceted. Many perspectives are possible. Data indicate that it is difficult to measure, change, and even to understand attitudes toward disabled persons. Even though these things are difficult, they must be done in order to improve the quality of life and status of persons with disabilities.

The field of attitudes toward disabled persons is becoming increasingly professional. There are fewer persons willing to discuss attitudes toward persons with disabilities based on their impressions, without being familiar with the extensive literature dealing with the topic. Similarly, there is increasing recognition of the importance of being knowledgeable about psychometrically adequate ways of measuring attitudes.

In the past 40 years there have been many studies dealing with attitudes toward persons with disabilities. Various measures of attitudes toward persons with disabilities have been developed. The early scales tended to be simple, often psychometrically inadequate, instruments which measured attitudes toward specific disabilities such as blindness or deafness. Then, beginning in the 1960s, more psychometrically adequate research instruments were developed. Two of the most used instruments, the Attitude Toward Disabled Persons scale (ATDP) and the Opinions about Mental Illness scale (OMI), both were developed in the early 1960s, and are still extensively used.

Despite the research that has been done there are still many unanswered questions. We need to investigate the sources of attitudes, seeking to specify the relative influence of variables such as culture, personal experiences, the teachings of significant others, and intrapsychic personality variables. We need also to obtain data pertaining to the attitudes of persons such as parents, rehabilitation and treatment personnel, teachers, friends, and classmates. Since members of each of these groups interact with and influence persons with disabilities, knowledge of their attitudes and the ways their attitudes and behaviors influence the behavior of disabled persons is of major significance.

There is also a need for research dealing with the relationship between attitudes and behavior. How do the attitudes of non-disabled persons influence their behavior toward disabled persons, and how do the attitudes of disabled persons influence their own behavior, their behavior toward disabled persons, and their behavior toward non-disabled persons? Programmatic research dealing with attitude change could be particularly informative. The programs should be multidimensional, using a combination of techniques. They should last more than a few hours or a few days, and should include follow up data.

All of these important types of research are dependent upon having psychometrically adequate measures of attitude. As indicated above, some of the measures developed in the past are pretty good, many are psychometrically inadequate. Before this volume was published, there was no single good source of information about the best and most used measures. Yuker, Block, and Young (1966) presented a brief review of instruments developed prior to 1964, but it related only to physical disabilities, and is out of date today. Shaw and Wright (1967) provided limited information and copies of a few scales. After that there was nothing. This volume represents the first attempt to summarize and describe the major research instruments that have been used. Each instrument is described in detail, its psychometric properties are specified and evaluated, and recommendations for its use are given. The authors' comments are useful and provide information about some of the inadequacies of each of the scales.

Attitudes toward persons with disabilities have changed over the years, at least partly as a consequence of legislation relating to discrimination against persons with disabilities, the mainstreaming of children in school, and, to a certain extent, the mainstreaming of disabled persons into society. Attitude measurement techniques also have changed. They have become increasingly sophisticated and currently the emphasis is on multidimensional scales. As Antonak and Livneh point out, these changes mean that some of the items on some of the older instruments are no longer meaningful or pertinent. This implies that it is necessary to either modify existing scales or develop new ones. In either case, the scales must be developed carefully, and their reliability and validity must be assessed. The new or modified scales should reflect the multifaceted nature of attitudes.

My belief is that it is better to try to improve old scales than to develop new ones. It is also less expensive and less time consuming. We should emphasize the cumulative nature of knowledge and build on the past, as is done in the sciences. As Antonak and Livneh point out in their final chapter, it is better to "refine rather than create scales," and to "update old scales."

This has often been ignored in the past. One of the disturbing characteristics of past attitude research has been the tendency of researchers to develop their own scales. This was particularly true of much of the doctoral research in the 1960s and 1970s. Although standardized scales were available, they were not often used. Few of the new scales that were developed used adequate procedures or were psychometrically evaluated for reliability and validity. Almost none of them were used more than once.

In the event that none of the existing measures are satisfactory, nor appropriately modifiable, this volume provides guidelines that can be used to develop new scales. It supplies information about the procedures to use in developing psychometrically adequate measures. If those procedures are followed, the new scale will be a good one. The procedures are, however, tedious, expensive, and time consuming.

The recommendations given in the last chapter are so important that they could profitably be read prior to reading the rest of the book. These recommendations include emphases on reporting the psychometric qualities and correlates of the scales, using multidimensional scales, and investigating attitude-behavior relationships.

This book is an excellent reference source. It should be useful to everyone engaged in research dealing with attitudes toward persons with disabilities. The information and commentary about the major scales currently being used, together with copies of the scales, and addresses of the scale authors will be of major value to researchers. By providing information about the current state of the field, this volume provides a good launching platform for future research and development in the area of attitudes toward persons with disabilities.

Harold E. Yuker

PREFACE

IN JUNE 1986, a conference on attitudes toward people with disabilities was held at Hofstra University. The conference agenda was organized by Professor Harold E. Yuker, the primary author of the Attitude Toward Disabled Persons Scale, and the Director of the Center for the Study of Attitudes Toward Persons With Disabilities at Hofstra University. This three-day conference brought together 22 theorists and researchers from across the United States and from three foreign countries. Over three days, these scholars discussed a range of theoretical, methodological, and practical issues involved in the measurement of attitudes toward disabled people. The majority of the presenters at the Hofstra University Conference submitted manuscripts to Professor Yuker who edited them into a publication (Yuker, 1987) which will be a significant resource for many years for researchers investigating topics in this attitude domain.

From our own research and reviews of the measurement literature in preparation for our presentations at the Hofstra University Conference there was an apparent need for a comprehensive source book of information on the availability and suitability of scales used to measure attitudes toward people with disabilities. This observation was confirmed by comments made in the addresses of several of the presenters, and through informal conversations with many of the participants. In all too many cases, important research questions are investigated with unsophisticated research designs using instruments of dubious psychometric adequacy. Any conclusion based on data obtained in such a study must be cautiously considered. In an attempt to provide the needed information, we offer this book as a modest contribution for researchers and practitioners in a variety of disciplines who are concerned with the measurement of attitudes toward people who are disabled. We hope that this book will be of value to those who are involved with the study and elimination of attitudinal barriers to the acceptance and integration of people who are disabled into our nation's schools, communities, and workplaces.

This book is divided into four parts. The first part, Attitude Measurement Methods, consists of five chapters. An introductory chapter provides a discussion of a variety of definitions of attitude, outlines reasons why the study and measurement of attitudes are important, and presents a brief history of the measurement of attitudes in general, and of attitudes toward people who are disabled in particular. Chapter 2, Fundamentals of Attitude Measurement, presents a taxonomy for the classification of various attitude measurement methods. Discussion of important measurement concepts will provide the reader with a foundation for understanding the remainder of the chapters in this first part of the book, and is indispensible for an understanding of the advanced measurement concepts presented in the chapters of Part II. The chapter concludes with guidelines for the selection of an appropriate scaling method.

Chapter 3, Direct Methods of Attitude Measurement, discusses those methods in which the respondents are aware that they are participating in an attitude measurement experiment. Ten direct methods are examined in detail: opinion surveys, interviews, rankings, Q-methodology, sociometrics, adjective checklists, paired comparison scales, semantic differential scales, probabilistic rating scales (summated ratings, consensual location, social distance, and scale discrimination), and deterministic rating scales (scalogram analysis and order analysis). A brief description of each method is presented, together with a general means for constructing a scale by that method. This is followed by examples of each method.

Chapter 4, Multidimensional Scaling, is an invited chapter provided by Professor Liora Pedhazur Schmelkin. This chapter first considers the limitations of the direct measurement methods, discussed in Chapter 3, which focus on unidimensional measurement paradigms. The newer multidimensional paradigms hold the promise of identifying salient organizing dimensions underlying the perceptions of disabilities and disabled people by focusing on a larger number of disabilities concurrently, and by using a methodology which is less constraining. The chapter then discusses nonmetric multidimensional scaling (MDS) procedures, and presents two examples of research using MDS to investigate perceptions of disabilities. The chapter concludes with a discussion of considerations relevant to MDS studies and suggestions for the use of MDS in disability attitude research.

The final chapter of Part I, Indirect Methods of Attitude Measurement (Chapter 5), begins with a discussion of the weaknesses of the direct attitude measurement methods discussed in Chapters 3 and 4. Indirect attitude measurement is then defined and its strengths and weaknesses discussed. This is followed by a presentation and discussion of four indirect measurement methods: projective techniques, disguised procedures, behavioral observations, and physiological methods. Illustrations of each method are provided.

Part II, Psychometric Guidelines for Attitude Scales, consists of three chapters concerned with the psychometric adequacy of attitude scales. The first of these chapters, Reliability (Chapter 6), begins with a definition of reliability and a taxonomy for the classification of various reliability estimates. This is followed by a discussion of indices in the following reliability categories: stability, equivalence, stability-equivalence, internal consistency, and inter-judge (or inter-rater). The chapter continues with a discussion of the concept of the standard error of measurement of scores and its interpretation and usefulness as a psychometric index. The chapter concludes with a discussion of the factors known to effect reliability estimates of an attitude scale.

Chapter 7, Validity, begins with a definition of validity and a taxonomy for the classification of various validity estimates. This is followed by discussions of indices in three validity categories: content, criterion-related, and construct. The chapter concludes with a discussion of the factors known to effect the validity estimate of an attitude scale. The second part of the book closes with Psychometric Characteristics of Attitude Scales (Chapter 8). This chapter presents detailed guidelines for the psychometric adequacy of rating scales. This presentation has two purposes: (a) to assist the researcher who is seeking a previously constructed rating scale in reviewing available scales, and (b) to assist the researcher who is unable to locate a rating scale in the process of constructing a new rating scale. The topics discussed in this chapter include: item preparation, pilot studies, item analyses, scale analyses (including investigations of the dimensionality of the scale), the influence of response styles on scale scores, and the presentation and use of normative data.

Part III, entitled Scales for the Measurement of Attitudes, is composed of five chapters. The purpose of the chapters in this part is to provide specific technical information on 22 attitude scales organized into five areas. Chapter 9, General Attitudes Toward People With Disabilities, presents and discusses six scales, all of which attempt to measure attitudes toward disabled people as a group. Chapter 10, Attitudes Toward Physical Disability Groups, presents and discusses four scales, all of which attempt to measure attitudes toward people who are disabled as a result of a physical impairment (e.g., blindness, deafness, epilepsy, and cerebral palsy). Chapter 11, Attitudes Toward Psychiatric Disability Groups, presents and discusses three attitude scales, while Chapter 12, Attitudes Toward People Who Are Mentally Retarded, presents and discusses four scales. The final chapter of Part III, Chapter 13, Societal Responsibilities to People With Disabilities, presents and discusses five attitude scales, all of which attempt to measure the extent to which respondents endorse premises concerning the responsibilities of society to the needs of people who are disabled. In particular, four of these scales attempt to measure attitudes to the special education practice of mainstreaming.

The final section of the book, Part IV, consists of a final chapter—Chapter 14, Summary and Recommendations. This chapter presents a summary of the preceeding 13 chapters as a framework for the reader to use for his or her study of the measurement of attitudes toward people with disabilities. The book concludes with a series of recommendations for researchers who are proposing to investigate the formation, structure, and correlates of attitudes toward people who are disabled.

We wish to thank these authors for making available copies of their attitude scales for review in Part III: Joan D. Berryman, Jacob Cohen, Emory L. Cowen, Jennifer Gan, Doris C. Gilbert, Sheldon A. Grand, Robert Harth, Barbara Larrivee, Liora Pedhazur Schmelkin, William M. Reynolds, Jerome Siller, and Harold E. Yuker.

We also thank Linda Filippelli, Rose Misuraca, and Audrey Thresher for their research and secretarial assistance.

And we acknowledge with deep appreciation the support and understanding of our families, friends, and colleagues throughout the time this book has been our preoccupation.

Richard F. Antonak
Hanoch Livneh

ABOUT THE AUTHORS

RICHARD F. ANTONAK received the BA degree in mathematics from Rutgers College (1969), and the M.Ed. (1970) and Ed.D. (1975) degrees in special education from Temple University. His first professional experience with people with disabilities was as a teacher of mentally retarded adolescents at the Woods Schools in Langhorne, Pennsylvania. From 1970 to 1973 he served as work-study coordinator at Penncrest High School in Media, Pennsylvania. While completing graduate study, he supervised teachers of exceptional children and taught special education courses for the Pennsylvania State University. He joined the faculty of the education department at the University of New Hampshire in 1975 where he designed and established the university's first special education teacher training courses and the Master's degree programs in developmental disabilities and special education. He is currently Professor of Education and the Coordinator of Special Education Programs at UNH.

Dr. Antonak's research specialties are in attitude measurement, psychometrics, multivariate statistics, and the history of mental retardation. He has published several research instruments to measure attitudes toward disabled people, including the Scale of Attitudes Toward Disabled People (SADP). He has authored research articles and statistical analysis programs, as well as monographs and book chapters on topics in attitude measurement and developmental disabilities. He has appeared as an expert witness on behalf of people with developmental disabilities and their advocates in court cases, and has served as a member or consultant to boards, agencies, and committees concerned with the provision of services for people who are disabled.

Dr. Antonak was elected to Phi Beta Kappa and Pi Mu Epsilon (the National Honorary Mathematics Society) while at Rutgers, and was advanced to Fellow of the American Association on Mental Deficiency (AAMD) in 1983. He was elected a member of the American Academy on Mental Retardation and the American Statistical Association. An incorporator of AAMD's Northeast Region X, he served as president in 1980 and is presently completing a second three-year term as secretary-treasurer. He is co-founder and incorporator of the New Hampshire State Chapter of AAMD which he serves as secretary-treasurer.

HANOCH LIVNEH received his BA degree in psychology from the Hebrew University, Jerusalem, Israel (1971) and his MA (1973) and Ph.D. (1976) degrees in Rehabilitation Counseling Psychology from the University of Wisconsin-Madison. In 1973, while doing his practicum and internship at the Division of Vocational Rehabilitation and the Dane County Mental Health Center, he counseled both physically and psychiatrically disabled clients. Also, during his doctoral studies, he supervised graduate students enrolled in rehabilitation counseling practicum courses. He joined the faculty of the Rhode Island College Counselor Education Department (later restructured and renamed the Department of Counseling and Educational Psychology) in 1977, as the Assistant Director of the Rehabilitation Counseling Program. In 1979, he became the director of the program and in 1980 led it to national accreditation by the Council On Rehabilitation Education (CORE). He is currently an Associate Professor of Rehabilitation and Counselor Education and the Director of the Rehabilitation Counseling Program at Rhode Island College.

Dr. Livneh's research interests are in attitude formation and measurement, adjustment to and coping with disability, psychiatric rehabilitation, and counseling and personality theories. He has authored theoretical and research articles and book chapters on attitude origination and measurement, adjustment to disability, the structure of anxiety and death anxiety, and rehabilitation models. He serves as a vocational expert for the Office of Hearings and Appeals, Social Security Administration. He served as consultant and peer counseling trainer for the Rhode Island Division of Vocational Rehabilitation, Rhode Island Institute of Mental Health, United Cerebral Palsy, and PARI Independent Living Center.

Dr. Livneh serves as a consultant reviewer for three journals—*Journal of Applied Rehabilitation Counseling, Rehabilitation Counseling Bulletin,* and *Journal of Social Behavior and Personality.* He is a Certified Rehabilitation Counselor, National Certified Counselor, and a Certified Vocational Expert.

CONTENTS

THE MEASUREMENT OF ATTITUDES TOWARD PEOPLE WITH DISABILITIES

Part I

ATTITUDE MEASUREMENT METHODS

THIS PART consists of five chapters. In the first chapter, we will begin with an introduction to the concept of attitude. The functions served by, and the importance of investigating, attitudes will then be discussed, followed by an explication of the importance of studying attitudes toward people who are disabled. Finally, the history of the measurement of attitudes in general, and attitudes toward people who are disabled in particular, will be traced. We will emphasize scales measuring attitudes toward a variety of disabling conditions which have been developed during the past quarter century.

In Chapter 2 we will provide an overview of basic concepts in attitude measurement, definitions of indirect and direct methods of measurement, and a discussion of the concept of scaling. A taxonomy for the classification of attitude measurement methods will then be proposed. A total of ten direct attitude measurement methods will be described in detail in Chapter 3. This will be followed by a discussion of nonmetric multidimensional scaling in the invited chapter written by Professor Liora Pedhazur Schmelkin. In the last chapter in Part I, Chapter 5, we will discuss indirect methods of attitude measurement, focusing on four methods: projective techniques, disguised procedures, behavioral observations, and physiological methods. The advantages of indirect methods in comparison to direct methods will be presented at the end of this chapter.

Chapter 1

INTRODUCTION

PROFOUND CHANGES in the provision of educational, psychosocial, and vocational services to people who are disabled have resulted from recent legislation (e.g., the Vocational Rehabilitation Act of 1973, P.L. 93-112, and its Amendments of 1974, P.L. 93-516; the Education for All Handicapped Children Act of 1975, P.L. 94-142; the Vocational Education for People With Disabilities Act of 1975, P.L. 94-482; the Comprehensive Rehabilitation Services Amendments of 1978, P.L. 95-602), litigation (e.g., lawsuits concerning institutional conditions, zoning restrictions, employment discrimination, access to services, the provision of special education), and research efforts (e.g., alternative communication systems for sensorially-impaired people, application of microcomputer technology to rehabilitation services, advanced diagnostic, medical, and surgical procedures to prevent, detect and correct disabling conditions). These changes are increasing the integration of children and adults who are disabled into the nation's schools, neighborhoods, and workplaces.

Full acceptance of people who are disabled by individuals who are not disabled will not occur, however, until subtle barriers can be eliminated. Most scholars and researchers agree that the attitudes of professionals, parents, peers, employers, coworkers, neighbors, and disabled people themselves compose one of the factors inherent in subtle barriers (Altman, 1981; Jones and Guskin, 1984). These attitudes are for the most part negative (Roessler and Bolton, 1978; Wright, 1983), and create or support negative expectations and behaviors which limit the successful rehabilitation, integration, and independence of disabled people in the community.

Siller (1984) has observed that "pinpointing attitudinal components will suggest differential change procedures and promote appropriate assessment of the effect of interventions" (p. 200). Similarly, Jones and Guskin (1984) have called for research efforts to create "a distinct framework for thinking about, investigating, and intervening in attitudes toward the handicapped" (p. 11). The framework to be adopted should allow researchers to examine the attitudes of individuals in various influential roles, and those of disabled people themselves. Answers to questions concerning the multidimensional and intricate interrelations of knowledge, attitudes, and behavior would, in turn, permit policy-makers and practitioners to design intervention strategies to change attitudes toward people who are disabled, to improve the training of personnel, and to remove barriers to services.

Investigations concerning attitudinal barriers to the rights of people with disabilities to participate in the benefits of society require psychometrically sound instruments which are reliable, valid, and multidimensional. Moreover, these instruments must allow for flexibility and differentiation in the definition, conceptualization, and measurement of attitudes. It is the intention of this book to assist researchers and practitioners in the fields of rehabilitation, special education, developmental and social psychology, and counseling to accomplish these important research objectives.

The present chapter begins by providing the reader with various definitions of attitude, its structure and dimensions. Next, the reasons why the study of attitudes per se is important will be presented, together with a discussion of the importance of attitude measurement. Particular emphasis will be placed on the measurement of attitudes toward people with disabilities. Finally, a brief history of the measurement of attitudes in general, and of attitudes toward disabled people in particular, will enable the reader to better understand contemporary measurement techniques. The chapter will conclude with a description of the goals for the remaining chapters of the book.

DEFINITIONS OF ATTITUDE

There are two main dimensions along which attitude definitions appear to vary: (a) a dimension represented by a continuum of abstractness, ranging from concrete (or operationally-defined) to abstract (or theoretically-conceptualized); and (b) a dimension represented by the extensiveness of the components (i.e., cognitive, affective, behavioral, or conative) included in the definition.

Abstractness

Attitudes are descriptive concepts which are inferred from observations of behavior; they are not themselves directly observable or measurable. Attitudes are often regarded as latent or inferred psychosocial constructs or processes which are postulated as residing within one's self. Furthermore, these constructs or processes lie dormant unless evoked by specific stimuli or referent objects (e.g., individuals, social groups, situations, events, social issues). These referents, by virtue of their perceived psychosocial value, are then capable of eliciting an attitude response from the subject. In this sense, attitudes may be conceived as mediators between particular observed environmental stimuli and specific behavioral responses (Allport, 1935).

The abstractness dimension, then, can be attributed to what Shaw and Wright (1967) called "the epistemological issue of specificity versus generality in the determination of behavior" (p. 2). The less the distance which the definer perceives from the mediating attitude to the observable behavioral response, the more concrete or specific the concept of attitude is defined. In other words, as attitudes are judged to be more proximal causes of behavior, the more affect they will be thought to exert on the ensuing behavior and the more specific the definition will become.

Examples of general (i.e., abstract or non-specific) definitions of attitude are provided by Katz (1960): "Attitude is the predisposition of the individual to evaluate some symbol or object or aspect of his world in a favorable or unfavorable manner" (p. 168), and by Allport (1935): "[Attitude is] the degree of affect for or against an object or a value" (p. 10). Examples of specific (i.e., concrete) definitions of attitude can be found in English and English (1958): "[Attitude is] an enduring learned predisposition to behave in a consistent way toward a given class of objects" (p. 50), and in Hilgard and Atkinson (1967): "[Attitude is] an orientation towards or away from some object, concept, or situation, and a readiness to respond in a predetermined manner to these, or related objects, concepts, or situations" (p. 583).

Extensiveness

The second dimension, which provides a basis for conceptualizing the content of attitude, is that of categorical structure. Three (at times four) categories or components are typically postulated: a cognitive component, an affective component, and a behavioral (or conative) component.

Cognitive Component. The cognitive component of attitude refers to the individual's ideas, thoughts, perceptions, beliefs, or opinions about the attitude referent. In other words, it reflects how the attitude referent is mentally conceptualized. Triandis (1971) posits that this component can be observed in the individual's use of critical attributes to categorize experience, such as in stereotypical perceptions (i.e., the belief that members of a particular racial, religious, or disability group possess certain common attributes). Cognitive responses are typically expressed through the use of verbal statements of opinions or beliefs and are measured accordingly. Statements suggesting desirable or undesirable qualities, characteristics, or attributes of the attitude referent are presented and the respondent is asked to indicate the degree of his or her agreement or disagreement with each statement. The cognitive component, viewed as an index of meaning (McGuire, 1960; Triandis, 1971), is ordinarily measured by such instruments as adjective checklists and by the activity and potency factors of the semantic differential. (See Chapter 3 for a discussion of these attitude measurement techniques.)

Affective Component. The affective component of attitude reflects the feeling or emotional underpinnings of the attitude, or the emotion that charges the idea (cognitive component) of the attitude (Triandis, 1971). This component is accordingly expressed unidimensionally in terms of feelings toward the attitude referent such as good-bad, pro-con, liking-disliking, or positive-negative (Insko and Schopler, 1967; Katz, 1960) expressed either through the use of verbal statements of affect or through physiological arousal (McGuire, 1969). Among the former indices are phenomenological measures such as the evaluative factor of the semantic differential and most attitude scales based on Likert's method of summated ratings and Guttman's scalogram technique (see Chapter 3). Among the later, measures of sympathetic autonomic nervous system responses (e.g., skin conductance, blood pressure, pupil dilation, heart rate; see Chapter 5) are often used (Ostrom, 1969; Triandis, 1971).

Behavioral Component. The third component of attitude's tripartite differentiation is that of the behavioral or conative component. Whereas some researchers perceive the two to be virtually indistinguishable (Rosenberg and Hovland, 1960; Triandis, 1971), others judge them to be independent (Fishbein and Ajzen, 1975; Ostrom, 1969). The conative element is conceived as the individual's intent or readiness to behave in a certain manner with respect to the attitude object. It is a preparatory tendency, orientation, or predisposition rather than the behavioral act itself. The behavioral element, on the other hand, consists of the actual (i.e., observed or overt) reaction toward the attitude referent. It is the instrumental act performed in the presence of that object. This may include expressions of what the individual would do, or recollections of past actions, in given situations involving the attitude referent (Ostrom, 1969). These behaviors signify goal-directed responses or activities which may take one of three general forms: approaching or seeking association with the object, avoiding contact or moving away from it, and moving against or fighting it (Horney, 1945; Triandis, Adamopoulos, and Brinberg, 1984). The behavioral component is usually measured by such means as the social distance scale (see Chapter 3), and through observations of how the individual actually behaves in situations involving the attitude referent (e.g., providing physical assistance to a disabled person or financial donation to a charity representing disabled people; see Chapter 5).

Examples

Although this component trichotomy serves a heuristic purpose, the three components of attitude are, both conceptually and empirically, highly intercorrelated (McGuire, 1969). Whereas several researchers seem to focus on a single component in defining attitude, others appear to include all three components. Examples of attitude definitions emphasizing the cognitive component include one offered by Allport in his classic 1935 paper: "[Attitudes are] individual mental processes which determine the actual and potential responses of each person in a social world" (p. 6), and the definition by Newcomb, Turner, and Converse (1965):

"Attitude is a state of readiness for motive arousal" (p. 40). Definitions denoted by their affective emphasis are those of Fishbein (1967): "Attitude is a learned predisposition to respond to an object or class of objects in a consistently favorable or unfavorable way" (p. 257), and Thurstone (1946): "Attitude is the degree of positive or negative affect associated with some psychological object" (p. 39). Finally, behaviorally-oriented definitions of attitude include the one originally suggested by Bogardus (1931): "An attitude is a tendency to act toward or against some environmental factor which becomes thereby a positive or negative value" (p. 52), and Campbell's (1950) observation that "[An] attitude is a syndrome of response consistency with regard to a set of social objects" (p. 31).

In contrast to these narrow definitions of attitude, a number of definitions have been proposed which incorporate two or even all three components. Allport's (1954) often-cited definition of attitude—"A mental and neural state of readiness (to respond), organized through experience, exerting a directive and/or dynamic influence upon the individual's response to all objects and situations with which it is related" (p. 451)—includes references to both the cognitive element ("a mental and neural state") and the conative element ("readiness to respond"). More recently, Krech, Crutchfield, and Ballachey (1962) defined attitude as: "An enduring system of positive or negative evaluations, emotional feelings, and pro or con action tendencies with respect to a social object" (p. 177). Both the affect and the behavioral components are clearly considered in this definition. Finally, Triandis (1971), in an all-inclusive definition which we will adopt for the remainder of this book, observes that:"An attitude is an idea [cognitive component] charged with emotion [affective component] which predisposes [conative component] a class of actions [behavioral component] to a particular class of social situations" (p. 2).

It is of interest that Shaw and Wright (1967) rejected the tripartite concept of attitude components. Instead, they offered their definition of attitude as: "A relatively enduring system of affective, evaluative reactions based upon and reflecting the evaluative concepts or beliefs which have been learned about the characteristics of a social object or class of social objects" (p. 10). In other words, Shaw and Wright narrow their definition to include only the affective reactions of the person. Furthermore, they view the cognitive and behavioral components as related temporally to attitudes. The cognitive component precedes the attitude by providing an evaluative basis for it, while the behavioral component follows (i.e., is predisposed by) the attitude, and constitutes the particular action taken toward the attitude referent.

To summarize, then, there appears to be a consensus among scholars and researchers that attitudes have the following elements: (a) attitudes are learned through experience and interaction with other people, social objects, and environmental events, rather than being inately determined, although the role of heredity or constitutional factors in attitude formation has not been fully investigated; (b) attitudes are complex, multi-component, structures; (c) attitudes are relatively stable (even rigid) as evidenced by their resistance to change; (d) attitudes have a specific social object as a referent (e.g., people, situations, events, ideas); (e) attitudes vary in their quantity and quality, possessing differing degrees of motivating force (intensity, strength), and direction (toward, against, away from the attitude referent); and (f) attitudes are manifested behaviorally via predisposition to act in a certain way when the individual encounters the attitude referent.

ATTITUDES AND RELATED CONCEPTS

Attitudes and Beliefs

Attitudes are often compared with such concepts as beliefs, opinions, and values, and related to behaviors. Beliefs are traditionally conceived as the cognitive component of attitudes. They are viewed as statements which indicate the probability that an attitude object possesses a particular characteristic, quality, or attribute (Fishbein and Ajzen, 1972, 1975). Beliefs are associated with the amount of information an individual has about a particular object. This informational base leads to the formation of a certain attitude toward the object, eventually directing the person to behave in a particular manner toward that object. Shaw and Wright (1967) argued that beliefs suggest a certain level of acceptance of a proposition (in probabilistic terms) with respect to characteristics presumed to be associated with the attitude referent. Eventually this proposition is accepted by the indivdiual as a truism regarding the object. These authors further claimed that a belief becomes an attitude when it is accompanied by the affective-evaluative component which links one's level of preference to the characteristics of that object. Put another way, attitudes are functions of beliefs and associated affects.

Attitudes and Opinions

Opinions are viewed as narrower in scope than attitudes and as similar to beliefs; primarily cognitive or non-evaluative in nature. Thurstone (1929) viewed opinions as the overt (both written and oral) expressions of the more covert or inferred attitudes. Bogardus (1933) perceived opinions to be the more rational, logical, and conscious aspects of beliefs, while suggesting that attitudes are the more irrational, illogical, or unconscious aspects of beliefs. Osgood, Suci, and Tannenbaum (1957), in a similar view, posited that opinions are more informational or factual in nature and are, therefore, observable concepts that can be verified and empirically tested. In contrast, they maintained that attitudes are a "matter of personal taste," tap the private world of the individual, and are virtually nonverifiable empirically. McGuire (1960, 1969) argued that opinions are beliefs associated with one's expectations or predictions regarding events or relationships, while attitudes are beliefs concerned with one's wishes and hopes regarding these same events or relationships. Further, he contrasted the concepts in two ways. First, opinions are beliefs with dynamic (drive) qualities, while attitudes possess both the dynamic and an additional directive quality. Second, opinions are beliefs that are measured by a single statement (an item), whereas attitudes are beliefs that are measured by an inventory or multi-item scale (a battery of items).

Attitudes and Values

Values are conceived as broad and abstract attributes which can be used to characterize a number of related attitudes (Eysenck, 1954; Rosenberg, 1956). They suggest a certain degree of worth ascribed by the individual to the referent (Shaw and Wright, 1967). Katz (1960) suggested that when specific attitudes (both positive and negative) are organized into a hierarchical structure, they create a value system. The more central the role of an attitude in an individual's value system, the more closely it is related to the individual's self-concept, and the more resistant it is to change.

Attitudes and Behaviors

The issue of the degree of consistency between attitudes and behaviors is highly complex and as yet unresolved. [Because a complete discussion of the relationship between the two is beyond the scope of this book, the reader is referred to the excellent treatises by Ajzen and Fishbein (1977, 1980), Cooper and Croyle (1984), and McGuire (1969).] As previously pointed out, attitudes are perceived as consisting of several related components. Due to their structural complexity and to the intricate social-environmental context in which attitudes are expressed, it would be epistemologically stultifying to expect attitudes to perfectly predict behaviors. Attitudes are neither a necessary nor a sufficient cause for behaviors (Triandis, 1971). They are, however, contributing factors to behavior, and under some conditions may strongly influence behavior. They exert both a directive (target-related) and a dynamic (energetic) influence on behavior (McGuire, 1969). As such, they may be viewed as mediating between environmental stimuli (i.e., the presence of the attitude referent) and the individual's response act. Behaviors, despite being affected by the chanelling force exerted by attitudes, are a function of a variety of other variables such as one's ability, effort and motivation, societal norms, past habits, prior exposure to the attitude referent, expectations regarding reinforcement and punishment, and personality factors.

WHY STUDY ATTITUDES?

Functions of Attitudes

Katz (1960), in his widely accepted analysis, stated that attitudes serve four main functions for the individual. First, attitudes perform an adjustive or utilitarian function. Viewed from a behavioral learning-theory perspective, attitudes maximize rewards in the environment, while minimizing potential penalities or punishments. They dispose the individual toward reinforcing objects and, at the same time, pave the way to satisfying one's needs by attaining valued goals. These utility values may range from acquiring objects in the physical world to attaining socially adaptive goals, such as initiating and maintaining interpersonal relationships with significant others.

Second, attitudes serve an ego-defensive function. As conceived by psychoanalytic or psychodynamic-oriented psychologists, attitudes protect the self from acknowledging certain painful triusms (e.g., unacceptable impulses, objectionable wishes, inner conflicts), or from the harsh realities of the external environment (e.g., outside threatening stimuli, rejecting social atmosphere). As such, attitudes serve to defend our self-image and enhance our self-esteem.

Third, attitudes facilitate value expressions. Ego psychologists often emphasize the role played by one's self-identity or self-realization. Expressing attitudes appears to involve gratification of the affective domain. The individual seizes the opportunity for both releasing inner tensions by externalizing them and also gaining social recognition by internalizing the values held by one's group. Asserting one's self adds to the realization of the person's identity and further serves as a vehicle for self-satisfaction.

Fourth, attitudes satisfy a knowledge or understanding function. They operate (as Gestalt theoreticians argue) to give comprehensible structure to one's universe. In striving to fulfill this function, attitudes help the individual to achieve a meaningful and well-organized system of perceptions and beliefs. Humans are curious beings constantly seeking to explain the world around them and satisfying their need to know. Attitudes provide clarity and consistency by setting the standards or frames of reference for organizing and understanding one's environment. McGuire (1969) argued that the knowledge function is embedded within a large economy function, whereby attitudes provide a parsimonious and practical manual for what constitutes appropriate behavior toward specific objects.

In addition to their functions of helping us adjust to the external environment, protecting our self-esteem, expressing our fundamental values, understanding the world around us, and interpreting its events, attitudes may also serve as reinforcers (Triandis et al., 1984). In this view, favorable attitudes are thought to increase the likelihood of certain behaviors reoccurring, while unfavorable attitudes may decrease the likelihood of other behaviors. Attitudes also function as stimuli evoking previously learned behaviors associated with these attitudes. Triandis et al. (1984) provided this example. When an individual has a favorable attitude toward people who are disabled, behaviors which were previously learned and already associated with the favorable attitude (such as donating money to a charity) may be invoked by making the attitude salient.

Attitudes Influence Behavior

The study of attitudes may also shed light on the controversy surrounding the relative importance of heredity and environment in determining one's behavior (Oskamp, 1977). Attitudes may be conceived as bridging elements, formed by an interplay of both genetic factors and experiential learning, which influence the individual's behavior. Shaw and Wright (1967), emphasizing the learning element, argued that since attitudes are acquired through experience, they represent the end products of the socialization process, and, accordingly, predispose one's responses to socio-cultural events and other people. The study of attitudes may enhance our understanding of the socialization process and the past events directly contributing to it. It may, likewise, contribute to our understanding of prejudice formation as acquired through identification with one's social group and assimilation of values held by one's parents and peers (Thomas, 1980).

Attitudes are also of importance in attempting to predict future behaviors, a cornerstone of psychological research. Finding out what a person's attitudes are (toward a given object, individual, group of people, or event), in conjunction with knowledge of various situational and other personality variables, may aid the researcher in better understanding, explaining, and ultimately predicting behavior toward the referent. Shaw and Wright (1967) went so far as to suggest that complex social behaviors cannot be predicted unless prior knowledge of one's attitudes was obtained.

Finally, if the mechanisms underlying the development and structure of attitudes are discerned, they may be used to alter people's reactions to various human interactions, such as those encountered in education, counseling, and psychotherapy. Consequently, the study of attitudes is of particular interest in the fields of rehabilitation and special education. Knowledge of the development and structure of attitudes toward people with disabilities is considered to be necessary for changing them, and thereby increasing the integration of disabled people into the larger society (Jones and Guskin, 1984).

Implications for Disabled People

Attitudes toward disabled people may be conceived as operating in three distinct yet interacting social circles or levels. The innermost circle comprises attitudes exhibited by the disabled person's relatives, friends, and peers. Attitudes of these groups influence not only the development of the disabled individual's self-concept but also the socialization of the individual into typical community activities (Altman, 1981).

The next attitudinal circle encompasses the relationships of the disabled individual and the rehabilitation professionals with whom he or she comes into contact. This group includes practitioners such as physicians, nurses, psychologists, counselors, social workers, teachers, clergy, and so on. In these roles, rehabilitation practitioners and educators are the providers of information, services, and stability. Their attitudes may have an enormous impact on both the medical and psychosocial processes of adjustment to disability as experienced by the disabled individual. Indeed, the attitudes of these professionals may strongly influence the attitudes of members of the first social circle—namely, family and peers—as well as the attitudes exhibited within the larger third circle, that of society at large.

The third and outermost circle is composed of attitudes of the general public. Society's negative attitudes toward its members who are disabled create real obstacles to the fulfillment of their roles and the attainment of their life goals. These detrimental attitudes are often covert, but may be detected in the use of media stereotypes, prejudicial beliefs, derogatory labels, or lack of care for the well-being of disabled people. These attitudes are also apparent in the work practices of employers. Employers' unfavorable attitudes toward people with disabilities often impede vocational possibilities and result in reduced opportunities for finding successful employment, diminished vocational training, and limited placement opportunities.

Yuker (1965) suggested that knowledge of attitudes of non-disabled people toward people with disabilities helps us to understand the nature of the interaction between the two groups. Studies measuring these attitudes may, therefore, shed light on the components of negative attitudes (e.g., avoidance, rejection) as well as positive attitudes (e.g., friendliness, interaction) toward disabled people. Furthermore, understanding the underlying dimensions of negative attitudes may suggest differential change procedures and promote appropriate assessment of the effects of these interventions (Siller, 1984).

MEASUREMENT OF ATTITUDES TOWARD PEOPLE WITH DISABILITIES

The study of attitudes toward people with disabilities clearly requires that these attitudes be measured. Since the measurement of attitudes toward disabled people is historically couched within the wider scope of measurement of attitudes in general, the present section briefly outlines a few measurement landmarks before assuming the more specific task of discussing the history of measurement of attitudes toward people with disabilities.

History of the Measurement of Attitudes

The scientific study of attitudes was initiated in Germany in the 1850s with the investigation of subjects' responses to certain classes of social stimuli (Triandis, et al., 1984). The term attitude was first used by the British psychologist Herbert Spencer in 1862 (Allport, 1935, p. 799). At the turn of the century, it was reasoned by most social psychologists that a person's thoughts and actions were strongly influenced by mental sets and attitudes. Baldwin in 1901 (reported in

Ajzen and Fishbein, 1980) offered a definition of attitudes as the "readiness for attention or action of a definite sort." Thomas and Znaniecki (1918) are often credited with originating the use of attitudes to explicate social actions. They suggested that attitudes, as cognitive processes, determine the individual's potential and actual responses. Similarly, Watson (1925) equated the field of social psychology with the study of attitudes.

As the concept of attitude gained increased popularity among theoreticians and researchers, attempts were made to construct psychometric techniques to measure it. One of the first, and most nobably successfully, research endeavors in the measurement of attitudes in the United States was the pioneering work of L.L. Thurstone (1927, 1928, 1929, 1931; Thurstone and Chave, 1929). Thurstone argued that attitudes toward a particular object could be measured on a single continuum ranging from most favorable or positive to most unfavorable or negative. The underlying continuum was that of affective disposition. Thurstone's frugal solution was to condense the abstract construct of attitude into a single score (based on the respondent's verbal report) reflecting his or her position on an affective dimension in regard to the attitude referent. Thurstone's method has come to be commonly known as the equal-appearing intervals (or consensual location) scale.

Rensis Likert (1932), seeking to decrease the complexity and reduce the laborious scale construction procedures of Thurstone's method, and to circumvent its tenuous statistical assumptions, proposed an alternative and simpler technique for the measurement of attitudes. Likert's method has since been used thousands of times by researchers around the globe to construct the ubiquitous summated rating attitude scale. A single score is derived, presumably representing the degree of favorableness (or unfavorableness) which the respondent ostensibly manifests toward the attitude referent.

Whereas the two previous methods, and most other early 20th century attitude research, viewed and defined the concept of attitude rather narrowly (i.e., emphasizing the person's affective response toward the attitude referent), E.S. Bogardus (1925a, 1925b, 1933) viewed the measurement of attitudes from a more conative-behavioral vantage point. He modified Thurstone's method and constructed his social distance scale by measuring the degree of endorsement of items suggesting differing levels of social proximity to an attitude referent (e.g., religious or racial groups, occupations).

In the 1940's, Louis Guttman (1944, 1947) contributed his scalogram technique. The cumulative scale of Guttman (1950) was designed to determine whether a series of items representing beliefs and attitudes could be arranged along a unidimensional and cumulative continuum from most favorable to least favorable. A decade later, Charles E. Osgood and his associates (Osgood et al., 1957) developed their semantic differential scales. Based on their original use as measures of the meaning of various concepts, these scales were quickly applied to the study of attitudes. This method consisted of a series of bipolar evaluative scales on which the respondent rated the attitude referent. (For more extensive treatment of these scaling methods in attitude measurement, the reader is referred to Chapter 3). The contributions of Q-methodology by William Stephenson (1953), adjective checklists by Harrison G. Gough (1960), and the unfolding technique of Clyde H. Coombs (1964) must also be noted.

History of the Measurement of Attitudes Toward Disabled People

Investigation of attitudes toward people with disabilities has concerned researchers for more than half a century, since the pioneering work of social psychologists such as Strong (1931) and R.G. Barker (1948). Although the designs of recent studies are more sophisticated and the statistical methods used to analyze the attitude data have changed substantially from simple descriptive statistics, the attitude instruments do not differ much from the three-option checklist used by Strong in his original investigations. They are, for the most part, designed for specific research situations, often are used only once (quite often for the completion of the dissertation requirements for the doctoral degree), and lack formal validation or detailed psychometric analyses.

Measures of attitudes of non-disabled people toward people who are disabled have ranged from subjective, informal, and (usually) psychometrically unsound instruments (e.g., open-ended or unstructured questionnaires or interviews) to more objective, carefully planned and developed, methodologically sound, and scorable instruments (e.g., semantic differential scales, summated rating scale). Most measuring scales, sadly enough, resemble the former type rather than the later. [See, for example, the discussion by Yuker, Block, and Younng (1970, pp. 5-12).] In the next paragraphs we will discuss the major research milestones in the brief history of the measurement of attitudes toward disabled people. The scales of measurement which have been developed for this research will be discussed and critiqued in Chapters 9 through 13.

One of the first attempts to objectively study the construct of attitudes toward disabled people was by Mussen and Barker (1943). Using a series of rating scales, these authors sought to describe the beliefs of non-disabled respondents regarding disabled (the actual term used was crippled) people's behavioral characteristics, and to measure the degree of favorableness of attitudes toward them. Twenty-four five-point rating scales were used to depict presumed personality characteristics (i.e., self-pity, friendliness, self-confidence) of both the physically disabled person and the so-called ideal person. Degrees of favorableness toward physically disabled people were derived from these ratings by computing the differences between the ratings of the ideal person and of the disabled individual on each of the scales.

Many of the attitude studies of the 1950s and early 1960s concerned the sensory disability of blindness. Rusalem (1950, 1965) was the first to use a device similar to an adjective checklist to study the physical, psychological, and social traits associated by respondents with blind people. Steingisser (1954) constructed a 100-item rating scale with three response categories (agree, neutral, disagree) to measure attitudes toward blindness. Basing their work on Steingisser's scale, and on Fitting's (1954) adjustment to blindness attitude scale, Cowen, Underberg, and Verillo (1958) developed what is probably the first psychometrically sound summated rating scale concerning attitudes toward a group of disabled people. Their Attitudes to Blindness (AB) Scale became a prototype of most of the attitude scales which followed it. At approximately the same time, Lukoff and Whiteman (1959) developed their own Attitudes Toward Blindness (A-B) Scale (see also Lukoff and Whiteman, 1961; Whiteman and Lukoff, 1962, 1964a, 1964b, 1965). Several of their items were selected from Cowen et al.'s (1958) scale and the remainder were selected from other previously constructed scales and questionnaires. Their diversified and multiple-item format (it included Likert-type items, as well as semantic differential scales and sentence completion items) resulted in an intricate and somewhat methodologically confusing scale. Factor and cluster analytic studies of data from the A-B Scale, together with their interpretations of the early work of Siller and his associates (Siller, 1963, Siller and Chipman, 1964), led them to conclude that attitudes toward people who are blind and toward people who are disabled in general, were complex and multidimensional, and could not be reduced to a single-scale format.

By the early 1960s, the measurement of attitudes toward other specific groups of disabilities was initiated. Horowitz, Rees, and Horowitz (1962, 1965) constructed an 88-item scale to measure attitudes and beliefs toward deaf people, while Cowen and his co-workers (Cowen, Bobrove, Rockway, and Stevenson, 1967) rewrote the AB Scale by using the referent deafness or deaf person, added new items, and constructed their Attitudes to Deafness (AD) Scale. Attitudes toward people with sensory impairments were not the only attitude studies conducted during that time period. Cohen and Struening (1959, 1960, 1962, 1963), using a series of factor analytic studies, developed their Opinions about Mental Illness (OMI) Scale to measure the attitude held by various groups of personnel employed in mental hospitals toward psychiatrically disabled people. Their five-factor scale gave support to the notion of multidimensionality of attitudes toward people with disabilities.

During the late 1950s and early 1960s, the majority of attitude studies adhered to conceptual and research methodologies emphasizing attitudes toward specific disability groups (e.g., blindness, deafness, mental illness). The thrust of this attitude research was shifted when three groups of researchers initiated their studies of attitudes toward general physical disabilities. Lukoff and Whiteman (1959) modified their A-B Scale to measure attitudes toward physically handicapped people in general (the P-H Scale), Roeher (1959) developed a 22-item scale to measure attitudes toward physically disabled people as part of his doctoral dissertation, and Yuker, Block, and Campbell (1960) published their Attitude Toward Disabled Persons (ATDP) Scale (Original, or Form-O). The ATDP Scale has since become the most widely used, and the most carefully studied, of all instruments measuring attitudes toward people with disabilities.

Although the ATDP Scale, with its extensive and supportive data (Yuker, et al., 1960), provided researchers with a new tool to use in their attitude studies, it soon became apparent that this scale, due to its unidimensional nature (i.e., it structured attitude along a linear affective continuum from positive to negative) would not yield the rich data afforded by scales emphasizing the multidimensional character of attitudes toward disabled people. The earlier factor and cluster analytic studies (e.g., Cohen and Struening, 1960; Whiteman and Lukoff, 1962) had indicated that these attitudes could be depicted as composed of a number of salient dimensions (usually three to five) accounting for most of the information contained in the data derived from the attitude scales. It remained for a research team to develop and present a general purpose multidimensional scale.

Based on their multi-component assumption of attitude structure, Siller and his colleagues and students (Siller, 1969; Siller, Chipman, Ferguson, and Vann, 1967; Siller, Ferguson, Vann, and Holland, 1967) sought to develop a series of attitude scales that would (a) rectify the problem of unidimensionality inherent in the ATDP Scale, (b) investigate the structure of attitudes toward specific disabilities rather than the obscure concept of the general referent "disabled people," and (c) explore the consistency of attitude components across the several physical disabilities. Following an extensive series of factor analytic studies, Siller's group presented the Disability Factor Scales (DFS), a collection of multidimensional instruments purporting to measure attitudes toward amputation, blindness, and cosmetic conditions. Also developed was a general form that encompassed attitudes toward nine disability types (e.g., amputation, paralysis, cancer). Maintaining that single-dimension, single-score scales (such as the ATDP Scale) tap a mixture of dimensions on a predominantly affective level, Siller and his coworkers structured their scales on a variety of attitude dimensions.

At the same time as these studies of attitudes toward physically disabled people were leading to the development of useful scales, another group of researchers were developing scales to measure attitudes toward another disability group. These scales, the Attitudes toward Mentally Retarded People (AMRP) Scale (Bartlett, Quay, and Wrightsman, 1960), the Attitudes Toward the Retarded (ATR) Scale (Efron and Efron, 1967), and the Multidimensional Attitude Scale on Mental Retardation (MASMR: Harth, 1974), were developed to explore the components of attitudes held by the general public toward people who are mentally retarded. In constructing these scales, the authors postulated that attitudes toward mentally retarded people share components in common with attitudes toward other minority groups (e.g., Blacks) and toward mentally ill people. As a result, the format and many of the items of the scales were borrowed from previously published scales measuring attitudes toward these groups (e.g., the OMI Scale).

The decade of the 1970s saw an attempt by Jordan (1971) to apply Guttman's structural facet theory to the study of attitudes toward three types of disabilities (i.e., deafness, mental illness, and mental retardation). Other than Jordan's scale (the Attitude Behavior Scale), this theory has not proven beneficial for the construction of scales in this attitude domain. The mid 1970s was also the start of the movement to reintegrate disabled children and adults into public schools, community residences, and typical workplaces. Researchers, consequently, turned their attention toward the possibility that the attitudes of teachers, neighbors, and employers might be a barrier to complete integration and acceptance of disabled people. As a result, scales to measure societal attitudes and responsibilities toward disabled people were proposed and constructed. The Opinions Relative to Mainstreaming (ORM) Scale of Larrivee and Cook (1979) was one of the first of these scales.

The early part of the 1980s witnessed a renewed interest among attitude researchers in the study of the factorial structure of the two most widely used attitude measures, namely the ATDP Scale (Antonak, 1980c; Livneh, 1982a), and the DFS-General Scale (Livneh, 1985c). In addition, the Scale of Attitudes Toward Disabled People (SADP) was developed by Antonak (1981a, 1982) to overcome several of the psychometric weaknesses of the ATDP Scale. The number of investigations of attitudes toward disabled people has increased tremendously through this decade, and had been benefitted by a number of carefully researched reviews of this measurement literature (e.g., Horne, 1980, 1985; Jones, 1984; Makas, 1981; Schroedel, 1979; Yuker and Block, 1986). The recent publication of a book containing state-of-the-art papers on theoretical, methodological, and practical issues in the measurement of attitudes toward people who are disabled (Yuker, 1987) will be a significant resource for many years.

SUMMARY AND PRELUDE

In this first chapter, we began with an introduction to the concept of attitude, ways of defining attitude, the functions served by attitudes, and the importance of investigating attitudes toward people who are disabled. This was followed by a history of the measurement of attitudes in general, and attitudes toward people who are disabled in particular. This history was focused on the scales which have been developed in the last 25 years to measure attitudes toward a variety of disabling conditions.

The remaining chapters in the first part of this book (Chapters 2, 3, 4, and 5) will present summaries of the basic methods available to measure attitudes, including direct, multidimensional, and indirect methods. This will be followed by a presentation in Part II (Chapters 6, 7, and 8) of the concepts of reliability and validity, and a discussion of psychometric guidelines for attitude scales. These chapters should help researchers to critically review available measures, as well as to carry out the complex and time-consuming process of creating a new attitude measure. The third part of the book (Chapters 9, 10, 11, 12, and 13) will organize 22 previously published scales by the attitude referent, and will present information on the psychometric adequacy of these scales. The book will conclude with a summary and our recommendations for research which uses measures of attitudes toward people who are disabled.

Chapter 2

FUNDAMENTALS OF ATTITUDE MEASUREMENT

MEASUREMENT

MEASUREMENT involves the assignment of a numerical value to the attributes or characteristics of objects, individuals, or events, according to a well-defined set of rules. The numerical values assigned (the data) are taken to represent the attributes or characteristics determined to be important in the particular measurement situation (Bolton, Lawlis, and Brown, 1976). While the values themselves are essentially meaningless, statistical manipulations are available which transform these data into information that can be both meaningful and useful for decision-making. The assignment rules used may be simple or complex, as long as they are applied consistently by the researcher to all elements of the sample. In some cases, the rules are fixed for all researchers in similar measurement situations (e.g., the standardized rules for administration and scoring which accompany certain tests and scales), whereas in other cases the rules are established by the researcher and may be unique to the particular research situation. Other researchers may follow these rules or not depending on the particular constraints in different situations.

The reader is referred to Anastasi (1982), Bolton (1976), Cronbach (1984), or Sax (1980) for comprehensive discussions of both the standardized and nonstandardized rules of measurement in the primary domains of education, rehabilitation, and psychology. Subsequent chapters in this book will discuss in detail methods to obtain these numerical values in attitude measurement (Chapters 3, 4, and 5), guidelines for the researcher who plans to construct a set of rules (a measuring instrument) to evaluate attitudes (Chapter 8), and the means by which the researcher can quantify his or her confidence that the values assigned are both error-free (reliable, see Chapter 6) and accurate (valid, see Chapter 7) representations of the attitude of interest. Our purpose in this chapter is to introduce some of the basic concepts of measurement, to define certain confusing terms, to apply these concepts to the domain of attitude measurement, and to introduce a classification taxonomy for the most widely used methods to measure attitudes.

Levels of Measurement

Four levels of measurement can be identified. In order of the amount of information which each presents, they are: nominal, ordinal, interval, and ratio. While higher levels of measurement provide more information on the attribute or characteristic of interest, these levels are not necessarily better in all cases. The appropriate level of measurement is determined by the research question which directs the research design and the selection of the measurement method. To put this another way, the method and level of measurement are determined after, and not before, the research question is specified.

Nominal Measurement. When we classify objects or events into unordered categories and then name the categories, we are engaging in nominal measurement. For example, the classification of people into categories by gender results in two categories, male and female. These two-category variables are also known as dichotomies. If the characteristic being classified is a naturally occurring duality, the dichotomy is known as a true dichotomy. For example, gender is a true dichotomy. However, dividing students in a classroom into two groups according to whether or not they are equal to or greater to 4 foot in height is an artificial dichotomy. We could just as easily divide the class at 4 foot 2 inches, or divide the class into three groups: those less than or equal to 4 foot in height, those greater than 4 foot but less than 4 foot 6 inches, and those equal to or greater than 4 foot 6 inches in height.

While the rules used to assign individuals to the categories are not arbitrary, the numerical values or labels assigned to the categories for statistical purposes are arbitrary. In the example concerning the height of our students, we may label the groups as #1, #2, and #3. These numerical labels merely discriminate the members of one category from another and do not express the value of the characteristic measured. Nominal measurement is most often expressed as frequency counts or percentages of the numbers of individuals or objects in each category.

Contrary to a popular misconception among students (and many researchers), there is a group of powerful statistical techniques which are appropriate for analyzing nominal data (see, for example, Marascuilo and McSweeney, 1977). These statistics allow the researcher to answer questions concerned with the distribution of objects into the categories, or the association of the distributions of objects in categories on two or more nominal variables. The chi-squared statistic is but one of these useful statistics.

Ordinal Measurement. When the individuals or objects studied can be ordered (ranked) on some dimension or according to some attribute or characteristic, then the values (ranks) assigned to the individuals or objects are known as ordinal measurement. The value assigned an individual on such a ranking represents the individual's position relative to the other individuals ranked; it does not represent the magnitude of the characteristic. For example, the researcher may rank the students in a class according to their height, from shortest to tallest, and then assign numerical values to the students' relative positions. The fact that Becky is assigned the value 4 and Chris is assigned the value of 8 does not imply that Chris is twice as tall as Becky. In fact, they may differ in height by only one-half inch.

Just as there is a set of powerful statistics useful for analyzing data derived from nominal measurement, there is also a set of statistical techniques available for analyzing data obtained from ordinal measurement (see, for example, Lehmann, 1975). Among the most widely known of these are the order statistics developed by Wilcoxon, Friedman, and Kendall.

Interval Measurement. In addition to the ability to rank individuals according to some characteristic, interval measurement also provides information about the magnitude of the characteristic present in each individual. In particular, data are said to be interval scaled if the difference between two adjacent numerical values is constant at all points on the scale. For example, the difference between the values of 33 and 34 is the same as the difference between the values of 11 and 12, or between 56 and 57.

Interval measurement allows the researcher to obtain data which can be manipulated statistically in all the same ways as nominal and ordinal data, but with the added advantage that algebraic operations are now permitted. For example, the average (in this case, the mean) of the values assigned to the members of the class on some variable can be calculated, and this average can be compared to the average of some other class of students who were also measured on the same variable with the same instrument or device. Because of this property, the original values can be rescaled by multiplying each value by a constant or by adding a constant to each value. This permits the comparison of the values obtained from two different measurement instruments since both can be converted to some common standard. [For example, both sets of values can be normalizd by subtracting the mean value from each and then dividing by the square root of the variance (the standard deviation.)].

A more important statistical characteristic of the values obtained from a sample of individuals is the variability of these values about some point in the distribution of values. If this point is selected to be the mean of the sample distribution, then we have the very useful statistic known as the variance of the set of values (the average variability about the mean). A powerful collection of statistical procedures has been developed to analyze this variance, procedures which include the analysis of variance, regression analysis, and factor analysis. The use of these procedures in attitude measurement is illustrated in Chapters 4 and 8.

Ratio Measurement. Ratio measurement differs from interval measurement in that the scale values include a true zero value (that is, a zero point which can be meaningfully defined). For example, the measurement of temperature on the Kelvin scale represents ratio measurement (0 degrees Kelvin is the point at which molecular motion ceases), whereas the measurement of temperature on the centigrade scale does not because 0 degrees centigrade is arbitrary (the point at which water freezes at sea level). Consequently, it is possible to have negative temperature on the centigrade scale. Because ratio scales include a true zero point, not only are the distances between any two points on the scale constant at any point on the scale, but the ratio of the values at any two points are constant. For example, 30 degrees centigrade is half of 60 degrees centigrade only when the arbitrary zero point is used to locate these two values [(30-0)/(60-0) = 30/60 = 1/2, but (30-10)/(60-10) = 20/50 = 2/5]. While many of the variables in the physical sciences are ratio scaled (e.g., temperature, mass, distance), very few variables in the social and behavioral sciences are measured on ratio scales. Time, a variable which appears frequently in behavioral research, is one notable exception to this generalization.

Representational and Index Measurements

There are a number of alternative measurement methods which are available to the researcher who wishes to assign a value representing the presence, strength, or direction of some attribute or behavior of a set of individuals (e.g., their attitude toward disabled people). Seldom, however, can the researcher devise a measure representing the internal state of the respondent which corresponds to, energizes, or directs the observed attribute or behavior. Some physiological measures, as we shall see in Chapter 5, may come fairly close to accomplishing this task.

Measures of internal states are referred to by Dawes (1984) and others as representational measures, in the sense that the value obtained by the researchers represents or substitutes for the attribute or behavior. Representational measures are considered to be interval measurement. Not only does this allow the researcher to rank different individuals on their attribute values, but it also allows the researcher to state the amount of the attribute, or the amount of the change of the attribute. Index measures, on the other hand, are those which require the researcher to assign a value to the respondent's attribute or behavior. The value is considered to be an index of the internal state. Dawes argues that index measurement is, at best, ordinal level measurement. This allows the researcher to rank different respondents based on their index value, and, therefore, to compare two different respondents or two different groups of respondents or the same respondent at two different times. The values derived from index measurement methods are often treated as if they were interval data, provided that certain assumptions about the distribution of the values can be made and supported by the researcher. The common practice of treating intelligence test scores as if they were data derived from representational measurement is a good example of this.

Both representational and index measurements allow the researcher to arrange a set of values, which are derived from the individuals' responses to a task or to a set of questions, into an ordered series. With this series (the norm or standard), the researcher can then measure the relative performance of other individuals asked to respond to the same task or set of questions. The majority of the methods to measure attitudes which are discussed in this book are index measurement methods.

Scales and Scaling

The terms which are associated with the products of the researcher's measurement effort (nouns), and the terms associated with the researcher's actions during this effort (verbs), create considerable confusion. The context in which the terms are used will, in most cases, determine whether the researcher is referring to the actions or to the products of those actions.

The arrangement of the numerical values derived from the measurement process (that is, ordinal or interval level measurement) is known as a scale (product—noun). Any measurement instrument which permits the researcher to construct such an arrangement of numerical values is also known as a scale (product—noun). If the responses are presumably directed and energized by an emotion-charged idea, then the researcher says that he or she has constructed an attitude scale. If the responses are directed and energized by cognitions, then the researcher says that he or she has created an intelligence scale. If the responses are attributes which are considered to distinguish and characterize the individual human being, then the researcher says that he or she has constructed a personality scale. An attitude instrument (a scale), then, permits us to create an ordered arrangement (a scale) of the values of the attitudes of a set of respondents toward a particular referent.

So much for the noun. The act of arranging the numerical values into a graded series is known as scaling and the researcher says that he or she intends to scale the respondents' values derived from the instrument (the attitude scale). The act of measuring or estimating the relative performance of an individual is also referred to by the verb to scale. The researcher, then, may say that he or she intends to scale a respondent's value on the attitude scale with reference to the scale derived from some norm group's values.

METHODS TO MEASURE ATTITUDES

The purpose of attitude measurement is to convert observations of a respondent's behavior into some index which represents the attitude presumed to underlie the behavior. As a basis for discussion in this section, we will use Triandis' (1971) definition of attitude as "an idea charged with emotion which predisposes a class of actions to a particular class of social situations" (p. 9). The class of social situations in this definition is known as the referent, and it is understood that this may be an object, a person, an event, or a construct (e.g., community integration of people who are disabled). The researcher measuring attitudes must begin with a set of assumptions about the respondent's internal state, the referent toward which the respondent directs his or her behavior, and the relationship between the respondent's internal state and external behavior. The methods available to accomplish this measurement task can be classified as either indirect or direct methods.

Indirect and Direct Methods

Indirect Methods. Indirect methods of attitude measurement, as you will learn in Chapter 5, have been developed for those experimental situations in which: (a) the act of measurement itself may create in the respondents an attitude toward a referent to which they were previously unaware (e.g., a questionnaire on attitudes toward meningomyelocele), (b) other methods may lead the respondents to respond in a way which is inconsistent with their true attitude (e.g., a course evaluation given by the instructor just prior to the final examination), or (c) the referent is so charged with emotion that the observed response is distorted by powerful personality characteristics (e.g., a scale to measure attitudes toward incest betwen fathers and daughters).

To illustrate these indirect measurement methods, let us suppose that a researcher is interested in measuring the attitudes of the general public toward people who are physically disabled. The researcher hypothesizes that if the respondents were aware that their attitudes were being measured, they might distort their responses to present themselves in the most favorable light (that is, as they interpret a favorable attitude toward physically disabled people). The researcher decides to devise a method in which the respondents are unaware that they are being measured.

For example, the researcher may create a situation in which the unwitting respondent, who is seated on a bench awaiting a bus, is joined by three confederates of the researcher. A woman (another confederate) who is obviously physically disabled—she is walking with a peculiar gait and using two canes—then approaches the bench. The respondent presumably may select any one among a class of personal actions in this social situation. The respondent may choose to ignore the woman by avoiding eye contact and remain seated, as the confederates do; or the respondent may remain seated, and stare at the woman without initiating verbal interaction; or the respondent may choose to remain seated, but ask the woman what happened to her legs; or the respondent may choose to get up and offer the woman a place on the bench. Each of these behaviors can be preceeded, accompanied, and followed by various facial expressions, gestures, movements, and vocalizations.

The researcher's task is to assign to the observed behaviors of the respondent some value which represents (measures) the emotion charged idea (attitude) presumed to have influenced the respondent's behavior in the experimental situation.

[Methods to assess the extent to which the assigned value faithfully represents the attitude to be measured (validity) will be discussed in Chapter 7.] If we have another occasion to observe the respondent's behavior in the same or an essentially similar situation, and if the respondent acts similarly, then we will have increased confidence in the value we assigned to the respondent's attitude toward this referent. [This and other means of quantifying the confidence that we have in our measurement (reliability) will be treated in Chapter 6.]

Among indirect measures of attitudes are: (a) those in which the respondents are unaware that they are being observed or measured (behavioral observations, as illustrated in the preceeding measurement example); (b) those in which the respondents are aware that they are being observed or measured, but they are unaware of or are unclear about the purpose of the measurement situation (projective techniques); (c) those in which they may be purposefully deceived as to the purpose of the measurement situation (disguised techniques); and (d) those in which they may be aware but inactive participants, as in the case of a physiological measurement.

In many situations, however, the researcher cannot observe or measure a respondent's behavioral reactions to the attitude referent. The researcher may not be able to devise a situation in which the behavior will be evident, such as in an investigation of attitudes toward capital punishment. Or, the researcher may not have the resources to commit to such an experiment, such as hiring confederates, arranging props, or purchasing and operating video equipment. Or, the researcher may not have the time needed to observe the behaviors of many respondents when interested in the general attitude of large groups of respondents, such as fourth graders' attitudes toward the integration of physically handicapped children into public school classrooms. In these and other cases, the researcher will typically select a direct measurement method.

Direct Methods. Direct attitude measurement methods are those in which the respondents are aware that they are participating in an attitude measurement experiment. For example, the researcher may ask respondents to react to a contrived situation and to report what they would do or how they feel about certain actions. To return to our previous example, the researcher may ask respondents to view a videotaped vignette depicting a physically disabled woman approaching a bench on a corner which is full of people seated waiting for a bus, and then stop the video and ask the respondents what they would do in that situation if they were one of the people sitting on the bench. Or the researcher may ask the respondents what the people sitting on the bench should do, or how they would react if no one arose and offered the woman a seat.

In another situation, the researcher may ask the respondents to read a description of a woman who is physically handicapped and then ask the respondents to state how they would act in various situations (Would they offer her their seat on a crowded bench?), or how they feel about certain characteristics of the woman (Are physically disabled people helpless?), or how they feel about certain societal provisions for the woman (Should at least one seat on all bus benches be reserved for disabled people?).

The researcher may select a direct measurement method in which the respondents are asked to read a list of 12 types of disabling conditions, and then select those conditions which, if they knew that a person had that condition, they would be willing to offer that person their seat on a crowded bus bench. Alternatively, the researcher may ask the respondents to rank the 12 conditions in an order which represents their willingness to surrender their seat to people with those conditions. Finally, the researcher may ask the respondents to express their willingness to surrender their seat to a person with each of 12 handicapping conditions on a six-point continuum, ranging from Very Unwilling (– 3), to Very Willing (+ 3). The methods illustrated in these examples are among the ten direct attitude measurement methods to be explained in detail in Chapter 3.

WHICH METHOD TO SELECT?

The type of measurement method which the researcher selects to study attitudes must be determined by the question which the researcher hopes to answer and by the parameters of the research situation. Among these parameters are time, cost, availability of respondents, availability of scales incorporating the measurement methods, and the researcher's competence and motivation. Some researchers are committed to only one type of measurement method (e.g., the summated rating scale), using it to answer all research questions—or rather, asking only those questions which can be answered by the data obtainable from the particular measurement method. Other researchers may avoid a particular type of measurement method (e.g., projective techniques)—perhaps because this method has not traditionally been a part of their professional discipline—even if it is the most appropriate method to obtain the data needed to answer the research question. It is Lemon's (1973) contention, as well as ours, that:

> The crucial question must always be whether a given technique constitutes an adequate operational definition of the underlying theoretical assumptions. If it does, then substantive conclusions can be drawn from it. If it does not, then the whole enterprise becomes a charade. (p. 27)

SUMMARY AND PRELUDE

This chapter provided an overview of basic concepts of attitude measurement, including: levels of measurement, representational and index measurement, and definitions of scaling. Indirect and direct methods of attitude measurement were then defined, and a taxonomy for the classification of attitude measurement methods was proposed.

In order to assist the researcher in selecting an attitude measurement method which can provide the data needed to answer the research question, 15 different measurement methods have been organized into a taxonomy composed of three primary categories. Ten of these are direct methods of measuring attitudes, and will be dealt with in the next chapter. The method of nonmetric multidimensional scaling is dealt with in Chapter 4. The remaining four of these are indirect methods of measuring attitudes, and are dealt with in Chapter 5. In some cases, methods are subdivided into subsets of well-defined methods. For example, probabilistic rating scales (a direct measurement method) include consensual location scales, of which one special case is the social distance scale.

The taxonomy used in the next three chapters is a synthesis of several previous attitude measurement taxonomies and classification systems. In particular, we have borrowed from the systems of Dawes (1984), Horne (1985), Lemon (1973), and Shaw and Wright (1967). Although we will present a comprehensive collection of attitude measurement methods, this collection is not exhaustive of the available methods. We have not included, for example, descriptions of Coomb's (1964) unfolding technique nor certain phenomenological scaling methods. The researcher who wishes to learn more about these methods is referred to Fishbein (1967), Lemon (1973), or Summers (1970).

The presentations to follow in the next three chapters begin with brief descriptions of each measurement method and the general means for constructing an attitude scale by each method. An example of a scale or, in some cases, a sampling of research which used the measurement method will be presented. The three chapters in Part II of this book present detailed information on the psychometrics of attitude measurement scales: that is, the topics of reliability, validity, and item and scale analyses.

Chapter 3

DIRECT METHODS OF ATTITUDE MEASUREMENT

DIRECT METHODS of attitude measurement are those in which the respondents are aware that they are participating in an attitude measurement experiment. These methods are by far the most widely known and used in measuring attitudes toward people who are disabled. Ten methods will be examined in this chapter: opinion surveys, interviews, rankings, Q-methodology, sociometrics, adjective checklists, paired comparison scales, semantic differential scales, probabilistic rating scales, and deterministic rating scales.

SURVEYS, INTERVIEWS, AND RANKINGS

Opinion Surveys

Opinion surveys ask respondents to express in writing their beliefs, attitudes, feelings, or intentions toward some referent by responding to a list of questions presented in a group situation or by mail. The researcher is not a part of the response process, although the researcher may be available to clarify a question. Because the respondent is aware of the purpose of the research, these methods are obtrusive and reactive measures. Respondents may change their responses in an effort to protect their privacy, or to provide the researcher with the data they think the researcher seeks. Opinion surveys may be structured (closed) or unstructured (opened).

In a structured opinion survey, the researcher may ask the respondents to elect from among a small set of possible responses the one which they consider to be the closest to how they feel about the referent. In some cases, the researcher may provide an option for the respondents to add other opinions to the list or to comment on the question itself. In a variant of this method, the respondents may be asked to select all of those responses presented in a list which apply, or those which they agree with, or those which they endorse. The opinion survey may also be structured as a forced choice between pairs of responses, so that the questions may read, Do you do X or Y? or Do you agree with X or Y? or Do you prefer X or Y?

An unstructured opinion survey permits the respondents wider latitude in the type of response they can provide, frequently by providing only a blank space after the question. Unstructured surveys often ask that the respondents provide not only an answer but also a justification or explanation for the answer. Comer and Piliavin (1972) explored the reactions of physically handicapped respondents in interactions with physically handicapped and physically normal interviewers using an open-ended question format. In an investigation of the reactions to disabilities of a group of 462 undergraduates, Linkowski, Jaques, and Gaier (1969) used an unstructured opinion survey in which the respondents were asked to list those disabilities they considered to be the most and least severe, and why they thought so. In addition, the respondents were asked a series of questions, such as: How would this disability affect someone's life? What would a person with this disability be able to do? Not be able to do? Other questions asked the respondents to provide information on their knowledge and contact with disabled people, and other demographic and experiential information. To analyze the resultant responses, the researchers used a technique they referred to a thematic analysis. Content units (i.e., single thoughts or ideas) in each respondent's answers were identified and sorted into content categories and valence (i.e., positive or negative tone) categories. The categories were then summarized and the results compared for various respondent groups. Insights from these analyses were presented by the authors, who suggested these insights be operationalized and tested in subsequent research using other direct measurement methods.

Interviews

Interviews require that the researcher interact directly and verbally with the respondent, although the interview may take place over the phone or through the use of field assistants who are carefully trained to conduct the investigation with respondents in various locations. The respondent's answers to a series of questions are recorded in writing, or on audiotape or videotape, for subsequent analyses. Although the interview may be conducted with more than one person at a time (for example, the parents of a disabled newborn may be interviewed together), typically a single respondent is the subject of the interview.

Structured interviews are organized according to a fixed set of questions of various types (agree-disagree, select those which apply, open-ended), called the interview protocol or schedule. The protocol is established in advance by the researcher and used in a fixed sequence with all respondents. Branching within the protocol may allow the researcher to skip over certain questions in the sequence depending on the respondent's answer to an earlier question, or to ask more detailed questions to investigate a particular response to a question. In a semi-structured or unstructured interview, the researcher is free to explore the respondent's attitudes and opinions in ways which presumably will contribute insight to the question being investigated.

In an early study, Ramsey and Seipp (1948) used a nine-question structured interview to study opinions of the general public in Trenton, New Jersey, related to mental illness and its causes. Lyth (1973) used a semi-structured interview protocol to investigate the attitudes of employers toward the employment of disabled people, while Philips (1975) used an unstructured interview procedure with employers to explore similar attitudes toward deaf people. Other examples of research using interview methods are Barngrover's (1971) investigation of 50 educators' views about the efficacy of special classes for mildly handicapped children; Mercer's (1966) investigation, using open-ended interviews to explore the attitudes, feelings, and motives of a group of parents of previously institutionalized mentally retarded children; and Conant and Budoff's (1982) study of the understanding of blindness by sighted people in five age groups (from preschool to adult). For more detailed information, the chapter on intensive interviewing by Williamson, Karp, Dalphin, and Gray (1982) is recommended.

Rankings

Ranking methods require the respondent to arrange a small set of terms or statements (typically 20 or fewer) into an order according to some specified criterion so that only one item is assigned to each of the ordinal positions. For example, Abroms and Kodera (1979) asked a group of 138 college students in introductory courses in special education to rank order a collection of 15 disability category labels presented to them in alphabetical order. The criterion which the respondents were required to use was the acceptability of the disability to them, a concept which was purposefully not defined. An analysis of the resultant data suggested that the respondents viewed acceptability of the disabilities along three dimensions: organic impairments (such as cancer or arthritis), sensorimotor impairments (such as blindness or cerebral palsy), and functional impairments (such as mental retardation or emotional disturbance). Ranking methods have been used frequently to compare various groups of respondents on their attitudes toward disabled people (e.g., Barsch, 1964; Orlansky, 1979), although the analyses of the scales and the resultant data are not often as sophisticated and detailed as in the case of the Abroms and Kodera (1979) study.

It should be noted that ranking methods can use other than paper and pencil response requirements, and, in this way, the method may be suitable for young respondents and for respondents who may not be able to read the scale or record their rankings in writing. For example, Richardson, Goodman, Hasdorf, and Dornbusch (1961) used a set of drawings of children with various types and levels of physical disabilities (e.g., a child seated in a wheelchair, or an obese child) to study the attitudes of handicapped and non-handicapped young children of various races and religions. This technique was subsequently used by Richardson and by others with a variety of other respondent groups, including cross-cultural comparison studies (e.g., Chigier and Chigier, 1968). Jones and Sisk (1967) also used a set of pictures to assess the attitudes of children between the ages of two and five years toward children with orthopedic handicaps.

Q-Methodology

Q-methodology, an advanced rank-ordering methodology developed by William Stephenson (1953), requires that phrases or statements (typically 50 to 150) presenting the characteristics of the attitude referent, be written on separate cards. The respondent is told to sort the cards into an ordered collection of piles according to some criterion, such as favorability, intensity of agreement, or descriptiveness. The number of piles is specified (typically, nine or fewer) and the number of items which the respondent may place in each pile is also specified (e.g., 100 cards are to be divided into nine piles as follows: 4, 8, 13, 16, 18, 16, 13, 8, 4 in order from least to most descriptive). The resultant ordered groupings are analyzed in various ways depending on the research question. There are, however, cautions which must be heeded with Q-sort data. Because of the ipsative nature of the data, the assumption of independence required for classical statistical analyses is not tenable.

The sorts of different respondents may be compared and analyzed to derive clusters of respondents with similar orderings. The content of the items in each pile for different clusters of respondents is examined in order to characterize the respondents. That is, the judges are clustered, not the items. The researcher may then assign a respondent to a group by comparing his or her orderings with those obtained in previous research. The clusterings may be examined before and after some event or intervention to discern changes in respondent's attitudes. For example, Shaver and Scheibe (1967) used Q-methodology (among other methods) in a pre- and post-test design to investigate the influence of an intensive camp experience on the attitudes of college students toward people with chronic mental illness.

If the items to be sorted can be written in such a way as to represent a particular theoretical perspective, the sorting requirements can be arranged to test that particular theory. For example, the results of the Abroms and Kodera (1979) study mentioned in the previous section could be explored with Q-methodology to test the tripartite model for the disability factors proposed by the authors. An early study by D.G. Barker (1964) used Q-methodology to accomplish such a test of a theoretical model of disability groupings. Respondents were asked to sort 16 sets of ratings of 20 disabilities, with the resultant collections analyzed to determine what similarities among the disabilities might emerge. Barker found that sorters used a bivariate model to sort the disabilities, with organic (physical) disabilities in one set (e.g., cancer, malaria, blindness) and functional (mental) disabilities in another set (e.g., alcoholism, neuroses). An early review of investigations using Q-methodology in psychiatric research is provided by Block (1961).

CHECKLISTS

Sociometrics

Sociometric techniques of attitude measurement are an attempt to operationalize the conative, or behavioral, component of the definition of attitude. The techniques are designed to determine how a person behaves or intends to behave toward a particular attitude referent when given a choice of behaviors. It is important that the respondents believe that their choices may have consequences for the referent, or that their choices may affect themselves. If not, then the respondents' stated intentions will differ little from a self-report questionnaire. The types of choices offered must be real and typical choices for the situation, such as asking school children who they want to eat with, or play with, or sit near, or date. The respondent may be presented with a roster of all the people in his or her class or group and asked: Which of your classmates on the list below do you most like to sit with in the lunchroom? Next most? . . . Least?

The resultant data can be analyzed to yield a sociogram illustrating the number of times a child, or group of children, is nominated or selected in various situations. The study by Jones and Sisk (1967) mentioned previously used a sociometric method. The selections of orthopedically disabled children as playmates and companions by 230 non-disabled children between the ages two and six years were obtained and analyzed. Sociometric techniques have been widely used with a variety of response modes and a variety of respondent groups (including disabled people) to determine which variables influence the integration of disabled children and adults in schools, communities, and workplaces (e.g., Bruininks, Ryners, and Gross, 1974; Force, 1956; Kleck, Richardson, and Ronald, 1974; Siperstein and Bak, 1985). Jay Gottlieb, a prolific contributor to the body of research on attitudes toward people who are mentally retarded, provides an excellent review of sociometric research techniques and results (Gottlieb, 1975). Altman (1981), and MacMillan and Morrison (1984) discuss sociometric research with a variety of others groups and areas within special education and rehabilitation.

Adjective Checklists

The original Adjective Check List (ACL) was constructed by Gough (1960) for the investigation of personality and self-concept. A list of 300 adjectives arranged alphabetically was presented to the respondents who were asked to select those adjectives which they felt descriptive of themselves. Factor and cluster analytic investigations led other researchers to derive a variety of scales from the ACL, presumably measuring various aspects of personality, such as achievement, autonomy, self-confidence, and personal adjustment. The ACL has been used in a tremendous number of research investigations (approaching 1,000), and has been modified many times for specific research purposes, including the measurement of attitudes toward disabled people. Cleland, Manaster, King, and Iscoe (1975) used the 300-word ACL with a sample of 215 respondents to determine differences in their perceptions of mentally ill and mentally retarded people. The 20 adjectives which were most often selected for each referent were examined and related to various theoretical models.

Typically, however, a subset of the ACL items is selected and arranged alphabetically on a scale, and the respondents are asked to select those which they feel characterize or typify different groups of disabled people. Siperstein, Bak, and Gottlieb (1977) used a total of 34 positive and negative adjectives in children's everyday lexicon to investigate the differences in children's attitudes toward their handicapped peers. The 100-item Personal Attribute Inventory (Parish, Bryant, and Sherazi, 1976), which was derived from the ACL, has been used in a number of studies of the attitudes of respondents of various ages to various groups of handicapped people. Parish and Taylor (1978) also developed a similar 48-item scale to be used with children. Recently, Williams (1986) used a modified adjective checklist procedure to investigate the perceptions of 373 college students of people who are mentally retarded. Other examples include a study by Goldstein and Blackman (1975), who used an 84-item checklist, originally designed to study attitudes toward ethnic groups, to study attitudes toward other devalued groups (i.e., the mentally retarded, mentally ill, criminals, alcoholics, and the physically disabled). A review of research using adjective checklists to measure attitudes toward mentally retarded children is provided by Gottlieb, Corman, and Curci (1984).

Paired-Comparison Scales

The method of paired comparisons, as the name implies, requires that the researcher present the respondents with all possible pairs of the objects or items which the researcher wishes to scale. The respondents are asked to select the item in each pair which they would rate higher in terms of a criterion presented by the researcher. As opposed to the ranking or Q-sort methods discussed previously, the respondents are required to compare all items to each other and to state a preference. The resultant data are analyzed to yield an ordering of the items for each respondent or for a group of respondents. Typically, all possible pairs are presented twice, the second time in reverse order, to determine the consistency of the respondents' selections. Because the method requires a total of n x (n-1) pairs, the method is usually reserved for a small sample of items (typically less than 15). Table 1 presents an example of some of the items in a hypothetical paired-comparison scale designed to measure the respondent's attitudes toward the seriousness of a set of impairments.

Table 3.1

Example of a Hypothetical Paired Comparison Scale

To Study Attitudes Toward the Seriousness of Impairments

Each item below presents two possible conditions which may impair a person. Please read each pair and circle the letter of the impairment which you believe is the more disabling. Continue to the end of the list judging each pair separately

1. (a) mental retardation
   (b) epilepsy

2. (a) blindness
   (b) cerebral palsy

.
.
.

13. (a) mental retardation
    (b) blindness

.
.
.

24. (a) cerebral palsy
    (b) blindness

.
.
.

Jones, Gottfried, and Owens (1966) presented a set of 13 group labels (i.e., 11 handicapped group labels, plus gifted and non-handicapped) to a sample of 189 high school students to scale their rankings of seven social situations (as a neighbor, as a visitor, etc.). Wicas and Carluccio (1971) investigated the attitudes of counselors toward the culturally different, ex-convict, and ex-mental patient by presenting these three group labels in a modified paired-comparison arrangement in each of 25 situations (employability, trust, etc.). Janicki (1970) used a total of 66 paired-comparison dyads to investigate the attitudes of 54 hospital employees to 12 different disability groups.

RATING SCALES

Rating scales require that the respondents indicate the strength of their agreement or disagreement with each item in a collection of items concerning the attitude referent. Some rating scales are graphic, requiring that the respondents place a mark on a line drawn with a series of intervals marked and anchored at the extremes by terms such as "Completely disagree" and "Completely agree." Other scales are numeric, requiring the respondents to mark a number on a continuum (e.g., − 3, − 2, − 1, + 1, + 2, + 3). Still others are verbal, requiring that a specific phrase or word be checked (e.g., YES! YES. YES? NO? NO. NO!).

Regardless of the response category format, the responses are completely structured by the researcher. There is no opportunity for respondents to add other statements, or to respond to a statement in any way other than that provided by the researcher. Because respondents are free to use any of the rating categories as many times as they wish, the rating assigned to one statement theoretically does not have any influence on the respondents' ratings of any other statement.

As stated in Chapter 2, the purpose of scaling is to assign an index value to observations of the respondent's behavior which represents the underlying attitude presumed to direct and energize the behavior. In any rating procedure, then, there are three elements: the respondents, the stimuli to which they respond, and the responses they provide to those stimuli. The index value obtained may be used to compose a distribution of the stimuli (i.e., an ordering of the items on the scale from those which the respondents endorse most frequently to those which the respondents endorse least frequently), or to obtain a distribution of the respondents (i.e., an ordering of the respondents from those who most endorse the attitude concept to those who least endorse the attitude concept). In either case, the index values are assumed to be distributed along a continuum, and the researcher's goal is to obtain the appropriate frequency distribution.

The obtained distribution of respondents, or responses, is an example of ordinal level measurement because many elements may be located at the same point on the distribution. To obtain more precision in the orderings, researchers often assign numerical values to the points on the item response continuum and then calculate the median of the distribution of responses of each respondent to a set of items, or the median of the distribution of responses of a set of respondents to each item. Because rating scale data are ordinal, the calculation and use of median index values is defensible. The calculation of a mean index value, however, requires that the data are interval level, which is clearly not the case. (Recall from Chapter 2 that this requires the scale points to be equally spaced and distributed along the continuum.) The precision obtained from interval data index values, and the statistical manipulations which can be performed on interval data (but not on nominal or ordinal data), led early researchers to search for measuring methods which would yield interval data index values from rating scales.

Semantic Differential Scales

The semantic differential method was developed by L.L. Thurstone in the late 1920's, but has come to be most closely associated with Osgood and his colleagues (Osgood, Suci, and Tannenbaum, 1957). In this method, a single concept (e.g., mental retardation) is presented on the top of a page and is followed by a set of scales (typically 7 to 20). Each scale is anchored at each end by bi-polar adjectives connected by a line marked in intervals, or by a series of blanks, or boxes (generally seven blanks, or boxes, or points are used). Respondents are asked to check the box or mark the line at a point which represents their rating of the concept on each scale.

In Osgood's original work, three clusters of scales emerged regularly from analyses of an original set of 50 scales. He termed these evaluative, potency, and activity scales. Other researchers, using different scales and different concepts, have derived other dimensions in addition to the original three. The data obtained are the ratings of the concept on each scale, as well as the mean rating or the sum of the ratings of the concept on all of the scales. A respondent's scores can be analyzed to determine their relationship to respondent characteristics, or they can be compared before and after some intervention, or they can be compared across concepts. The scores of different groups of respondents to different concepts can also be compared. Table 2 presents an example of a hypothetical semantic differential scale to rate the concept of mental retardation.

Golin (1970) used 11 seven-point semantic differential scales to study the attitudes of respondents who were asked to read fictitious stories about disabled people which varied by the amount of information they contained and the favorableness of the information. Examples of other studies which compared semantic differential ratings for groups of disabled people are the studies conducted by Panda and Bartel (1972), and by Rapier, Adelson, Carey, and Croke (1972). Begab (1970) used the technique to measure the change in attitudes of students following training, Jaffee (1972) studied changes before and after team conferences concerning mentally retarded children, Sadlick and Penta (1975) studied changes

Table 3.2

Example of a Hypothetical Semantic Differential Scale for the Measurement of Attitudes Toward Mental Retardation

Please indicate your perception of the concept of mental retardation by placing a check on one of the seven spaces on each of the continuua presented below.

MENTAL RETARDATION

good	___ :	___ :	___ :	___ :	___ :	___ :	___	bad
hot	___ :	___ :	___ :	___ :	___ :	___ :	___	cold
soft	___ :	___ :	___ :	___ :	___ :	___ :	___	hard
slow	___ :	___ :	___ :	___ :	___ :	___ :	___	fast
ugly	___ :	___ :	___ :	___ :	___ :	___ :	___	beautiful
small	___ :	___ :	___ :	___ :	___ :	___ :	___	large
strong	___ :	___ :	___ :	___ :	___ :	___ :	___	weak

in nurses' attitudes toward physically disabled patients after training using television, and Stude (1973) studied changes of rehabilitation counselors' attitude toward people with epilepsy following training.

Probabilistic Rating Scales

Another set of rating scale methods are based on a probabilistic measurement model. It is assumed that the response to any item on the scale is not determined by the latent attitude which the respondent holds, but rather the respondent's attitude is assumed to increase the probability that a particular response to an item will be selected. The most widely known and used (or, perhaps, we should say abused) of these methods is the summated rating scale method developed by Rensis Likert (1932). This was not, however, the first of the probabilistic scaling methods. In fact, Likert proposed his method as a way of constructing reliable rating scales while avoiding the statistical assumptions which are required by the consensual location (or equal-appearing intervals) method proposed earlier by L.L. Thurstone (1928). The use of Thurstone's method by Bogardus (1933) led to the creation of the social distance scale. This is not a type of scale nor a scaling method, although it is often presented as such. It will be discussed in the context of Thurstone's method. In 1948, Edwards and Kilpatrick proposed their scale-discrimination method which incorporated elements from both Likert's and Thurstone's methods to enable a researcher to create a scale of items.

Summated Rating Scales. In Likert's model, the items which comprise the universe of items characterizing the attitude referent are assumed to be arrangeable on a monotonic continuum determined by the probability that a respondent who holds the attitude will endorse or agree with the statement. The respondents are asked to indicate the extent of agreement (endorsement) with each item, and numerical weights are assigned to each response category (successive integers, typically 1 to 6, or − 3 to + 3). The highest numerical value is usually reserved for the response category representing the strongest endorsement of the item.

As will be discussed in detail in Chapter 8, the researcher begins with a pool of items which are refined and then presented to a sample of respondents in a pilot study. Their responses to the complete set of items and to each individual item are examined statistically and a final set of items with the best psychometric properties is retained. The index value (or score) for each respondent is determined by summing the weighted responses to the items. If the researcher wishes to investigate more than one aspect of the attitude referent, a set of subscales can be constructed in a similar fashion.

While many so-called "Likert-format" scales have been used in research on attitudes toward disabled people, in most cases these scales are not summated rating scales. Although the items are in the appropriate form, they have not been selected according to the summated scaling procedure and are of dubious quality. They certainly do not provide the interval level data required for the sophisticated analyses subsequently performed by the researcher. The results of any study using a "Likert-format" scale for which scale development information is not provided should be cautiously considered. Perhaps the paradoxes, confusions, and contradictions noted in the literature by reviewers such as Gottlieb (1975) may be explained by the failure of researchers to adhere to the psychometric requirements of summated rating scales.

The precursor of all summated rating scales is the Attitude Toward Disabled Persons Scale developed by Harold E. Yuker and his colleagues at Hofstra University (Yuker, Block, and Campbell, 1960; Yuker, Block, and Younng, 1966). (The 1960 publication used the singular attitude, the 1966 publication used the plural attitudes, while other publications use both. We will use the singular because Yuker argues that the scale is a unitary measure of attitude toward disabled people considered as a group.) Examples of other scales which have been carefully developed are the Scale of Attitudes Toward Disabled Persons (SADP: Antonak, 1981a, 1982, 1985a, 1985b), and the Opinions about Mental Illness (OMI) Scale (Cohen and Struening, 1959, 1960). These scales, as well as a number of others, will be presented and discussed in detail in the chapters in Part III of this book.

Consensual Location Scales. Basing his work on psychophysical research methods, Thurstone (1927) sought a method of attitude scaling in which an index value could be assigned to any item characterizing the attitude referent. The respondent's attitude would then be estimated from the median of the index values of those items which he or she selected to endorse. This model assumes that the dispersion of responses to any item is normal, and that the item's index value (median of the item response dispersion calculated from a large panel of judges) is the true index value for the item. The researcher constructs a scale by selecting a small number of items of suitable dispersions and index values covering the continuum from complete agreement to complete disagreement.

Consensual location scaling requires that the researcher collect 100 to 150 items concerning the referent and submit them to a large number of judges (typically 100). Each judge is asked to sort the items into piles (typically 9 or 11), or to rate each of the items on a scale (of 9 or 11 points), representing the degrees to which the item expresses favorability to the referent. Note that the judges are not asked to rate the items on the extent of their agreement with them. The dispersion of the judges' ratings is obtained, the median is calculated, and those items (30 to 50) with values which cover the full continuum are selected for a second-stage analysis. The items are presented on a second scale to a second sample of judges, and the dispersion of their responses to the items is analyzed for consistency (minimum variability). Approximately 20 items are retained with index values fairly equally spaced along the continuum (hence, the other name for the method, equal-appearing intervals), and randomly arranged on the final scale. The respondents in any subsequent investigation are asked to select the one item which they endorse, and the index value for this item is taken to be a measure of the respondents' attitude toward the referent.

Thurstone and his colleages used this method to derive scales expressing attitudes toward a variety of social practices and institutions, including the church, war, and capital punishment. In 1933, Bogardus used a modified version of Thurstone's method to refine his earlier work (Bogardus, 1925a, 1925b) and developed the prototype social distance scale. This scale consisted of seven equal-appearing intervals to measure attitudes toward various religious, ethnic, and occupational groups. A hypothetical example of a social distance scale to measure attitudes toward different groups of disabled people is presented in Table 3.

Table 3.3

Example of a Hypothetical Social Distance Scale for the Measurement of Attitudes Toward Various Disability Groups

For each of the groups of impairments listed below, select the one level of social contact which expresses your feelings of personal-group distance and mark the appropriate space. Please provide your first reaction in every case. React to each impairment as a group. Do not give your reaction to the best or worst members of the group that you have known or can imagine.

	1 Would marry into group	2 Would have as close friends	3 Would have as next door neighbor	4 Would work in same office	5 Would have as speaking acquaint-ances only	6 Would have as visitors only to my nation	7 Would debar from my nation
Amputation	--	--	--	--	--	--	--
Blindness	--	--	--	--	--	--	--
Cerebral Palsy	--	--	--	--	--	--	--
Deafness	--	--	--	--	--	--	--
Emotionally Disturbance	--	--	--	--	--	--	--
Mental Retardation	--	--	--	--	--	--	--
.							
.							
.							

In 1970, Tringo combined the work of Bogardus with a new set of items expressing social distance from people who are disabled, analyzed the resultant data according to Thurstone's method, and created the nine-item Disability Social Distance Scale (DSDS) (see Chapter 9). Horne (1978), using Thurstone's method, created the Perceptions of Social Closeness Scale to measure pupil and teacher attitudes toward other class members. Tringo's scale and Horne's scale have been used in a number of studies of attitudes toward different disability groups (e.g., Harasymiw, Horne, and Lewis, 1976; Hollinger and Jones, 1970; Leyser and

Abrams, 1982; Rickard, Triandis, and Patterson, 1963). Other scales have been developed which purport to measure the social distance which respondents desire from people who are disabled. These scales were not, however, developed with Thurstone's method and generally do not report the scale development and analysis of data necessary to inspire confidence in their validity and usefulness. In fact, many of these so-called social distance scales are essentially self-report questionnaires composed of the ubiquitous "Likert-format" items, and are of dubious quality.

Scale Discrimination Method. Edwards and Kilpatrick (1948) proposed an alternative scale development model which used the best of both of the preceeding probabilistic scaling methods (i.e., summated rating scales and consensual location scales). A large pool of items is created and each is written on a separate card. This collection of cards is given to a large sample of judges who are asked to sort the items into piles according to Thurstone's method. The dispersions of the judges' responses are examined to eliminate inconsistent items and to derive index values for each item. The remaining items are arranged as six-point Likert scales with response categories from "Strongly disagree" to "Strongly agree." A second sample of respondents is asked to evaluate each item, and the total scale scores and item scores are analyzed to select those items with the best discriminating power at each interval along the continua.

Perhaps because of the large number of judges and respondents which are required for this procedure, and the resultant time and effort requirements, no scales measuring attitudes toward disabled people have been found which were developed using this composite scale-discrimination method.

Deterministic Rating Scales

The final set of rating scale methods to be considered are based on a deterministic measurement model in which it is assumed that the response to any item on the scale is completely determined by the latent attitude of the respondent. The probability that a respondent will endorse an item with an index value which represents a point on the attitude continuum above the respondent's attitude is therefore zero, while the probability that the respondent will endorse any item with an index value at or below the point on the continuum representing his or her attitude is one. Hence, any respondent's attitude toward the referent can be measured by presenting a set of items of known index values to the respondent and locating the one item which he or she is willing to endorse. Of course, this method requires the assumption of no error or no inconsistency in responding, and the assumption that a set of items of known index values can be written.

The most widely known and used deterministic scaling method is scalogram analysis (Guttman, 1944). This method was originally developed to determine whether a set of items comprised a unidimensional linear scale. More recently, William Bart and his colleagues (Bart and Krus, 1973) have proposed their method of ordering-theoretic data analysis to generate multidimensional and nonlinear scales of items.

Guttmann Scaling. The task for the researcher who wishes to use a Guttman scale to measure attitudes is to select items which, as a group, will be scalable; that is, they will form a unidimensional continuum which spans the range of favorability to the attitude referent. Based upon a respondent's score on the scale, it will then be possible, with a perfect scale, to reconstruct the respondent's responses to each item. The matrix of endorsements (the scalogram) of five respondent types to four attitude items presented in Table 4 is a perfect Guttman scale. (It is assumed that endorsement represents a favorable attitude and is scored as 1, and that failure to endorse represents an unfavorable attitude and is scored as 0.) An asterisk (*) has been placed in cell (i, j) if and only if subject type i endorses item j. Endorsement of one item in the scale implies endorsement of all other items lower in the ordering; and conversely, failure to endorse an item implies failure to endorse all items higher on the linear scale. The respondent's score (the number of items he or she endorses) is a measure of the respondent's attitude toward the referent. Respondent type 1 has the most favorable attitude, represented by a perfect score of 4; respondent type 2 has the next most favorable attitude, represented by a score of 3; and so on.

The general rule is that item *a* can be ordered above item *b* (*a* expresses a more favorable attitude than *b*) if, and only if, all people who endorse item *b* also endorse item *a*. All items which elicit identical response patterns are considered identical, and all items which elicit no endorsement are considered irrelevant. The item endorsements of the next respondent allow the researcher to place the respondent on the continuum of favorableness to the attitude referent by determining where in the ordering of people the respondent falls. That is, all people who present an identical endorsement pattern are considered to hold an identical attitude toward the referent.

The perfect scale represented by the triangular arrangement of asterisks in Table 4 indicates that all responses are completely predicted from the score. This is rarely found in practice because there are typically one or more endorsement patterns in which the stringent rule does not hold, so that the resultant ordering matrix of the items and people is inconsistent. A statistic known as the coefficient of reproducibility has been proposed which expresses the degree to which the scale items present the perfect ordering. A coefficient of .85 or better is generally considered to indicate a satisfactory Guttman scale.

The procedure for constructing a Guttman scale is an iterative one. The researcher starts with a pool of items which represent the range of attitudes toward the referent. (The researcher may use the scale-discrimination method described previously to generate the initial pool of items.) A small number (12 to 15) of these items is presented to a large sample of respondents and the matrix of endorsements is constructed and analyzed for consistency. Certain items are removed and

Table 3.4

Responses of Five Respondent Types to Four Attitude Items for a Perfect Guttman Scale

Respondent Type	Item a	Item b	Item c	Item d	Respondent Score
1	*	*	*	*	4
2	*	*	*		3
3	*	*			2
4	*				1
5					0
Item Score	4	3	2	1	

Note. Asterisk (*) denotes endorsement

the data from this second version of the scale are reanalyzed. The final version of the scale is proposed after several such revisions and the coefficient of reproducibility is reported. To verify that the items do form a scale, data from a new sample of respondents are obtained and analyzed. If the hypothesized ordering appears, then the scale may be used to measure the attitudes of subsequent samples of respondents.

Several cautions are in order. A deceptively large value of the coefficient of reproducibility can be obtained from a small sample of respondents (15 or fewer). Because the coefficient is calculated after the data are collected, and is therefore sample dependent, a chance ordering of the items of a small number of people is probable and may be taken to be a good scale. Second, guidelines for an acceptable minimum value for the coefficient of reproducibility have not been agreed upon by statisticians although a rule of thumb (.85) has been proposed. Third, the coefficient may be adequate, but the unidimensionality of the items may be questionable. That is, the items may not be a homogeneous set of characteristics of the attitude referent. The construct validity of the scale must be carefully examined to determine if the items represent a homogenous set of items. Fourth, it is extremely unlikely that a researcher can obtain a reproducible scale with more than eight items (there are 40,320 possible different orderings of eight items, and over 1.3 trillion different orderings of 15 items).

Perhaps because of these difficulties, few examples of Guttman scaling in research on attitudes in general, and research on attitudes toward disabled people in particular, are available. Several investigations have used the method to analyze data from Bogardus' social distance scale to study prejudice toward various groups (Triandis and Triandis, 1965). Cohen (1963) used the scalogram technique to investigate attitudes of employers toward hiring mentally retarded people. Yamamoto and Dizney (1967) constructed a six-item Guttman scale of social tolerance and help sources to order respondents on a continuum of rejecting attitudes toward five types of mental illness. Yamamoto and Wiersma (1967) later used this scale in a study of the relationship of self-concept to tolerance of disability.

A final criticism of even the ideal (perfectly reproducible) Guttman scale is that it is restricted to the identification of linear and unidimensional orderings of the items, in which one and only one item may be placed at any level of the hierarchy. Most experts on attitude measurement, however, argue that attitudes are best considered as nonlinear and multidimensional (Jones and Guskin, 1984; Siller, 1984). Linear scales ignore the fact that attitudes have multiple, interrelated antecedents, and that the behaviors they predispose the individual to display have multiple facets. Scalogram analysis has been extended to several dimensions (Lazarsfeld and Henry, 1968; Lingoes, 1963); however, the constraints of small item pool and a large sample, and the issue of what is an acceptable coefficient of reproducibility still apply.

Ordering Theory. Ordering theory is a deterministic measurement model that extends scalogram analysis to include nonlinear item orders in unidimensional as well as multidimensional configurations (Airasian and Bart, 1973; Bart and Krus, 1973; Krus and Bart, 1974; Krus, Bart, and Airasian, 1975). Using Boolean algebraic analysis methods (Krus, 1975, 1977), the ordering-theoretic analysis of bivalued response patterns identifies prerequisite relationships among a set of items.

The prerequisite relationship is derived from formal logic: Item i is a prerequisite to item j if, and only if, the response pattern (0, 1), where 0 represents a failure to endorse item i and 1 represents endorsement of item j, occurs

Table 3.5

A Response Pattern Data Matrix to Determine the Hierarchical Relationship Between Two Items

Item i Response	Item j response 0	1
0	a	b
1	c	d

Note. a + b + c + d = n

infrequently. That is, the response pattern (0, 1) is considered a disconfirmation that endorsement of item i is prerequisite to endorsement of item j. For any pair of items, a matrix of responses, such as that presented in Table 5, can be constructed for a sample of n respondents. A frequency of 0 in the (0, 1) cell ($b = 0$) indicates that no respondent endorsed item j, yet failed to endorse item i. If cell $c = 0$ as well, so that $a + d = n$, then item i and j are considered to be equivalent. Finally, an essentially random distribution of responses into the four cells is indicative of independence of the items.

To overcome the limitation, shared with other deterministic measurement models, of dealing with random error in the item-response patterns, ordering-theoretic data analysis identifies a prerequisite relationship between two items only if the frequency of disconfirmatory response patterns is less than or equal to the frequency of such response patterns established by an error tolerance level selected by the researcher. For a sample of n respondents, a researcher who selects a five percent error tolerance level is willing to accept a frequency of at most $.05 \times n$ in the (0, 1) cell identifying a prerequisite relationship between item i and item j. All possible 2×2 item response tables are constructed from the respondent data and examined to specify the relationships among the items. It should be noted that different item hierarchies are constructed for different tolerance levels. As the error tolerance level approaches zero percent, fewer prerequisite relationships are found and the resultant hierarchical ordering becomes compressed into fewer dimensions.

Examples of the use of ordering theory in attitude research include the studies by Bart (1972a, 1972b) investigating attitudes toward the environment and toward certain species of animals, and the study by Thede and Antonak (1981) investigating the structure of women's attitudes. Antonak (1979a) reported an ordering-theoretic analysis of data from 150 university students who responded to the Attitude Toward Disabled Persons Scale. The resultant hierarchical ordering was examined and insights were suggested for experiments concerning attitude formation and modification. In an investigation of the ordering of statements expressing attitudes toward the school integration and community integration of 11 groups of exceptionality and the normal, Antonak (1980b) showed that attitudes toward the integration of disabled people are multidimensional and involve separate factors for different disability groups.

Using a procedure similar to that outlined for Guttman scales, the ordering-theoretic method can be used to construct multidimensional nonlinear attitude scales. Replication of the ordering with subsequent samples is supportive of the validity of the scale. As an alternative, ordering-theory can be used to confirm a theory of attitude structure. A set of items is composed which are derived from the theory and the presumed relationships among the items are specified. Respondent data are then examined to determine if the hypothesized hierarchical ordering can be established. Antonak (1985c) used ordering-theoretic data analysis as a follow-up to a multivariate statistical test of data from a questionnaire given to 150 service providers. The research question was whether, as predicted from Finkelstein's (1980) conceptualization of the problems faced by people who are impaired, service providers endorse the premise that components of society contribute to the disablement of people with chronic health, emotional, mental, physical, and sensory impairments. The resultant orderings showed the endorsement of the premise for the different impairment groups and the relationship of endorsement of the premise to respondents' characteristics. Ordering-theoretic methods can also be used to generate higher-ordered multidimensional scales from clusters of attitude scales derived from factor analyses or latent partition analysis (Antonak, 1985a).

SUMMARY AND PRELUDE

In this chapter, our attention has been focused on ten direct methods of attitude measurement: opinion surveys, interviews, rankings, Q-methodology, sociometrics, adjective checklists, paired comparison scales, semantic differential scales, probabilistic rating scales, and deterministic rating scales. Probabilistic rating scale methods were subdivided into three types: the method of summated ratings, consensual location scaling, and the scale discrimination method. Deterministic rating scale methods were subdivided into two types: Guttman scalogram analysis and ordering-theoretic data analysis.

There is considerable diversity in the types of direct measurement methods available to the researcher who is seeking to answer questions concerning attitudes toward people who are disabled. Among the ten methods discussed in this chapter, the rating scales have been used most often by social and behavioral scientists. All of these methods, however, share a number of weaknesses.

On the one hand, the small and fixed number of items or stimuli on these scales and checklists means that a considerable amount of subtle information concerning the respondents' attitudes may be lost. An anology, perhaps, would be looking at the stars with a pair of binoculars. Moreover, the data obtained from most of these methods are at best ordinal level data and, therefore, not suitable for the more sophisticated inferential statistical analysis techniques. Finally, by focusing on only one disability, or a very small number of disabilities one at a time, it is not possible to determine the commonalities that may exist in the respondents' attitudes toward different disability groups. In response to these limitations, multidimensional scaling procedures have been developed. These procedures will be discussed, and their strengths illustrated, in Chapter 4.

Chapter 4

MULTIDIMENSIONAL SCALING

By

LIORA PEDHAZUR SCHMELKIN

THIS CHAPTER will present and illustrate a particular scaling approach, multidimensional scaling (MDS), that can be applied to assess the perceptions of and attitudes toward people with disabilities. Before beginning the discussion of MDS, however, it is useful to clarify the distinction between perceptions of and attitudes toward a referent.

Considerable overlap and confusion exists between the concepts of perception and attitude. Some authors maintain that they are one and the same concept, other authors distinguish between them, and still others view perception as one aspect of attitude (e.g., the cognitive component of the tripartite definition of attitude presented in Chapter 1). For the present purposes, a distinction will be made between perceptions and attitudes, with the former focusing on the objects of attitudes.

In order to understand why people react as they do to disabilities and to people with disabilities (i.e., their attitudes), we need to gain a better appreciation of what aspects of the stimuli they attend to (i.e., their perceptions). The presentation of multidimensional scaling that follows focuses on perceptions of disabilities because the methodology is particularly well-suited to the study of perceptions, and because most of the applications to date have been in this area. The methodology can also be adapted and applied to the measurement of attitudes (Livneh, 1983; Napior, 1972).

Some research endeavors are oriented toward answering attitudinal questions, while others address perceptual concerns. Frequently, the research can provide information relevant to both perceptions and attitudes. For example, research on disability preference hierarchies has typically focused on the affective nature of attitudes. Yet, placing disabilities on a continuum may provide information on the

Liora Pedhazur Schmelkin is an Associate Professor in the Department of Counseling, Psychology, and Research in Education at Hofstra University, Hempstead, Long Island, New York.

underlying organizing dimensions used by the respondents. In other words, in addition to assessing which disabilities may be more accepted by a respondent, the particular placement of the disabilites may be used to ascertain the meanings, categories, perceptions, and stereotypes that are attached to the various disabilities, and to detect any commonalities or differences that may exist among them. This approach leads to questions such as: What are the perceptions that subjects have of disabilities and people with disabilities? What are the organizing categories or dimensions that are used in these perceptions? What are the stereotypes that underlie these perceptions?

While MDS applications within the disability and rehabilitation literature are relatively recent (for a review see Schmelkin, in press), the general MDS literature has grown in the past 20 years, both in methodological advances and in the range of topics to which it has been applied. This chapter will provide an intuitive, non-technical introduction to some of its uses, focusing on nonmetric multidimensional scaling. For more technical discussions of MDS methods and applications, see the publications of Coxon (1982), Davison (1983), Kruskal and Wish (1978), Romney, Shepard, and Nerlove (1972), Schiffman, Reynolds, and Young (1981), and Shepard, Romney, and Nerlove (1972).

The chapter begins with a discussion of the limitations of traditional scaling approaches, such as those discussed in Chapter 3. This is followed by an overview of the purposes and nature of MDS. Two examples are then provided, both of which use the computer program ALSCAL (SPSS, 1986), one of several programs available for the analysis of MDS data. For more information on the various computer programs, see Kruskal and Wish (1978), and Schiffman et al. (1981). The chapter concludes with some suggestions for various MDS applications in the study of psychosocial aspects of disability.

LIMITATIONS OF TRADITIONAL SCALING APPROACHES

Traditional approaches to the study of perceptions and stereotypes of disabilities, as well as attitudes toward people with disabilities, have either focused on global attitudes (e.g., studies using the scales to be reviewed in Chapter 9), or have been directed to a specific disability group (e.g., mental retardation, blindness, deafness, learning disability, psychiatric disability). Within the latter approach, research can be classified into two broad categories. The first has concentrated on one or a very few disabilities at a time, and is typified by studies which use the scales to be reviewed in Chapters 10, 11, and 12. The other line of research has focused simultaneously on a wider group of disabilities in an attempt to assess the overall organizing dimensions of perceptions and attitudes (e.g., a study which asks the respondent to rank a set of disability labels in terms of the impact of the disability on employment potential). In all of these classes of research, however, the measurement approach used has been limited almost exclusively to the direct methods presented in Chapter 3 (e.g., rankings, adjective checklists, semantic differential scales). These methods impose several, oftentimes severe, limitations on the research results and subsequent interpretations.

Dimensionality of the Data

To begin with, different scaling methods are based on different models of the relationship between a latent or underlying continuum (e.g., unfavorable vs. favorable attitude) and the probability of a respondent agreeing with a specific item or statement. Moreover, most of the methods are based, either explicitly or implicitly, on the assumption of unidimensionality of the data structure. For example, ranking disabilities, or using a summated rating scale, implies that there is only one underlying continuum that is important to the respondents. In many instances, this is an unrealistic assumption and, as a result, these methods may not be able to adequately scale the complex phenomena with which they deal.

Even when the responses to scale items are factor analyzed, and the results indicate that more than one underlying factor is appropriate for the interpretation of the data, researchers may modify or eliminate items so as to reduce the structure to a single factor or dimension. More often, they may ignore the results altogether and proceed to sum the responses to all of the items into a total score. They are thus treating the domain they are measuring as if it were unidimensional even though the results of the factor analysis have demonstrated otherwise. As Baird and Noma (1978) aptly described the situation:

> Throughout most of its history, experimental psychology has concentrated on the scaling of stimuli along a single dimension . . . However, the concept of a multidimensional psychological space is probably as old as experimental psychology . . . More recently, there has been renewed interest in multidimensional scales, or rather in the placement of stimuli in a multidimensional space. Part of the motivation for this revival is the implausibility of psychological mechanisms that must be invoked for evaluating stimuli on a single . . . scale. (p. 177)

Multi-Disability Comparisons

Another concern with the direct measurement methods is the way perceptions of disabilities have traditionally been studied. This concern relates to the difficulty of ascertaining the commonalities or differences that may exist in the perceptions of various disabilities. Many studies attempt to make comparisons among disabilities or between a particular disability and what is considered to be normal or average. In most instances, respondents are asked to assess each of the disabilities individually (e.g., by using ratings or checklists). Then, depending on the focus of the study, correlations may be derived among all the disabilities, differences between ratings of the disabilities may be tested, and so forth. The important point is that, with the exception of ranking methodology, the comparisons among the disabilities are obtained after the fact. It is assumed, often inappropriately, that each of the individual assessments is equally as applicable and conveys the same meaning for each of the disabilities.

As an example, consider a typical study using the semantic differential method to compare several disabilities. The various disabilities serve as the concepts of the study and a set of scales is provided. What is oftentimes overlooked is that the meaning of the scales is dependent in part on the particular concepts being used. Moreover, the correlations between pairs of scales may change from concept to concept. Such a situation would result in concept-scale interactions rendering comparisons among concepts problematic.

Researcher's A Priori Conceptions

A third limitation of the traditional measurement approaches is that they impose upon the respondents the researcher's conceptions of the relevant dimensions and constructs of the attitude domain. As a result, the universe of potential dimensions is restricted or constrained by the scales that are used. For example, in a study which uses adjective checklists, a predetermined list of adjectives is provided, while in a study with rating scales, a predetermined set of scales is provided. The results obtained will be dependent upon the researcher's judgment as to the important constructs, as reflected in his or her choice of adjectives or scales. A related difficulty is that "some dimensions may not be amenable to effective articulation by any a priori unidimensional scale, whether defined verbally, behaviorally, or physically" (Carroll and Wish, 1974, p. 394). Consequently, it may not be possible to determine what part of the resultant structure is due to respondents' perceptions and what part is due to the constraints placed on them by the researcher.

To clarify this point, consider the study of stereotypes of ethnic groups by Ehrlich and Rinehart (1965) in which responses to an adjective checklist were compared with responses to an open-ended questionnaire. The two measurement methods produced different lists of salient traits for the referents of the study. In addition, those subjects responding to the adjective checklist assigned more traits to the various ethnic groups and exhibited greater consensus than did the subjects who responded to the open-ended questionnaire. The methods of response elicitation in this study may have forced the subjects to think in generalizations that they did not normally consider. In another study, Funk, Horowitz, Lipshitz, and Young (1976) concluded that research into stereotypes which uses only traditional direct measurement methods, such as rating scales or adjective checklists, may yield detailed descriptions of the stereotypes based on subtle distinctions of the referent's characteristics which subjects seldom make in "real-life" situations.

NONMETRIC MULTIDIMENSIONAL SCALING

Purposes of MDS

MDS consists of a set of methods which are designed to: (a) explore the internal representation or psychological structure underlying a set of stimuli; (b) determine whether, in fact, that structure is unidimensional or multidimensional; and (c) discover the salient dimensions in as unconstrained a way as possible. MDS is particularly suitable for unraveling stereotypic perceptions of different groups studied simultaneously and in relation to each other. It provides for a direct comparison of the stimuli within a frame of reference used by the respondents. Furthermore, the researcher's solutions can be presented graphically, which often enhances interpretation.

To elucidate some of the basic concepts of MDS, let us assume that it is known in advance that the underlying structure of a particular stimulus set is two-dimensional. One obvious example is to consider a map (see, for example, Coxon, 1982; Kruskal and Wish, 1978; or Rabinowitz, 1986). Suppose that we randomly sampled 30 cities in the United States. The location of these 30 cities on the map can be described in terms of their positions on the east-to-west and north-to-south axes or dimensions (e.g., latitude and longitude). Knowledge of these two coordinates is sufficient to construct a map showing relative positions (as crude as that map may be), and distances between all pairs of cities can be computed in a straightforward manner.

Now suppose that the situation was presented in reverse. That is, the positions of the 30 cities on the two dimensions are not known in advance, but a matrix presenting estimates of the distances between all pairs of cities is available. Can these estimated distances be used to construct a map of the locations of the 30 cities? In fact, that is precisely what MDS attempts to do. Given some measure of distance, the two primary purposes of MDS are to determine the appropriate number of dimensions that underlie a set of stimuli (the dimensionality), and to determine the pattern of the stimuli on these dimensions (the configuration). Consequently, it may be possible to interpret the nature of the underlying dimensions and to infer the traits or characteristics attributed to the stimuli, as well as their relative importance for the perceiver.

MDS of Perceptions

Unlike the map example, the number of relevant dimensions and placement of the stimuli on these dimensions is rarely known in advance. In fact, MDS methods are particularly useful in domains of study where neither the dimensionality nor the specific configuration is known in advance, domains where traditional direct measurement methods are least likely to yield meaningful data. Jackson (1969) suggested that it is precisely when we know little about the underlying dimensions that it is most hazardous for the researcher to attempt to specify these to the respondents.

Rather than specify the dimensions in advance, an assumption is made that respondents have some type of internal representation of the stimulus set, known as a psychological map. The stimuli can be coded on this map along several continuously scaleable dimensions. These dimensions need not be explicit or conscious, nor limited to two as was the case in the map example. Rather, it is entirely possible, indeed probable, that there are three, four, or even more dimensions underlying perceptions of the type of complex social stimuli that we are concerned with in disability research.

In the case of constructing a map, it was suggested that the distances between selected cities could be used to generate a good representation. Rather than thinking of distance in terms of kilometers, MDS requires that we think of distance in terms of psychological units. The units of psychological distance are derived from the concept of similarity, one of the fundamental concepts of psychological relations (Carroll and Wish, 1974). Two stimuli located in close proximity to each other on a respondent's psychological map are presumed to be perceived more similarly than stimuli located further apart from each other.

Using a measure of similarity to ascertain the dimensions of the respondent's perceptions is predicated on the notion that the characteristics which they used to define similarity can be discerned (Attneave, 1950). Thus, an analysis that uses MDS requires an interpretation of the dimensions that are retained. In the map example, the interpretation of the east-to-west and north-to-south dimensions is rather easy. In psychological research, on the other hand, the interpretation of the dimensions which are discovered may not be as clear-cut. Nevertheless, the aim is "to identify physical or other correlates of these psychological dimensions or to specify their psychological meaning in some way" (Carroll and Wish, 1974, p. 393).

General MDS Procedures

Various straightforward approaches can be used to assess the respondents' perceived similarity among the stimuli. One of the simplest and most commonly used techniques is to pair every stimulus with every other stimulus in the set and to ask the subjects to rate the similarity of the stimuli. Alternative approaches include the presentation of triads of stimulus pairs, various sorting procedures, and magnitude estimation methods. [See Shepard (1972) for a taxonomy of types of data and methods for analysis. Other sources include Coxon (1982), Davison (1983), and Schiffman et al. (1981).] One of the advantages of MDS is that the data-gathering procedure requires subjects to perform a simple task. The issue of whether the data are representative of the respondents' perceptions or of the researcher's conceptions is essentially avoided. By not providing subjects with a narrow set of scales or adjectives, MDS reduces experimenter contamination and is a relatively unconstraining methodology (Schiffman, et al., 1981).

The nature of the relationship between similarity judgments, on the one hand, and the distances between all pairs of stimuli, on the other hand, depends on the assumptions made about the scale properties of the data. In order to perform the nonmetric multidimensional scaling proposed by Shepard (1962a, 1962b) and refined by Kruskal (1964a, 1964b), all that is required of the similarity data is that they be ordinal in nature. It should be noted that the stimuli themselves are not ranked. Rather, what are rank ordered are the pairwise similarity ratings from the most similar pair to the least similar pair. The number of pairs is equal to $[n \times (n-1)]/2$, where n is the number of stimuli. In the map example with 30 cities, there would be 435 pairs, rank ordered from the pair that consisted of the closest of the two cities to the pair that consisted of the two cities that are farthest apart.

Given a rank ordering of the pairwise similarities, what is sought is a monotonic relationship between the similarities and the distances derived from the configuration. A monotonic relationship is described by any curve that follows a rising or a falling pattern, depending upon whether the data are dissimilarities or similarities, respectively. This is a relatively nonrestrictive assumption which is satisfied as long as the rank order of the computed distances parallels the rank order of the similarities which serve as the input data.

While the focus up to now has been on similarity ratings, other measures could be used to assess distances. Therefore, the term proximity, which encompasses both similarities and dissimilarities, as well as conditional probabilities, indices of profile similarity, and the like, will be used in the discussion of the general case which follows.

Classical MDS Procedures

The first step in a typical nonmetric MDS analysis, also called classical MDS, is to obtain proximities for all pairs of stimuli. A stimulus-by-stimulus symmetric data matrix can be constructed with the rows and the columns of the matrix referring to the same stimuli. Because the matrix is square and symmetric, the values in the upper right hand triangle are a mirror image of the values in the lower left hand triangle.

Because it is usually not known in advance how many dimensions underlie the data set, solutions are typically sought in several dimensions. For each r-dimensional solution (e.g., in the map example $r = 2$, and the solution is two-dimensional), there is an initial or starting configuration of the proximity values. While the various MDS computer programs approach the calculation of this starting configuration differently, for our purposes it is convenient to think of it as a random starting configuration. In two-dimensional space, we could use the analogy of throwing darts at a target. Each stimulus could be represented by a different colored dart and the darts thrown onto the target at random.

Given the starting configuration, the interpoint distances between all pairs of stimuli can be calculated. For each pair of stimuli, a matrix of target values, called disparities or fitted distances, is also constructed. How these disparities are derived depends on the particular type of MDS model adopted. Within a classical nonmetric framework, these values are derived through the application of monotone transformations (i.e., movements up and down a linear scale) which need only maintain the rank order of the proximities. The discrepancies between these fitted distances and the interpoint distances are then used to assess the goodness-of-fit of the MDS solution. Various goodness-of-fit measures exist, of which the most common is *stress* (Kruskal, 1964a).

Stress is perhaps more appropriately conceived as a badness-of-fit measure, in that the larger the value of the index the poorer the solution. The goal of MDS, therefore, is to minimize stress. The computer program used for the examples in this chapter computes an index called *s-stress* similar to stress, but which is defined in terms of squared distances and disparities. ALSCAL also reports a measure called *RSQ*. *RSQ* is the proportion of the variance in the disparities which is accounted for by their corresponding distances.

The process of searching for a solution with a minimum level of stress for a given dimensionality is iterative. Following the calculation of stress based on the initial configuration, the configuration is altered by moving the stimuli according to some predefined criterion in an attempt to improve the fit of the model to the data. The distances are recalculated, a new set of disparities is constructed, and stress is reevaluated. The iterative procedure terminates when there is no further improvement in the fit of the model (i.e., reduction in stress).

Confronted with solutions is several dimensions, the user must now make a choice. Determination of the most reasonable dimensionality of the solution in MDS from the various *r*-dimensional solutions is arrived at not only on the basis of statistical considerations but also on the basis of substantive interpretability of the dimensions. Strict adherence to statistical goodness-of-fit measure may result in an uninterpretable structure. The decision as to the number of dimensions to retain is usually made by trying to achieve a balance between "parsimony, stability, and visualizability, on the one hand, and overall goodness-of-fit to the data on the other" (Shepard, 1972, p. 9).

A Classical MDS Example

Schmelkin (1982) designed a study of perceptions of disabilities which used a stimulus set consisting of 13 disability concepts: behavior disorder, brain injury, communication disorder, emotional disturbance, exceptionality, health impairment, learning disability, mental retardation, multiple handicaps, normal, physical disability, slow learning, and social maladjustment. Respondents were asked to rate the similarity of each of the 78 pairs of the 13 concepts on a 9-point scale, where 1 indicated "Not at all similar," and 9 indicated "Extremely similar." The order

Table 4.1

Input Data Matrix for MDS Example 1

4.55											
5.00	5.40										
7.05	4.70	4.90									
4.45	5.25	4.40	4.75								
3.05	4.95	3.35	4.35	3.55							
4.45	6.20	6.00	4.85	5.45	3.45						
4.15	5.65	5.55	3.95	5.95	3.80	4.85					
3.40	4.90	3.85	4.25	5.25	5.85	3.80	3.70				
2.20	2.30	3.10	2.60	3.15	2.60	3.10	1.70	2.20			
2.95	4.55	3.10	3.20	5.20	6.75	3.80	2.80	5.55	2.85		
3.85	6.25	5.40	4.10	4.45	3.05	6.45	5.65	4.85	3.15	2.70	
7.20	4.40	4.90	6.55	3.70	3.30	4.30	4.35	4.05	2.75	3.75	4.25

of the presentation of the paired concepts followed the procedure developed by Ross (1934) to maintain the greatest possible space between pairs and to avoid regular repetitions. Subjects were instructed to use their own frame of reference for similarity. The responses of 20 subjects were averaged, yielding a matrix of mean similarities which is presented in Table 4.1.

The s-stress, stress, and *RSQ* values for four separate dimensional solutions are presented in Table 4.2. All three indices reflect an improvement in goodness-of-fit from the one-dimensional to the two-dimensional solution. There is no appreciable improvement, however, beyond the three-dimensional solution. It is clear that on the basis of these indices a one-dimensional solution does not provide as adequate a representation as would a solution of higher dimensionality. In other

Table 4.2

Selected Results of MDS Example 1

No. of Dimensions	S-Stress	Stress	RSQ
1	.279	.428	.618
2	.158	.187	.863
3	.123	.096	.937
4	.091	.081	.940

words, a simple linear rank ordering would obscure the fact that a complex representation is more appropriate. An examination of the two-dimensional, three-dimensional, and four-dimensional solutions (see Schmelkin, 1982) revealed that the three-dimensional solution was the most interpretable.

The coordinates for the 13 stimuli on the three dimensions were then used to construct plots for interpretation. The plot of Dimension 1 versus Dimension 2 (one of three pairwise plots from the three-dimensional solution) is presented in Figure 4.1, with abbreviations used to indicate the location of each concept. The dashed lines superimposed on the plot and labeled Dimension 1' and Dimension 2' indicate the position of the axes following rotation to increase the interpretability of the dimensions.

Dimension 1' is anchored at one end by the concepts most often associated with physical impairment (i.e., health impairment, physical disability, multiple handicaps). At the other extreme of this dimension is the concept normal. Disabilities that do not obviously convey physical impairments are situated closest to the concept normal. Therefore, this dimension was named Physical Impairments (vs. their absence). The concept normal has an extreme projection on one end of Dimension 2', while mental retardation serves as an anchor on the other side. This dimension was, therefore, called Cognitive Impairments (vs. their absence). Note the close proximity to mental retardation of disabilities more often associated with educational problems.

Other techniques are sometimes used as an aid to the interpretation of the

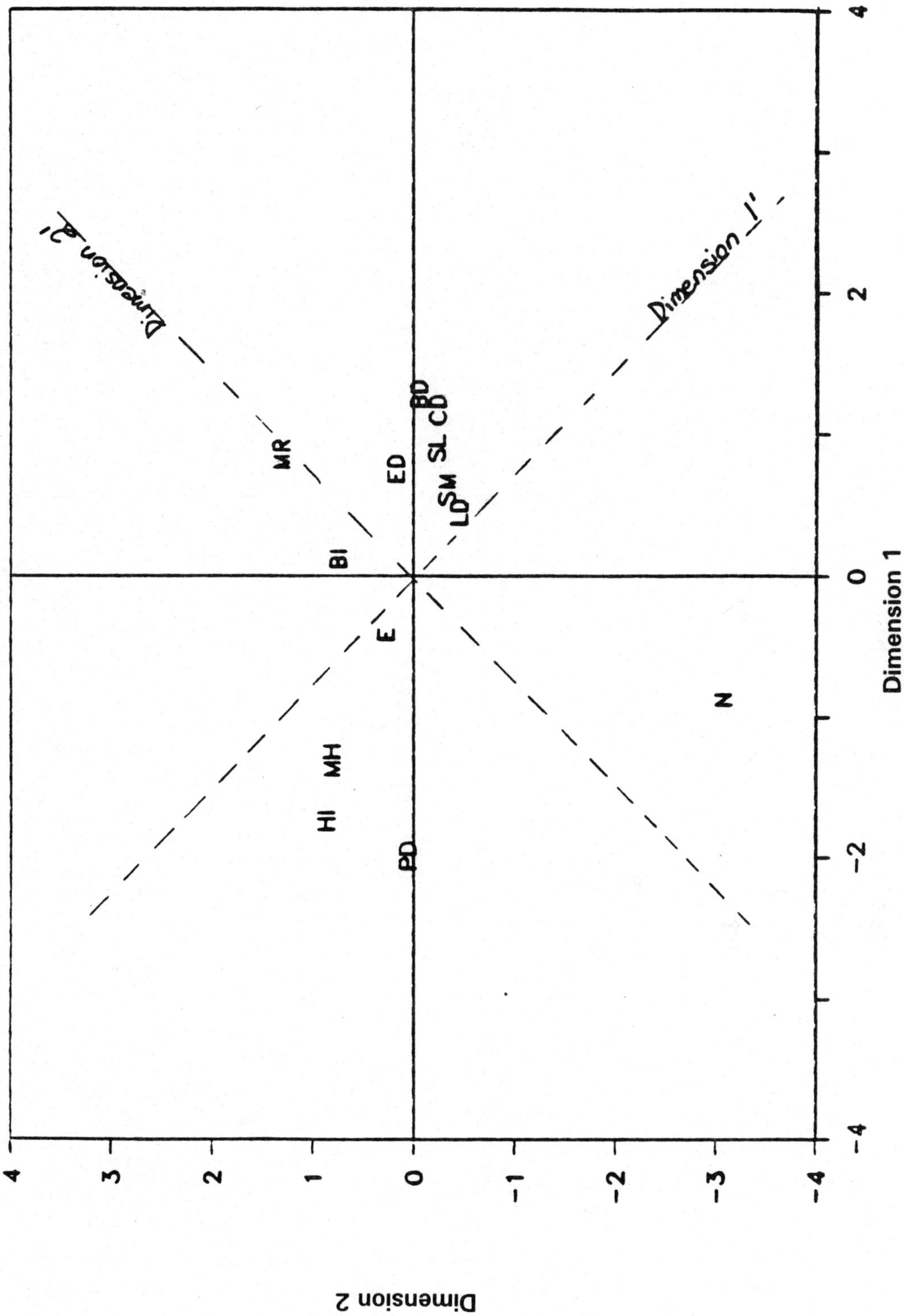

Figure 4.1. Plot of Dimension 1 vs. Dimension 2 from the three-dimensional MDS solution of Example 1.

plots, in order to verify or objectify the process of naming the dimensions. One such approach relates the MDS dimensions to various unidimensional rating scales (usually given to another group of respondents) using a multiple regression analysis (i.e., by regressing the latter data on the former). [See Kruskal and Wish (1978) and Schmelkin (1985) for examples of this procedure.] In addition, the results of cluster analysis of the data are often used to aid in the interpretation of the MDS plots.

Individual Differences MDS

The discussion of classical MDS was limited to an analysis of a single data matrix. Such a model is typically used to uncover the structure underlying responses to a stimulus set obtained from a group of respondents with no attention focused on the particular individuals in the group. (It could, alternatively, have focused on a particular individual by using as the single input matrix that individual's data.) It is possible, however, that the obtained structure of the group space is not equally applicable to the various individuals that compose the group. Different group members may pay different attention to the perceptual dimensions that they share as a group. That is, different individuals attach different importance to different dimensions of the stimuli (Carroll and Wish, 1974).

Several three-way (stimulus by stimulus by subject) models have been proposed to account for individual differences. The most common of these models introduces the notion of subject dimension weights (as proposed by Carroll and Chang, 1970); hence the name *weighted* MDS. This model produces a group stimulus space similar in nature to the one produced by classical MDS (with the exception that it is not rotatable), as well as a subject space. The latter space represents the salience or importance of the dimensions for the individuals under study. Thus, the model can accommodate variations within the group. Alternatively, the different matrices could represent different occasions or conditions, rather than individuals. The weights would then reflect the relative importance of the dimensions on the various occasions or under the various conditions.

An Individual Differences MDS Example

Recall that Example 1 described a data set derived from the subjects' perceptions of 13 stimuli. The responses of the 20 subjects that provided pairwise similarity ratings were averaged and the resultant matrix of means was analyzed. Rather than analyzing this matrix of means, an individual differences scaling analysis begins with the 20 separate data matrices (i.e., one for each subject). The output that is produced by an individual difference scaling includes the stress and *RSQ* values for each matrix, as well as individual weights for each subject on each of the dimensions of the solution, and plots of the subject space.

The data for Example 1 were reanalyzed using and individual differences MDS procedure. Similar to the outcome of the analysis of the data in Example 1,

Table 4.3

Representative Subject Information for

6 of the 20 Subjects for MDS Example 2

			Dimension		
Subject	RSQ	Weirdness	1	2	3
A	.725	.279	.384	.656	.384
B	.807	.282	.356	.590	.576
H	.798	.044	.594	.483	.460
K	.331	.173	.436	.270	.259
M	.661	.504	.746	.222	.237
T	.577	.281	.316	.463	.512
	Overall Importance of Each Dimension		.265	.204	.158

a three-dimensional solution was retained as the most appropriate weighted solution. Table 4.3 presents selected results for six of the 20 subjects in the original study. An inspection of this information shows that there is considerable variability within the group in the individual perceptual spaces.

While the average of the *RSQ* values for the 20 subject matrices was .627, the individual *RSQs* ranged from a low of .331 to a high of .801. This reflects the fact that the three-dimensional solution provides a better fit for some subjects than it does for others. The overall importance of each dimension to the group (the average of the squared weights in each column) indicates that the first dimension is the most important for the group of subjects, followed by the second and then the third dimensions.

An examination of the individual subject weights reveals the existence of different patterns of salience for these six subjects. For example, the most important

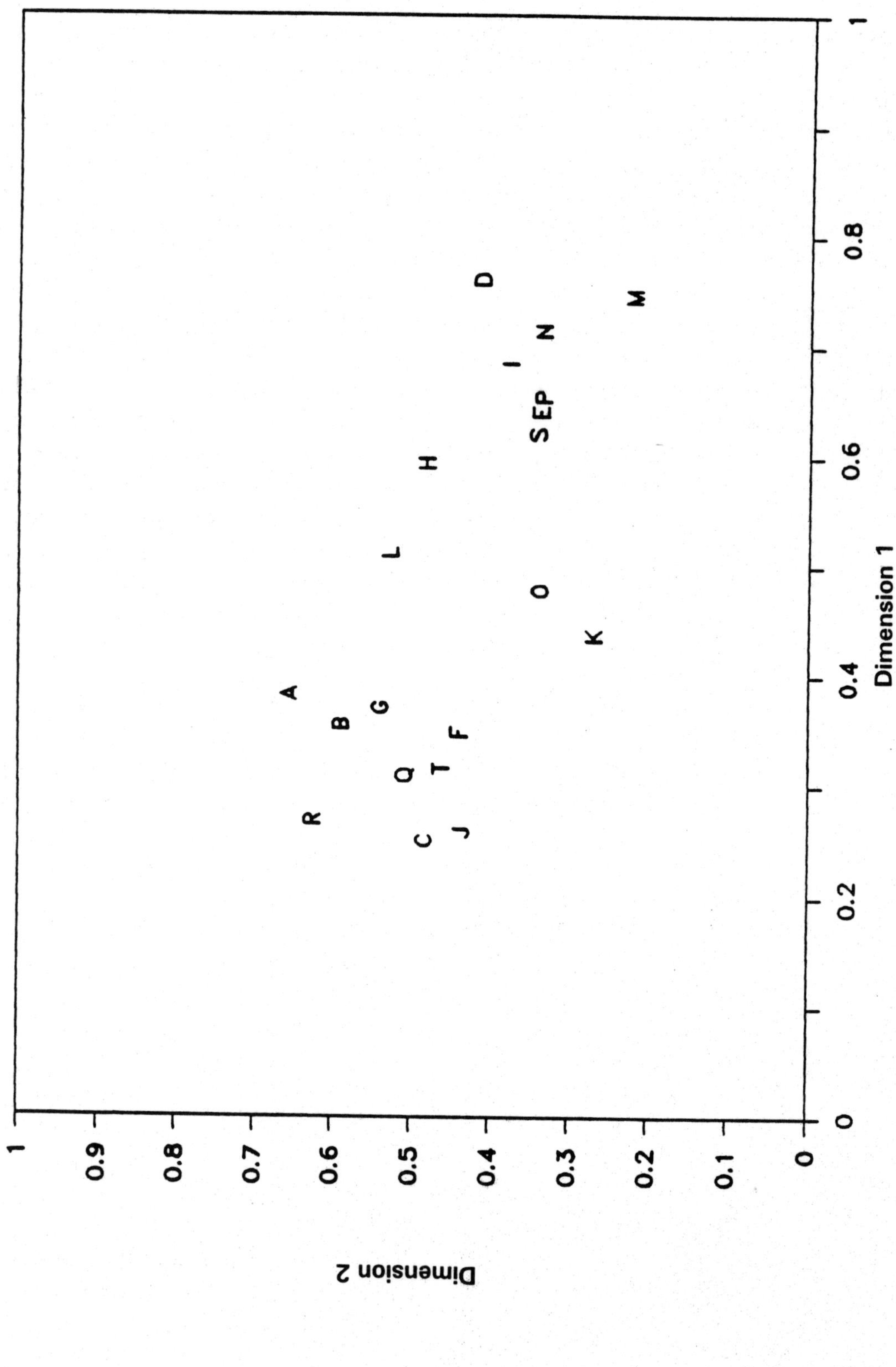

Figure 4.2. Plot of subject weights for Dimension 1 vs. Dimension 2 for the three-dimensional MDS solution of Example 2.

dimension for subject A is the second dimension, with dimensions 1 and 3 being weighted approximately the same but less than dimension 2. Subject M, on the other hand, places primary importance on the first dimension, with dimension 2 and 3 carrying relatively little weight. A different pattern exists for subject T who weights the third dimension the highest, followed by the second and then the first dimensions. The column labeled *weirdness* indicates the extent to which the subject weights for individuals are proportional to the average weights for the group. Subjects whose weights are proportional to the average weights have a weirdness value near 0 (e.g., subject H), while subjects who have one large weight and several low weights have a weirdness value near 1. Of these six individuals, subject M's data has the highest weirdness value.

The individual perceptual saliences can be applied to the group stimulus space in order to produce a personal space for each respondent. This is accomplished by differentially stretching or shrinking the dimensions of the group space according to each individual's pattern of weights. Finally, one can examine the plots of the subject weights to discern if there are any readily identifiable clusters of subgroups who have similar patterns of weights. Figure 4.2 presents an example of such a plot. Tests of subgroup differences could also be applied (see Schiffman, et al., 1981).

ISSUES AND CONCERNS IN THE USE OF MDS

MDS techniques are potentially powerful methods for the study of perceptions and attitudes. In applying MDS, however, users will need to address various issues and concerns which have not been elaborated upon in this introductory chapter.

Subject Selection

The number of subjects and the way they are selected need to be considered. MDS methods are generally powerful and do not require a very large sample size as compared to other multivariate techniques such as factor analysis. The choice of the number of subjects is related to the MDS approach selected (e.g., classical or weighted MDS), the number of anticipated dimensions, and other concerns. As an example, Davison (1983) recommends that when proximities are averaged over the judgments of several people (as in Example 1), the number of judgments averaged for each pair should be at least $(40^*r)/(n-1)$, where r is the number of anticipated dimensions, and n is the number of stimuli.

Questions related to the characteristics of the subjects and how they are selected need to be raised and addressed as well. For example, are the subjects familiar enough with the stimuli? Are they selected in such a manner that their responses are representative of the group to which the researcher would like to make inferences?

Data-Related Questions

Various decisions must be made with regard to the data. While MDS methods are less constraining than other scaling procedures, solutions are constrained by the particular choice and number of stimuli in the set. A narrower set would, of necessity, produce a different structure than would a stimulus set that is more representative of the universe of stimuli under study. This concern is also related to particular questions that arise when large data sets are used. Because the elicitation of all pairwise similarity ratings would be too demanding a task due to the large number of such ratings required, various methods for handling large data sets have been described (Golledge and Raynor, 1982).

The form and type of stimulus presentation also need to be considered (e.g., pairwise rating, sorting, preference data), as well as the order of presentation of the stimuli. Strategies for dealing with incomplete designs and missing data need to be mastered as well (MacCallum, 1979; Spence, 1982). Once the data are collected, they may require preprocessing (e.g., derived measures of proximities may need to be calculated). Finally, the shape of the input data matrix (i.e., whether it is square or rectangular, symmetric or asymmetric), and whether or not there is more than one matrix, are also important questions whose answers influence the MDS model used.

Model and Computational Concerns

Assumptions about the data will determine, in part, whether the scaling should be nonmetric or metric, and the appropriate form of the metric (e.g., Euclidean distance, city block). Additionally, the available computer programs differ in the way they approach various MDS models. Computational problems such as the lack of convergence and degenerate solutions may also arise and require resolution.

Interpretation Concerns

Various ways of interpreting the obtained dimensional solutions are possible, and aids in this activity need to be explored. Whether, and how best, to rotate the primary axes must also be decided by the researcher during the interpretation phase of the investigation.

Group Comparisons

Differences among groups can be investigated using diverse approaches. For example, the data for all individuals (from all groups) could be entered into an individual differences analysis, and differences among subject weights for the groups assessed. Alternatively, the matrices of means from the groups could serve as input data into a pseudo-individual differences analysis. Another approach would be to compare the solutions arising from separate analyses.

Confirmatory MDS

Methods have been advanced to test explicit assumptions and constraints relating to the data and the resulting solutions (e.g., Borg and Lingoes, 1980; Ramsay, 1977). Using these methods, the MDS solution which a researcher selects can be verified and confirmed in subsequent investigations. Such a process can contribute significantly to theory-building in attitudes to disability research.

SOME SUGGESTED USES OF MDS IN ATTITUDES TO DISABILITY RESEARCH

As stated at the outset of this chapter, applications of MDS to disability research are still in their infancy. Due to the relatively unconstraining assumptions and methods of response elicitation required, these methods may be particularly useful for investigating questions in the complex areas of attitudes, perceptions, behaviors, and interactions among individuals with and without disabilities.

To date, many of the applications have been within the educational arena, focusing on teachers and administrators in both regular and special education settings. The perceptions and attitudes of other groups need to be investigated as well. For example, due to the relative simplicity of the response mode required for MDS techniques, their use with children appears particularly promising. The important aspects underlying children's attitudes and perceptions could be assessed. Moreover, developmental studies, both cross-sectionally and longitudinally, can address questions related to the origins of perceptions and attitudes, how they develop, and what type of interactions may affect them.

A great deal of research using sociometric methods has explored the social status of children with disabilities (see Gottlieb, 1975). MDS techniques provide an unconstraining alternative approach to conventional sociometric methods for studying group structure. In addition, they can be used to predict sociometric choices from perceived group structures (Davison and Jones, 1976).

Studies of communication patterns between disabled and nondisabled people also lend themselves to analysis with MDS (Wish, 1975, 1976; Wish, D'Andrade, and Goodnow, 1980). The results of these approaches may reveal the nature of interactions among individuals with and without disabilites and focus on situational and other determinants of these communications.

SUMMARY AND PRELUDE

This chapter has focused on a methodology that shows promise for studying perceptions of and attitudes toward disabilities and people with disabilities. Limitations of traditional direct methods of measuring attitudes were reviewed, focusing primarily on the constraints of the unidimensional assumptions and of the researcher's a priori conceptions of the important dimensions. As an alternative, an overview of nonmetric multidimensional scaling was presented, augmented by two examples illustrating the methodology and results. Various considerations relevant to MDS studies were then summarized and suggestions for the use of MDS in attitudes to disability research were presented.

A significant criticism, however, can be leveled against both the traditional measurement methods discussed in Chapter 3, and the multidimensional scaling methods discussed in this chapter. Despite the methods used to analyze the data, the data themselves may not be true measures of the attitude construct under study. That is, the respondents may be aware of, and react to, some aspect of the measurement process itself so that the data are contaminated by extraneous and irrelevant factors. In response to this criticism, indirect measurement methods have been developed. We will turn our attention to these methods, and illustrate their value, in Chapter 5.

Chapter 5

INDIRECT METHODS OF ATTITUDE MEASUREMENT

THE DIRECT methods of measuring attitudes toward disabled people considered in Chapters 3 and 4 are all subject to several threats to the validity of the resultant measurements, despite efforts to control invalidation sources, such as assuring anonymity, separating experimental and measurement sessions, varying the context of the item presentation, and using a forced-choice response format (Cook and Selltiz, 1964). To avoid these threats, measurement experts have suggested the creation or selection of an attitude measurement method which is not plagued by attitude-distorting influences (Campbell, 1950; Webb, Campbell, Schwartz, and Sechrest, 1966). Taken together, these methods are referred to as indirect measurement methods.

This chapter will begin by discussing three classes of threats to the validity of research conclusions based on direct measurement methods. This will be followed by an examination of four indirect methods of attitude measurement: projective techniques, disguised procedures, behavioral observations, and physiological reaction methods.

VALIDITY THREATS OF DIRECT METHODS

The plausible threats to the validity of direct measurement methods may be classified into three groups: (a) sensitizing the respondent to an attitudinal domain of which he or she was previously unaware, (b) eliciting a reactive response from the participant by neglecting to consider the transparency of the purpose of the measurement method used, and (c) tapping irrelevant personality characteristics, such as response styles and social desirability tendencies.

Respondent Sensitization

Direct methods of measuring attitudes may sensitize respondents to a particular attitude domain of which they were previously unaware or had, at best, only a nebulous conception. In essence, the mere process of responding to one of these direct measures may transform a non-existent attitude to an existing one, or create a transient attitude in the respondent which the researcher, quite erroneously, interprets as meaningful in some way.

For example, the researcher may construct a scale to measure attitudes toward people with a relatively rare disorder, such as meningomyelocele (a hernial protrusion of the meninges through a defect in the vertebral column), neurofibromatosis (the "elephant man's" disease), or any other uncommon physical or psychiatric impairment. The researcher proceeds to construct a set of well-defined and domain-representative items which appear to meet the requirements for a valid and reliable attitude scale. The researcher then administers this scale to a group of naive or uninformed respondents, who, on the whole, have no knowledge of the attitude referent and consequently have no particular disposition toward individuals who have this type of disorder. When the data are finally gathered and analyzed, the researcher may present in his or her report an elaborate, but erroneous, description of the attitudes of lay people toward people with that particular disorder. Gottlieb and Siperstein (1976) discussed a related phenomenon in their study of the effects of attitude referent specificity on attitudes toward people who are mentally retarded.

Reactivity

A second threat to the validity of direct attitude measurement concerns the subject's realization that his or her attitudes, opinions, or values are being measured. This realization, stemming from the apparentness of the measuring instrument's purpose or the transparency of its implications (Cook and Selltiz, 1964), may create a discrepancy between the respondents' privately-held attitudes and their overtly-admitted attitudes. In other words, by becoming aware that they are being assessed, the respondents may modify or distort their privately-held attitudes. Responses such as these, that are partially determined by the subject's awareness that his or her attitudes are being evaluated, are referred to as reactive responses (Campbell and Stanley, 1966; Dawes, 1984).

Triandis (1971) discussed four mechanisms that may underlie the respondent's reactive responses. First, he or she may attempt to please the experimenter in his or her responses. Second, the respondent may try to give a good impression of himself or herself. Third, he or she may seek to sabotage the study by purposefully disclosing inaccurate attitudes. Finally, the respondent may attempt to appear as an open-minded, sophisticated, or enlightened person by second guessing how such people would respond to the instrument. The first two mechanisms (pleasing the experimenter, and giving a good impression of one's self) are together referred to as the social desirability tendency of respondents, and will be discussed later in this section.

To illustrate, consider a study designed to measure attitudes toward people with a spinal-cord injury. If a subject perceives that he or she is in a testing situation, then he or she may alter his or her true feelings regarding this referent group. The respondent's awareness may arise from an inadvertent use of a wheelchair-bound experimenter, or the subject may have prior knowledge of the researcher's interest or of the measuring scale, or may have been informed about the researcher's purpose from a friend who previously participated in the study. An attempt, therefore, to interpret the results yielded by using that particular scale under those particular circumstances could lead to erroneous conclusions about the respondent's attitudes.

Response Styles

The final source of potential invalidity of direct measurement methods is the confounding of an unrelated personality characteristic with the intended attitudinal domain. That is, certain factors may exert distorting influences on the respondent's professed attitudes. Within the fields of psychometrics and measurement theory, the term response style and response set have been used somewhat interchangeably to refer to this collection of factors. Rorer (1965) argued, and we agree, that the two terms—style and set—are not synonymous and should be distinguished.

> When used within the psychometric area in a manner consistent with usage in other areas, the term "set" connotes a conscious or unconscious desire on the part of the respondent to answer in such a way as to produce a certain picture of himself. In this traditional usage, an individual may have a set to dissimulate, to malinger, to appear aggressive, to fake good, to get a job, etc. To say that a respondent has a set in this sense is akin to saying that he is motivated. (p. 133)
>
> Style, in the sense in which it is used here, refers to the tendency to select some response category a disproportionate amount of the time independently of the item content. For this reason styles have sometimes been termed "contentless." Styles include yeasaying, naysaying, or any preference for a certain response category. (p. 134)
>
> The term "bias" will . . . usually be synonymous with style. (p. 134)

The respondent may demonstrate an acquiescence response style (Couch and Keniston, 1960) in which all, or almost all, the items are answered in the affirmative (e.g., "Agree," "Yes," or "True"). This group of respondents is referred to as the "Yeasayers." Similarly, respondents may answer all, or almost all, the items in the negative (e.g., "Disagree," "No," or "False"). This group of respondents is termed the "Naysayers."

Other types of often-detected response styles include the respondent who endorses only those statements on the attitude scale which he or she believes to represent the socially appropriate or culturally sanctioned response. This tendency has been referred to as a social desirability response style (Edwards, 1957b). Finally, the respondent may select response alternatives according to their extremeness. In so doing, a respondent may choose only (or never) the most extreme alternative or may prefer only moderate alternatives (i.e., the central positions on an attitude scale's response continuum). This tendency has been referred to as an extreme position response style (Nunnally, 1978). If the researcher cannot demonstrate that the measurement method is independent of these confounding variables, then the resultant measurements will not be valid representations of the respondents' true attitudes toward the referent.

INDIRECT METHODS

Projective Techniques

The rationale underlying all projective techniques is that the presentation of unstructured or ambiguous stimuli or tasks will elicit responses or feelings of which the individual may be unaware. Hence, when a respondent is confronted with a task or set of stimuli (e.g., inkblots, characters, scenes, or incomplete sentence stems) of which he or she has only provided with dim clues regarding their nature, his or her psychological guards will be lowered. This, in turn, may lead to the externalization of otherwise well-hidden values, beliefs, attitudes, feelings, needs, wishes, desires, impulses, and motives (the person's private or inner world). More specifically, because the probability of conscious response distortion is considerably lessened, the respondent is expected to project his or her true attitudes onto the attitude measurement task. This projection can then be interpreted or scored by a clinically trained professional.

Projective techniques can be classified by the type of task stimuli presented or, alternatively, by the type of response which is elicited (Lindzey, 1959). The five major projective procedures often cited are:

Association Techniques, which require the subject to respond with the first thing that comes to mind at the presentation of a stimulus. Included here are techniques such as the Rorschach (1942) inkblot test, the Holtzman (1968) inkblot technique, and a variety of word-association methods, such as those of Jung (1910), Kent and Rosanoff (1910), and Rapaport, Gill, and Schafer (1946).

Construction Techniques, where the focus is on the output produced by the subject. Here, the respondent is required to construct a story or a picture. Examples include the Thematic Apperception Test (TAT; Murray, 1938), Rosenzweig's (1950) Picture-Frustration Study, the Draw-a-Person Test (Machover, 1949), and the House-Tree-Person Test (Buck, 1948), to name just a few.

Completion Techniques, in which the subject is supplied with an incomplete stimulus (e.g., a sentence or story), and is required to complete it as he or she wishes. These are perhaps the least disguised (most obvious in their intent) of the projective techniques. Examples of these techniques include Rotter's Incomplete Sentences Blank (Rotter and Rafferty, 1950), and several story and discussion completion tasks (e.g., Loevinger, Wessler, and Redmore, 1970).

Choice or Ordering Techniques, which require the subject to choose from among several alternative items (e.g., pictures, photographs, colors, or designs) the ones which appear most relevant, correct, or otherwise personally gratifying. Included here are the Szondi Test (Deri, 1949), the Color Pyramid Test (Schaie, 1963), the Luscher (1969) Color Test, and the Lustig (1965) Color Vector Test.

Expressive Techniques, similar to construction techniques, which require the subject to form a product out of raw material. The emphasis, however, is on the manner in which the respondent does this or the process that he or she uses. In doing so, the subject may manipulate or interact with one of a variety of materials, including toys (e.g., the World Test; Lowenfeld, 1939), pencils, crayons, paints, dolls, and even other people (e.g., role-play or psychodrama techniques).

While projective techniques have been used extensively for the investigation of psychological adjustment to a variety of physically disabling conditions (e.g., Plummer, 1976; Shontz, 1971), they have been used infrequently for the measurement of attitudes toward disabled people. One of the earliest efforts to use a projective procedure in measuring attitudes toward disabled individuals was reported by J.R. Thurston (1959). He developed a semi-projective procedure, the Thurston Sentence Completion Form, consisting of 45 incomplete sentences presumably tapping the attitudes and emotional reactions of the parents of handicapped children in seven general areas (e.g., the child's satisfaction and discomfitures, the treatment setting and its staff, and the parents' hopes and expectations). Parents' responses (which were usually accepted at their face value) were transcribed onto a specifically-designed interpretation sheet for scoring.

Ford, Liske, and Ort (1962) also used a sentence completion technique in their study of the attitudes held by medical personnel toward people with chronic illnesses. Clinical faculty members and medical students were given a form of 30 items referring to both personal feelings toward patients having chronic illnesses and general aspects of medical care. The responses of the participants were scored on orientation tendencies (favorableness/approach vs. unfavorableness/avoidance), as well as comprehensiveness indices (breadth and depth of thought). Although a variety of favorable feelings were expressed by the medical staff toward diagnosis and treatment, situations associated with treatment of severely physically disabled and hopelessly ill patients elicited unfavorable feelings and avoidance tendencies.

To investigate the attitudes of non-disabled elementary school children toward their physically disabled peers, Billings (1963) used two specifically-adapted projective techniques ("Tell me a story," and "Complete this sentence"). The story telling technique required the respondent to write a story about two pictured seven-year-old girls, one of whom was portrayed as a "little crippled girl," and the other as able-bodied. The differences in narrative between the two stories were used as a measure of the respondent's attitudes toward disabled youngsters. The sentence completion technique used ten sentences of which three related to disabled individuals. Responses were assessed by judges as to their social qualities (i.e., on a worthy-to-devalued scale). The overall findings of the study indicated that: (a) the attitudes of able-bodied children toward children with disabilities were significantly more negative than their attitudes toward able-bodied children, and (b) the attitudes of able-bodied children toward disabled children became more negative as the able-bodied children became older.

Moed, Wright, Feshbach, and Sandry (1963) developed a projective procedure entitled the Children's Seashore House Picture Story Test to investigate children's psychological reactions to physical disability. The sample consisted of 100 inpatient children hospitalized for a physical disability, a control group of 100 non-disabled school children, and a group of 50 formerly hospitalized children. The subjects were required to make up a story about each of 19 pictures presented to them. The stories were scored on a variety of categories, including recognition of disability, sympathy, self-pity, attitude toward disability, and need for achievement. The inpatient children were found to differ from the control children on most categories. Former child patients, for the most part, responded in ways similar to the controls. An unexpected finding was the high incidence of negative attitudes toward disability expressed by the former patients. The authors speculated that the former patients, seeking identification with normal and able-bodied children, tended to overcompensate by rejecting the disabled group to which they previously belonged.

A final illustration is the study reported by Noonan, Barry, and Davis (1970) who investigated personality correlates of negative attitudes toward people with visible disabilities (e.g., amputations, disfigurements). The authors used as their criterion measures the ATDP Scale-Form A (see Chapter 9) and the Granofsky (1956) Picture Test (GPT), a TAT-like projective technique in which visibly disabled people are portrayed in 12 social interaction scenes. Scoring of the responses to the GPT pictures was based on a seven-point scale, ranging from complete rejection to complete acceptance of the disabled individual portrayed. The authors found a significant correlation between the ATDP-A and the GPT measures in a sample of female college students. Furthermore, acceptance of the disabled person on the GPT was significantly negatively related to authoritarianism and cultural conformity, and significantly positively related to body satisfaction.

Disguised Procedures

In disguised procedures, the respondent is not aware of, or unclear about, the real purpose of the investigation, or the respondent may be told that the purpose of the investigation is other than what it actually is (sometimes referred to as duping), or he or she may be led to believe that no control can be exerted over one's responses (Dawes and Smith, 1985). These disguised procedures differ from the projective techniques of the previous section in several respects. First, there is an inherent structure to the task performed by the respondent. Second, a deliberate attempt is made to direct the respondent's attention away from the attitude for which a measurement is being sought. Finally, whereas projective techniques assume the operation of certain psychodynamic (mainly ego defensive) processes as the basis for the respondent's reaction, the disguised procedures make no such claim.

In applying disguised procedures to the measurement of attitudes, the researcher may present the respondent with a specific task which has no clear purpose. For example, the respondent may be asked to sort a random sample of photographs of people into two (or more) groups, those who are liberals and those who are conservatives. Some of these photos may be of disabled people involved in various activities. Similarly, the researcher may direct the respondent to sort the photographs according to specific nationalities, religious groups, or other characteristics.

A task lacking a clear criterion of success may involve asking respondents to classify individuals in terms of their group membership without stating what characteristic defines the groups (Cook and Selltiz, 1964). For example, the participant is provided with a set of photographs of individuals differing in sex, age, race, disability, and other visible recognizable demographic characteristics, and merely asked to select those photographs which "belong together." Respondents may classify the photographs into groups based on a number of privately held perceptions, thus reflecting the salience of each characteristic in their attitude structure. For example, if two groups are created, one containing only nondisabled people and the other containing all, or mostly, disabled people, it may be inferred that disability, or lack thereof, is the most salient characteristic for that particular respondent.

Other disguised techniques present the respondent with a clear criterion for success but hide the true purpose of the investigation. For example, the respondent may be asked to select an answer from among three (or more) provided to a set of questions presented as a test of knowledge or skill regarding some domain. In fact, all of the answers are wrong, but they are written in such a way as to covertly reflect varying degrees of favorableness or unfavorableness to the attitude referent. These so-called error-choice tests (see Table 5.1) may include real items in order to disguise the true purpose of the investigation.

In a memory distortion procedure, the respondent is first shown a picture or is asked to read a vignette, and then asked to recall specific details or answer questions, some of which concern events which were not originally presented. For example, a picture taken of a classroom of children during free play may be shown to the respondent for a brief time interval, and the question may then be asked "What was the child in the wheelchair doing?" where no such child was included in the picture. Similarly, the respondent may be given a story to read about a day's events in a sheltered workshop. At the completion of this task he or she may be

Table 5.1

Example of Two Items from an Error-Choice Test To Measure Attitudes Toward Eugenic Sterilization of Mentally Retarded People

---

1. In 1986, how many millions of dollars were spent in the United States to provide public services (such as day care, food stamps, and rent subsidy) to the offspring of mentally retarded parents?

   a. $.5 million

   b. $50 million

   c. $175 million

2. What is the average number of children who are born to unmarried mentally retarded women in the United States?

   a. less than 1 child

   b. 1.5 children

   c. 4.0 children

---

asked "What were the activities that the mentally retarded person successfully completed?"

Although the disguised procedures illustrated in this section appear to hold promise for research on attitudes toward disabled people, no studies using them could be located in the existing research literature. A form of measurement duplicity which has been used to study attitudes toward disabled people is the bogus pipeline procedure (Jones and Sigall, 1971).

In this procedure, the subject is positioned in front of an ominous looking machine (usually a large electronic device), and is led to believe that he or she is being connected to it. The respondent is told that the machine measures the direction and intensity of one's emotional response toward a particular referent through the analysis of involuntary muscle movements that accompany the responses he or she gives to questions presented by the experimenter. The hypothesis underlying the bogus pipeline procedure is that the respondents' answers in the experimental setting will be more indicative of their true feelings, thereby giving a more accurate self-report of their attitudes in these deceptive circumstances.

Carver, Glass, and Katz (1978) used the bogus pipeline procedure to investigate the feelings of subjects toward handicapped interviewees. Undergraduate female students participating in the study rated interviewees (a nonstigmatized person, a Black male, and a handicapped person) on a series of 11 descriptive dimensions. Contrary to the authors' expectations, no differences emerged between the subjects' ratings of the handicapped person under the control and the bogus conditions. However, overall evaluations, under both conditions, were significantly more positive toward the handicapped person than toward the nonstigmatized interviewee.

Another indirect approach seeking to camouflage the real purpose of a study is to divert the participants' attention through the presentation of a fictitious cover story, directions, or instructions. Comer and Piliavin (1975) asked subjects (both physically disabled and non-disabled) to give their first impressions of two men—one disabled and one able-bodied—whose photographs they were provided. The introductory paragraphs (the cover story) to the questionnaire concentrated on techniques used by television commercial advertisers to form attitudes and sell their products, thus distracting the participants' from what was actually being measured. To further disguise the study's intentions, the subjects were asked to rate a photograph of an able-bodied Black man. Most interesting was the finding that recently disabled people demonstrated a lowering of their previously-held positive attitudes toward disabled people, while also lowering their attitudes toward physically normal people. Finally, people who had been disabled for a longer period of time demonstrated less favorable attitudes toward other disabled people, but at the same time manifested improved attitudes toward physically normal people.

Behavioral Observations

The concept of behavioral disposition is an integral part of all definitions of attitude. This is so because attitudes cannot be measured directly, but must be inferred from a variety of verbal and nonverbal behaviors which the respondent is predisposed to display. In other words, the behavior that the respondent displays toward an attitude referent in natural settings is considered to be a direct operationalization of his or her attitude. It may be unequivocally argued, of course, that all of the techniques and procedures discussed in Chapter 3 and 4, and so far in this chapter, are samples of the respondent's behavior. These other direct and indirect measurement techniques, however, are more artificial since they are applied within the standardized conditions of the attitude scale's administration (i.e., removed from one's typical or natural setting).

The behavioral observation methods to be discussed next can be classified into two sets: (a) those in which the respondent voluntarily engages in a specific behavior in a natural setting (e.g., helps a disabled person, or donates money to a charity organization serving a particular disability group), and (b) those in which the respondent is asked to participate in a role playing exercise where he or she is to simulate a real-life situation in a natural setting.

Behavioral Observations in Natural Settings. Several of the studies using behavioral observations to measure attitudes toward disabled people have created innovative research situations in natural settings. Pomazal and Clore (1973), for example, arranged for the experimenter, in the process of jacking up a disabled car on a highway, to wear a white knee brace on the right leg and a white cloth sling on the left arm. Although this dependency-creating manipulation yielded many offers for help from passers-by, the difference in help offered was not significant when compared to a low dependency condition (i.e., when no physical impairment was portrayed). In a related experiment, the authors (Pomazal and Clore, 1973) used a physically disabled hitchhiker with and without a knee brace and arm sling for their high dependency condition. Contrary to expectations, the number of rides offered to an able-bodied hitchhiker was significantly greater than the number of rides offered to the physically impaired hitchhiker.

Samerotte and Harris (1976) had unaware adult shoppers approached by an adult male confederate carrying a stack of envelopes. The confederate either brushed against the shopper, dropping the envelopes (subject-responsible condition) or merely dropped the envelopes approximately one foot from the shopper (subject-not-responsible condition). The confederate assumed three separate roles: a disfiguring disability (an eye patch and an extended facial scar), a non-disfiguring disability (a bandage wrapped around the forearm), and a control condition (neither eye patch and scar, nor bandage around the forearm). The findings supported the authors' hypothesis that people with a mild disability are helped more by others than people with a disfiguring disability, both of whom are helped more than the non-disabled person. Subjects who were led to believe that they were responsible for the confederate's misfortune also helped more than subjects believing in their innocence for the occurrence.

A different field research approach was used by Baker and Reitz (1978) to investigate whether blind people would be assisted more than sighted people. Over 400 adults were randomly chosen from a telephone book by an individual caller who identified himself or herself as either blind or sighted in a situation which elicited either high or low need for assistance. The authors reported that assistance was offered more frequently to the blind caller than to the sighted one in both situations, and more frequently to the caller in the high need condition. Females offered more assistance than males to both the blind and the needy callers. Similarly, Pancer, Adams, Mollard, Solsberg, and Tammen (1979) used a woman who appeared to be crossing an uncontrolled intersection in one of four conditions. She was either disabled (i.e., confined to a wheelchair) or not, and either carried a bag of groceries or not. The disability factor was found to be significant in that fewer cars passed by the disabled woman than the nondisabled woman before one stopped so that she could cross the intersection.

Finally, Willis, Feldman, and Ruble (1977) explored the differential conditions under which children donated money to charities for disabled children and disabled adults. Forty-eight children, recruited through newspaper advertisement, divided into a younger (ages five to six years) and an older group (ages eight to nine years), participated in this study. More generousity, in terms of the actual sums of money donated, was expressed toward disabled children than toward disabled adults. Only slight age differences in the level of participants' generosity were found. Girls donated to charity consistently more than boys did.

Another class of behavioral observations in natural settings is that of interactions among disabled and non-disabled children in school. McCauley, Bruininks, and Kennedy (1976), for example, compared interactive behaviors of hearing impaired children and non-handicapped children in a classroom. A modified version of the Pupil Observation Schedule (Wood, 1972) was used to collect data on positive, negative, verbal, and non-verbal social behaviors directed by both hearing impaired and hearing children toward both teachers and peers. The results showed that hearing impaired children relied to a greater extent on their teachers as a source of rewarding positive and verbal interactions in the classroom. Hearing children, on the other hand, used their peer group as a source of rewarding social interactions.

Bryan and associates (Bryan, 1978; Bryan, Wheeler, Felcan, and Henek, 1976), after monitoring learning disabled children's conversations, concluded that their communicative interactions differed from those of their average achieving peers. The learning disabled child was less likely to be the recipient of considerate communication, and was more likely to emit more competitive and less considerate statements. These results suggested that handicapped children may experience communication difficulties in their interpersonal relationships with other children, resulting in negative evaluations of these children by their peers, and perhaps by their teachers. The results of a study by Dunlop, Stoneman, and Cantrell (1980), who examined the social interactions between handicapped and nonhandicapped children in an integrated preschool classroom, did not confirm Bryan's (1978) conclusion. An observation instrument was specifically developed for the study which contained four major categories of behavior: solitary activity, direct interaction—dominance, direct interaction—cooperation, and adult-child interaction. No differences were observed between the two groups of children across categories of interactions examined.

Behavioral Observations in Simulated Situations. A second class of behavioral observations explores interactions between disabled and non-disabled people in a variety of simulated social and academic settings. The researcher typically creates an experimentally-controlled interaction between participants in an attempt to model real-life interpersonal situations.

Kleck and his associates (Kleck, 1968, 1969; Kleck, Buck, Goller, London, Pfeiffer, and Vukcevic, 1968; Kleck, Ono, and Hastorf, 1966), in a series of innovative experiments, set out to investigate the face-to-face interactions between disabled and non-disabled people in an interview-like situation. In their prototypical research design (Kleck, et al., 1966), undergraduate students were directed into an interviewing room where they were greeted by either a disabled (wheel-chair bound) or an able-bodied confederate. Analyses of these interactions revealed that subjects interacting with the physically disabled confederate terminated the interaction sooner and demonstrated more stereotyped behavior.

In a later study (Kleck, 1968), structured interactions between a physically disabled person (a confederate simulating a left leg amputation necessitating the use of a wheelchair) and an able-bodied person were achieved by having both parties exchange information concerning their attitudes on such topics as participation in sports, academic achievement, and so on. The results showed that the presence of a physical disability had an impact on the behavior of non-disabled high school-aged participants. Subjects interacting with the disabled confederate exhibited more motoric inhibition yet formed more positive impressions of him as measured by an adjective checklist. Similar studies of attitudes inferred from observations of participants' behavior were reported in a study of the interaction of college students with a confederate perceived to have epilepsy (Kleck et al., 1968), and in a study of the interaction of college females with a confederate assuming the role of a left leg amputee confined to a wheelchair (Kleck, 1969). A similar interactional study using confederates simulating a hearing disability (Wilson, 1971) extended this research design to the investigation of attitudes toward individuals who are deaf.

In an insightful study designed to investigate the discrepancy often noted between privately and publicly held attitudes toward disabled people, Snyder, Kleck, Strenta, and Mentzer (1979) theorized that most people desire to avoid contact with physically disabled people, but they are not willing to admit to it. They argued further that if non-disabled people were given the opportunity to avoid the presence of disabled people by choosing on some other and unrelated basis (i.e., given an alternative motive), they would do so. Undergraduate students were directed to enter a room in which two confederates, one wearing a metal leg brace and sitting near metal crutches, and the other playing the role of an able-bodied person, sat on opposite sides of a partition with an empty chair beside them watching different movies on television monitors. The results showed that the subjects avoided the presence of the disabled confederate more often when the decision to do so was made parallel to their decision to choose between the two movies. Such a decision, according to the authors, was based on the wish to avoid the disabled person by camouflaging it as a preference for one movie over the other.

To study the general hypothesis that attitudes toward stigmatized people are highly ambivalent (sympathetic and aversive at the same time), Katz and his associates (Katz, Glass, Lucido, and Farber, 1977; Katz, Katz, and Cohen, 1976) instructed volunteer female subjects to deliver either a mild or loud noise to a female confederate who was either confined to a wheelchair or able-bodied. Subjects were also required to evaluate the confederate's personality before and after administering the noxious stimulus. As anticipated, the greatest amount of post-experimental personality denigration of the target occurred under the wheelchair—loud noise condition. The researchers concluded that causing harm to a disabled person results in guilt feelings which were reduced by lowering the worth of the disabled person.

In a study designed to verify this ambivalence-guilt-response amplification hypothesis, Gibbons, Stephan, Stephenson, and Petty (1980) had undergraduate students work with a disabled confederate on an experimental task and then evaluate the confederate on several personality variables. The authors found that under the condition of high relevance, amplified negative and positive reactions toward the disabled individual did occur. That is to say, subjects evaluated the disabled confederate more negatively under failure conditions and more positively under success conditions.

In a series of experiments, Farina and his co-workers (Farina, Holland, and Ring, 1966; Farina and Ring, 1965; Farina, Sherman, and Allen, 1968) used a variety of observational measures with duping techniques to measure attitudes toward both mentally ill and physically disabled individuals. In general, the results of these studies revealed that a subject's behavior toward, and evaluation of, people believed to be disabled is strongly, and negatively, influenced. Confederates who played the roles of disabled people were blamed for inadequacies in performance, were shocked more for failure in experimental learning situations, and were avoided more often than confederates playing roles of non-disabled people. In a study similar in design to those of Farina and his associates, Titley and Viney (1969) found that able-bodied male high school students aggressed more toward disabled confederates, while able-bodied female high school students aggressed more toward nondisabled than toward disabled confederates.

Finally, Langer, Fiske, Taylor, and Chanowitz (1976), using a set of several behavioral observations, investigated the hypothesis that the wish to explore a novel stimulus (i.e., staring at a physically disabled person), in the presence of social norms disallowing such behavior, would result in conflict leading to feelings of discomfort. Male and female subjects who viewed photographs of disabled (novel) and able-bodied (familiar) people engaged in more staring at the photographs of disabled people when they were convinced that they were not being observed. In an actual interaction with a disabled or an able-bodied partner, on the other hand, the subjects preferred to sit closer to the able-bodied confederate. Subjects who were first given the opportunity to observe the confederate through a one-way mirror, thereby reducing the stimulus novelty, demonstrated reduced avoidance of the disabled confederate.

Other behavioral observation techniques include the study of written records (e.g., the voting records of local or state politicians on bills concerning the attitude referent), analyses of laws and public policies, reviews of media presentations, and naturalistic observations of respondent's behaviors in various settings (e.g., Gottlieb and Budoff, 1973; Webb, et al., 1966). For a detailed summary of these and other so-called qualitative research methods, the reader is referred to the book by Bodgan and Biklen (1982).

Physiological Methods

Physiological methods are those which purport to measure reactions over which the respondent has no conscious control. They are often regarded as being the most straightforward measures of attitudes (Mueller, 1970; Triandis, 1971). Furthermore, physiological reactions are considered by many (Cialdini, Petty and Cacioppo, 1981; McGuire, 1969) to reflect subtle responses to an attitude referent that the individual is either unwilling or unable to report accurately. In contrast to the phenomenological approach (direct and conscious verbal or written responses or introspection), the physiological approach (response activation on an autonomic or unconscious level) mainly taps the affective realm of one's attitudes (McGuire, 1969; Mueller, 1970).

Among the indices used in attitude measurement regulated by the autonomic nervous system are: galvanic skin response (GSR, previously known as psychogalvanic reflex or PGR), pupillary dilation (or constriction), heart rate, finger-pulse volume, blood pressure, perspiration, salivation, blinking, and voice pattern. These physiological measures all assume that the magnitude of the physiological reaction is directly and positively associated with the extent of the autonomic arousal or the intensity of the underlying attitude (Cook and Selltiz, 1964; McGuire, 1969). The direction of the corresponding attitude (e.g., pleasurable or unpleasurable, favorable or unfavorable), on the other hand, cannot be assumed with clarity, although it is often inferred that the greater the magnitude of the emotional arousal, the more unfavorable the attitude.

The most widely used procedure to measure autonomic activation has been the electrical conductiveness of the skin (Mueller, 1970). This galvanic skin response is said to occur in individuals who are apparently anxious, nervous, worried, tense, or otherwise emotionally aroused. It is assumed that when strongly held negative attitudes are aroused in the subject they are accompanied by a physiological activation lowering the level of skin resistance. For example, studies of racial prejudice (Porier and Lott, 1967; Vidulich and Krevanick, 1966) have used the GSR to measure subjects' attitudes toward Black people.

Despite the popularity of the GSR method in measuring attitudes toward racial groups, it has been meagerly used in studying attitudes toward disabled people. Kleck et al. (1966), in a study discussed previously, arranged for their experimental subjects to interact with both disabled and non-disabled confederates. The authors reported that the subjects who interacted with the wheelchair—confined confederate showed significantly greater electrodermal changes in the direction of lowered skin resistance (as measured by the GSR method) than did the subjects who interacted with the able-bodied confederate. The authors interpreted this physiological change as a sign of emotional conflict or stressful reaction attributed to the interaction with a disabled individual. Zych and Bolton (1972) studied subjects' responses to a variety of photographs using both direct (ATDP-Form B Scale) and indirect (GSR) attitude measurement methods. No significant differences in skin conductance were found between high and low ATDP Scale score groups when viewing photographs of the able-bodied person. When viewing the photographs of the disabled person, however, the difference in GSR scores between the high and low ATDP Scale score groups was significant. In a more recent study, Weslowski and Deichmann (1980) monitored both skin conductiveness and heart rate responses while subjects viewed three different scenes; namely, people with a visible disability, physically normal people, and neutral scenery. The two measures were found to discriminate among the three types of photographs.

A second physiological method used in attitude measurement is pupillary dilation elicited by emotional arousal to affective stimuli (Mueller, 1970; Nunnally, Knott, Duchnowski, and Parker, 1967). Hess and his co-workers (Hess, 1965; Hess and Polt, 1960; Hess, Seltzer, and Shlien, 1965) consider pupil dilation as a sign of favorable, pleasant, or positive reaction toward an observed referent, while pupil constriction is viewed by them as signaling an unfavorable, aversive, or negative response. Although these researchers have studied a wide range of reactions to aversive and abhorrent stimuli, including bodies of dead soldiers on a battlefield, corpses of concentration camp victims, and so on, they have not attempted to study pupillary reflexive responses to visible disabilities.

A third line of investigation is that of measures of heart rate, on the premise that heart rate is a valid indicator of one's level of state anxiety. Marinelli and Kelz (1973) and Marinelli (1974) hypothesized that subjects showing more negative attitudes toward visibly disabled (i.e., facially disfigured) people, as measured by the Disability Factor Scale-Cosmetic (see Chapter 9), will manifest more state anxiety, as measured by heart rate, in interactions with them than subjects who show more positive attitudes toward the same group. Results showed that subjects whose attitudes toward the cosmetically disfigured person were more negative, did show more state anxiety than subjects whose attitudes were more positive when interacting with a confederate assuming this role.

In a study of the attitudes of teachers toward teaching disabled children, Gargiulo and Yonker (1983) found a statistically significant difference between novice and experienced regular and special educators in the magnitude of change of pulse rate after viewing slides of individuals with various disabling conditions. A self-report rating measure, however, failed to differentiate the groups. The authors suggested that the psychophysiological measure adopted succeeded in depicting the educators' true attitudes toward teaching exceptional children whereas the self-reported measure failed due to its transparency of purpose.

The final application of physiological reaction measures to the study of attitudes toward physically disabled people which we will discuss was reported by VanderKolk (1976a, 1976b). Using the Psychological Stress Evaluator (PSE)—an electronic device that purportedly measured the person's level of stress by charting his or her vocal modulations from an audiotape recording—VanderKolk (1976a) studied respondents' reactions to 11 different groups of physically, mentally, and emotionally disabled people. Subjects demonstrated significantly higher levels of stress, as measured by the PSE, for all of the disability groups as compared to a normal situation stress level. In addition, discrepant rankings of subjects' willingness to acquire each disability were found between stated preferences and the order in which they were actually experienced (i.e., level of discomfort). VanderKolk (1976b) aruged that people have differential levels of physiological reactions to disabled people, and further asserted that the able-bodied individual's stress reaction to the disabled person results from threat to one's intact physical body image while in the presence of an unfamiliar or different person.

In general, physiological measures propose a unique and creative line of inquiry. But because their reliability and validity have not been conclusively demonstrated [see the discussions by Kidder and Campbell (1970, pp. 369-375) and by Mueller (1970, pp. 546-548)], they should be adopted cautiously and considered as experimental methods until further data can be accumulated and analyzed.

SUMMARY AND PRELUDE

As a result of the susceptibility of direct methods of measurement to the influence of respondent sensitization and response styles, and the robustness of the indirect methods when faced with these threats to validity, it comes as no surprise that the latter methods have gained considerable popularity in attitude research in the past quarter century. The use of indirect methods to measure attitudes toward people with disabilities may be expected to have an even greater impact if the sophistication and ingenuity witnessed in recent research designs are taken as indicators.

Regardless of the measurement method selected by the researcher investigating attitudes toward disabled people, certain fundamental psychometric characteristics of the method must be investigated, and their adequacy assured, before confidence can be placed in the researcher's conclusions. In the next part of this book, we will turn our attention to two of these characteristics: reliability and validity. While validity is considered the more important of the two characteristics, reliability will be discussed first. This is because no method can be considered to be a valid measure of a construct unless it is first shown to be a reliable measure of the construct. The third chapter of Part II will present detailed information on the psychometric characteristics of the most widely used attitude measurement method: the rating scale.

Part II

PSYCHOMETRIC GUIDELINES FOR ATTITUDE SCALES

THIS PART consists of three chapters which provide comprehensive guidelines for the psychometric adequacy of attitude scales. These chapters will be useful to the researcher who is searching for a scale to measure attitudes toward disabled people when the guidelines are used for the review of published scales. Moreover, these chapters will be useful for the researcher who, unable to locate a suitable or adequate attitude scale, proposes to undertake the tasks necessary to create a new scale.

A discussion of the concept of reliability is the focus of Chapter 6. Reliability concerns both the degree of consistency of scale scores over time, as well as the precision with which a scale samples the attitude domain of interest. Estimates of both types of reliability, as well as composite indices, will be presented, and factors known to affect a scale's reliability will be detailed.

Validity refers to the capability of the scale to achieve its desired measurement aims. Three classes of validity estimates will be presented and discussed in Chapter 7: content, criterion-related, and construct validity. Factors known to affect the estimate of a scale's validity will also be presented.

Because rating scales are the most widely used method to measure attitudes toward people who are disabled, Chapter 8 will be devoted to a detailed examination of the psychometric characteristics of these scales. This examination will suggest a sequence of steps which the researcher should follow when developing a new scale. Part II will conclude with a discussion of the needs for, and the means to establish and present, normative data for the interpretation of a respondent's scale score.

Chapter 6

RELIABILITY

THERE ARE numerous, albeit comparable, definitions of reliability. According to Nunnally (1978), "reliability concerns the extent to which measurements are repeatable—by the same individual using different measures of the same attribute or by different persons using the same measure of an attribute" (p. 172). Bolton (1974), more parsimoniously, views reliability as "the *precision* of a measurement" and reliable measurement as "a *consistent* procedure" (p. 46). Similarly, Mehrens and Lehmann (1978) defined reliability as "the degree of consistency between two measures of the same thing" (p. 88). In the present context, reliability is concerned with whether a respondent's score on an attitude scale is a consistent and precise measure of his or her true attitude.

From a psychometric point of view, reliability may be conceived as the accuracy with which an observed score represents the true status of the person on that aspect on which he or she is being measured. A person's true score on a test is composed of his or her observed score minus an error score, which is considered to be random in nature. Therefore, the variance of the set of true scores of a group of individual test takers equals the variance of the set of observed scores minus the variance due to error which is inherent in the measurement process. Reliability is defined, accordingly, as the ratio of the true-scores variance to the observed-scores variance. [For an extensive discussion of test-scores theory, the reader is referred to Cronbach, 1984; Guilford, 1954; Mehrens and Lehmann, 1978; and Thorndike, 1976.]

METHODS TO ESTIMATE RELIABILITY

Several methods to estimate the reliability of a set of test scores exist. They are: (a) test-retest (stability) measures, (b) alternate-forms (also called parallel-forms or equivalent-forms) measures, (c) measures of both stability and equivalence; (d) internal consistency measures (which include a variety of estimates such as the split-half, Kuder-Richardson coefficients, Cronbach's coefficient, and Hoyt's method), and (e) inter-judge (or inter-scorer or inter-rater) measures (Bolton, 1979; Carmines and Zeller, 1979; Mehrens and Lehmann, 1978).

Test-Retest Reliability Estimates

In order to obtain an estimate of an attitude scale's stability, the instrument is administered to a group of individuals at a specific point in time and is then readministered to the same group of individuals at a later point in time (usually after a one or two-week interval). The scores of the individuals on the two separate occasions are then correlated to yield a test-retest reliability coefficient. A positive and statistically significant correlation coefficient is indicative of the scale's stability over time.

One of the problems inherent in the use of test-retest reliability estimates is pretest contamination, or the influence of the original testing on the retest scores. Test takers are subject to a memory effect, where they merely repeat their choices or answers on the second occasion. This problem is particularly prevalent under conditions where only a short period of time elapses between the two test-taking occasions. A second problem which may beset a stability coefficient is due to a change in the test-taker's attitudes as a result of either gaining additional information between the two occasions, or the unintentional effect that the first test's answers may have on forming a certain attitude in the test taker who was virtually neutral or even ignorant of the particular topic tested. As discussed in Chapter 5, the very process of measuring one's attitudes toward a specific topic may result in a change or adoption of that attitude. Whereas memory, or recall, effects tend to result in overestimation of the reliability coefficient, the effects due to topic sensitization (called reactivity effects) often result in underestimation of the scale's reliability.

Estimates of the test-retest reliability of the ATDP Scales (see Chapter 9) may be found in Yuker et al. (1966) who reported eight estimates of stability for the ATDP Scale Form-O (ranging from $r = +.66$ to $r = +.89$), one estimate for Form-A ($r = +.78$), and two estimates for Form-B ($r = +.71$ and $r = +.83$). The time intervals ranged from two weeks to 18 months. For example, 84 non-disabled subjects who were retested on the ATDP Form-A after a time interval of two weeks resulted in a stability coefficient of $r = +.78$.

Alternate-Forms Reliability Estimates

When an estimate of a scale's sampling of content adequacy is required, the researcher uses the approach known as alternate-forms (or equivalent-forms) estimation. In contrast to the test-retest method, the alternate-forms reliability estimate is arrived at when the same group of individuals is administered two parallel forms of the same scale within a reasonably short time interval. The scores of the individuals on the two separate (i.e., parallel or alternate) forms are then correlated to yield a reliability coefficient. A positive and statistically significant correlation coefficient suggests that the two scale forms are representative of the same item domain.

Problems that often best alternate-forms reliability estimates include the practical difficulty of constructing a second scale form that is equivalent to the original one. The researcher may not have the time or resources, or may not be able to devote the energy necessary to develop a second attitude scale. (See Chapter 8 for details on scale construction.) A second problem stems from the short time interval required between the administration of the two scale forms. Contamination due to memory effects, even though items on parallel forms are different, or phrased differently, may still result in spuriously high reliability coefficients. The researcher constructing alternate forms must also attempt to increase the representativeness of the items sampled (Bolton, 1979) and to ascertain the statistical equivalence of the two measures (i.e., equal or nearly equal item means, item variances, total score distributions, item difficulty distributions, and item intercorrelations).

Estimates of alternate-forms reliability of the ATDP Scales, based on ten studies in which the three forms (i.e., Forms A, B, and O) were intercorrelated, ranged from $r = +.57$ to $r = +.83$ (Yuker et al., 1966). For example, 234 disabled individuals were administered Forms A and O and the resultant reliability coefficient was $r = +.61$.

Test-Retest and Alternate-Forms Reliability Estimates

The researcher who combines the two reliability estimates discussed so far is adopting the test-retest alternate-forms reliability estimate (also referred to as the delayed alternate-forms or stability-equivalence reliability method). This procedure allows the researcher to measure both the changes in subjects' scale scores due to the passage of time (i.e., instability of attitude structure) and the changes in scores due to the inconsistency of the specific items chosen to sample the item domain (i.e., the unrepresentativeness of the scale's items). Despite a deflated reliability estimate, most experts (Bolton, 1979; Nunnally, 1978) feel that two or more alternate forms, each administered to the same group of subjects at approximately a two-week interval, provide the best estimate of a scale's reliability. It should be pointed out, however, that a researcher constructing alternate forms to be administered at different time intervals should be cautious of the pitfalls of both the test-retest and the alternate-forms reliability estimates.

Yuker et al. (1966) report five studies of the stability-equivalence reliability of the ATDP Scales. These reliability coefficients ranged from $r = +.41$ (Forms A-B, 58 non-disabled subjects over a six-week interval) to $r = +.83$ (Forms O-B, 81 non-disabled subjects over a six-week interval). Two studies reported reliability coefficients of $r = +.73$ and $r = +.76$ (Forms A-B) for five-month intervals.

Internal Consistency Reliability Estimates

All internal consistency methods allow for the estimation of reliability from a single administration of the scale to a single group of individuals. The various internal consistency estimates to be described are all, in reality, measures of the scale's item homogeneity. In theory at least, these reliability estimates are assumed to be the average of all possible ways of subdividing the entire set of scale items in order to calculate a reliability coefficient for the particular scale (Bolton, 1979).

Split-Half Reliability Estimate. The split-half method of estimating reliability is a variant of the alternate-forms methods previously discussed. The items on the scale are divided into two comparable parts—which are actually alternate forms of each other—and the respondents' scores on these two subscales are then correlated.

One common procedure is to split the scale into odd-numbered items and even-numbered items, and then to correlate the scores on the two subscales for the entire sample of subjects. If the items were randomly arranged on the scale, and if all were of approximately equal difficulty level; this procedure is considered appropriate to yield two equivalent subscales. However, the correlation coefficient under these conditions estimates the reliability for only half the total scale rather than the entire scale. Since reliability coefficients are affected by the length of the scale (i.e., reliability of a scale increases as the number of items on it increases), the reliability coefficient calculated with this procedure underestimates the true reliability coefficient. In other words, the derived correlation coefficient is an estimate of a scale only half as long as the original one. A statistical correction is applied to obtain an estimate of the reliability of the original scale. This statistical correction, known as the Spearman-Brown prophecy formula (see Guilford, 1954 for details), allows the researcher to adjust the correlation so that it predicts the value which would have been obtained for a scale twice the length. If there are an odd number of items on the scale, so that the halves will not have equal numbers of items, then an adjustment proposed by Horst (1966) can be made to the calculation of the correlation coefficient. Alternatively, one of the items may be randomly eliminated to create an even number of items.

Two factors which may inflate split-half reliability estimates are unequal variances of the scale halves and lack of temporal fluctuations. Because the scale is administered at only one point in time, respondents' changes over time are not taken into account in these estimates.

Estimates of the split half reliability for the ATDP Scales are reported by Yuker et al. (1966). For the A form (seven studies), reliability coefficients ranged from $r = +.73$ to $+.89$; for the B form (seven studies), coefficients ranged from $r = +.72$ to $+.87$; and for the O form (six studies), coefficients ranged from $r = +.75$ to $+.85$. For example, using 553 non-disabled subjects, the authors found a split-half reliability coefficient of $r = +.83$ for the ATDP Form O.

Kuder-Richardson Reliability Estimates. Because the type of split used (i.e., first-half items vs. second-half items, odd-numbered items vs. even-numbered items, matched or unmatched randomly chosen items) could affect the correlation coefficient, and because as the number of items on a scale increases the number of different possible splits increases immensely, other methods of estimating the internal reliability that do not require splitting and still require only a single scale administration were developed. Two such methods are the Kuder and Richardson (1937) formulas 20 and 21 (abbreviated as K-R 20 and K-R 21). These formulas are considered to be estimates of the average correlations obtained from all possible split-half reliability estimates (Guilford, 1954; Mehrens and Lehmann, 1978).

It is noted that the Kuder-Richardson formulas require dichotomous scoring of the items. Dichotomous scoring involves assigning a value of 1 or 0 to a subject's response to an item, depending upon whether the subject expresses, or does not express, the particular attitude being measured. The assumptions underlying both the K-R 20 and K-R 21 formulas, in addition to dichotomous scoring, include that all scale items have equal correlations with all other items, and that they measure the same property or construct (Thorndike, 1976).

The essential distinction between the two formulas stem from an additional assumption underlying the K-R 21 formula. That is, it is assumed that all scale items are of equal difficulty. If the item difficulties are unequal, then the K-R 21 formula will yield a lower value than the K-R 20 formula, thus underestimating the scale's reliability. The K-R 21 formula requires less computational time and effort than the K-R 20 variant (only the means and variances of the scale items are computed). As was true with the split-half method, the K-R 20 and K-R 21 formulas do not take into account temporal fluctuations in respondents' measured characteristics.

No K-R 20 and K-R 21 internal reliability estimates are reported for the ATDP Scales. It may, however, be assumed from viewing the split-half coefficients that the scales' reliability coefficients would fall within the range of $r = +.70$ to $+.80$.

Cronbach's Coefficient Alpha Reliability Estimate. The coefficient alpha internal consistency index, first introduced by Cronbach (1951), is an extension of the K-R 20 formula. The major distinction between the two estimates is that in the K-R 20 formula the variances of the scale's individual items, summed over all the items, are based on dichotomous scoring. In the coefficient alpha formula, this summation of item variances is based on continuous scoring of each scale item. This procedure can also be extended to estimate internal consistency of scales composed of several parts (i.e., subscales). In this case we arrive at a measure of the homogeneity of the total scale, or the extent to which the subscales measure a single construct. If a scale is found to be non-homogeneous, the computed alpha coefficient will result in an underestimation of the scale's reliability. The alpha coefficient requires more computation time than any of the previously discussed reliability estimation methods. No coefficient alpha reliability estimates are reported for the ATDP Scales.

Hoyt's Analysis of Variance Reliability Estimate. Another extension of the K-R 20 formula was proposed by Hoyt (1941) who, by using analysis of variance, generalized Kuder and Richardson's dichotomously scored scale item formula to one suitable for items of multicategorical format. Hoyt perceived the matrix of the respondents' item scores to be but a version of a two-way analysis of variance design where each item is considered as a level of treatment condition and each respondent is measured at all levels (Thorndike, 1976). The K-R 20 formula, Cronbach's coefficient alpha, and Hoyt's method all yield similar internal consistency (i.e., homogeneity) estimates when computed for the same scale data. As with the alpha coefficient, computing Hoyt's estimate requires considerable time and effort of the researcher. No reliability studies of the ATDP Scales were found that reported Hoyt's analysis of variance estimate.

Inter-Judge Reliability Estimates

Although most attitude measurement uses scales constructed as objective, self-administered, paper-and-pencil instruments which do not require the use of outside raters or judges, there are occasions in attitude measurement when scoring by observers has been adopted. For example, when judging or inferring attitudes from certain observed behaviors of participants in the presence of a referent (e.g., a person with a specific disability), the need to ascertain the observers' scoring accuracy and consistency is clearly indicated. Similarly, when measures of attitudes are derived from such procedures as projective techniques (e.g., the Rorschach or TAT) or literary narratives (e.g., stories or books), it is of utmost importance to achieve a level of agreement and consistency among all individual scorers. In other words, the source of error due to variability between observers or judges should be eliminated or controlled by the researcher. (These and other indirect attitude measurement methods were discussed in Chapter 5.)

The inter-judge reliability estimate is simply the correlation coefficient computed between the ratings of two (or more) observers or judges on a specifically designed attitude measure. The level of data (i.e., nominal, ordinal, or interval) will determine the exact type of correlation coefficient which needs to be calculated (i.e., phi, rho, or product-moment). If the researcher is interested in a reliability estimate summed over the ratings of two judges, he or she could apply the Spearman-Brown prophecy formula (or its general extension to ratings of three or more judges). For a more in-depth discussion of the reliability of ratings, often referred to as intraclass correlation reliability, the reader is referred to Guilford (1954).

STANDARD ERROR OF MEASUREMENT OF SCORES

The standard error of measurement statistic provides an estimate of the amount of error present in an obtained score. In line with test-scores theory mentioned previously, it may be considered to be the amount by which a respondent's obtained score on a test or scale differs from his or her hypothetical true score due to errors of measurement. The standard error of measurement (variously denoted as *s.e.m.*, *SEM, SEmeas,* or *Se*) is a statistic of intra-individual variability theoretically arrived at through repeated and independent testings of, or ratings by, an individual with the same scale. In reality, the *Se* is estimated from group data using a specific formula (see Nunnally, 1978, p. 218).

The *Se* provides an index of the absolute stability of measurement. This is in contrast to the reliability coefficients which are indices of relative stability (Thorndike, 1976). The relationship of reliability to standard error of measurement is an inverse relationship: the smaller the standard error of measurement (i.e., as error variance decreases) the more reliable is the scale, and the more reliable the scale (as *r* approaches 1) the smaller is the standard error of measurement (*Se* approaches 0). Moreover, as the reliability coefficient of a scale approaches 0, the estimate of the standard error of measurement approaches the standard deviation of the scale's scores. The *Se*, unlike the reliability coefficent, is not directly affected by the range of the scores of the group tested (i.e., the variance).

FACTORS AFFECTING RELIABILITY

There are several factors which individually, or in combination, may affect the reliability estimates of a given scale, several of which have been discussed in preceeding sections. Because it is imperative that the researcher become aware of these factors when reliability coefficients are calculated, these factors will be summarized in this last section of the chapter.

Group Homogeneity

Group homogeneity refers to the range of the measured characteristic (e.g., ability, personality trait, attitude) possessed by the sample of respondents. In general, as the heterogeneity of the group increases (i.e., the score variance increases), so does the scale's reliability coefficient. This is simply a reflection of the definitional formula of reliability. Scales to measure attitudes toward individuals with disabilities may report high reliability values if they included some respondents who were known to have highly positive attitudes and other respondents who were known to have highly negative attitudes toward the particular disabled populations.

Scale Length

As previously discussed in the section on estimating the reliability of a scale with the split-half method, the longer the scale (i.e., the more items there are on it), the higher is its reliability coefficient (other things being equal). This can easily be illustrated by introducing gradually increasing numbers of items into the Spearman-Brown prophecy formula. There is, however, a point at which the increase in the reliability coefficient will taper off as the number of items is increased. The most appropriate length of a scale is, therefore, based upon a trade of between reliability and practicality (e.g., cost and time to administer).

Difficulty of the Items

The level of an item's difficulty (actually, easiness) is defined as that proportion of the subjects who respond correctly to the item (range from 0.00 to + 1.00). Averaging the difficulty values of the scale's items leads to an estimate of the total scale's difficulty level. Reliability tends to increase for scales with more items in the middle range of difficulty (approximately + .40 to + .60), but it tends to decrease as extremely easy items (in the case of attitude scales, commonly held attitudes) or extremely difficult items (rarely held attitudes) are included. In other words, as item difficulty values become more heterogeneous (i.e., the scale difficulty approaches the 0.00 or + 1.00 values), the reliability estimate tends to decrease.

As mentioned previously, reliability estimates depend on scale score variability. That is, scales with higher score variability result in higher reliability coefficients than scales of little score variability. Whereas increased sample homogeneity (i.e., low score variance on the scale) results in decreased reliability estimates, increased item homogeneity (i.e., concentration of items in the middle range of difficulty) results in increased reliability estimates.

Discrimination of the Items

Item discrimination is defined as the capability of a scale item to differentiate between a person possessing much or little of the attitude, ability, or trait being measured. Several methods of measuring item discrimination exist (see Baker, 1985; Lord, 1980). The most common method is the correlation of the item to the total scale score (see Chapter 8). Other things being equal, as the average item discrimination index increases, the reliability of the scale tends to increase. A scale with a larger number of items that differentiate between people holding negative attitudes and those holding positive attitudes toward a particular referent group is generally more reliable. The item discrimination factor, obviously, bears a strong relationship to the group homogeneity factor previously discussed.

Content of the Scale

Whereas the first factor influencing a scale's reliability dealt with group homogeneity, this factor refers primarily to the scale's item homogeneity or breadth of topic coverage (Thorndike, 1976). As the content of the scale become more narrow (i.e., as only a narrow range of attitudes or behaviors is measured), the reliability of the scale tends to increase. If a scale constructor inadvertently includes a composite of several attitude dimensions in his or her score, the reliability estimate, especially internal consistency coefficients, will be quite low. Factor or cluster analyses of the scale are recommended when the researcher seeks to reassure himself or herself of content homogeneity (see Chapter 8).

Time Limits

A speed test is one in which every subject can theoretically answer all the items correctly. That is, all item difficulty levels equal approximately 1.00. However, due to administrator-imposed time limitations, no subject is allowed enough time to complete all the test items. Speed tests are often contrasted with power tests, which allow enough time to complete all the items. Due to increasing difficulty of the items, however, usually no person correctly answers all items on a power test. Estimating the reliability of speed tests through methods of internal consistency is inappropriate since by definition they assure all subjects of correct answers and, therefore, result in internal consistency coefficients approaching 1.00. This concern is typically irrelevant in the case of attitude measures which are rarely constructed as speed tests.

Objectivity of the Scale

The more objectively a scale is scored, the higher will be its reliability estimate. Attitude scales that are scored objectively (i.e., most paper-and-pencil instruments) clearly have the potential to behave in a more consistent fashion than attitude measures that are based on observations and inferences made by several judges or raters from such sources as projective test data or story narratives.

Uniformity of Testing Conditions

The more uniform the conditions under which subjects are tested, the higher will be the scale's reliability. Other things being equal, an attitude scale administered to one group of subjects, located at one setting, at one specific point in time, will result in higher reliability estimates than if the scale was administered to subjects located at a variety of settings (e.g, home, work, school) on different days and periods of the day.

SUMMARY AND PRELUDE

Our discussion of the concept of reliability began with a definition of the concept and a taxonomy of ways to estimate a scale's reliability. Five types of reliability estimates were then discussed: test-retest, alternate forms, combined test-retest and alternate forms, internal consistency, and inter-judge reliability. The concept of the standard error of measurement of scores was related to the concept of reliability of a scale. Finally, eight factors known to affect the estimate of a scale's reliability were detailed.

In the next chapter we turn our attention to the concept of validity, or the capability of a scale to achieve its desired measurement aims. It will be noted that assurance of the reliability of a scale is a necessary, but not a sufficient, condition for the assurance of the validity of a scale.

Chapter 7

VALIDITY

VALIDITY is concerned with the extent to which a particular instrument (e.g., an intelligence test, personality test, or attitude scale) measures what its developer intends for it to measure. In other words, a specific scale possesses validity if it measures what it purports to measure or if it is capable of achieving certain predetermined goals. A scale may, then, be valid for one particular purpose (e.g., measuring attitudes toward people who are physically disabled), but not for another purpose (e.g., measuring attitudes toward individuals who are mentally retarded). Similar to reliability, the validity of a scale is not a dichotomous concept but rather a continuum-based concept. Even though validity is commonly expressed numerically as a correlation coefficient, validity is, more correctly, inferred from accumulated evidence rather than specifically measured (Messick, 1980).

Both the validity and reliability of a scale are crucial to the establishment of how well-designed a scale is, but the relationship between these two concepts is not reciprocal. A scale may be highly reliable (i.e., it is consistent in what it measures), but it may be only marginally valid (i.e., it does not accurately measure what it aims to measure). As an example, a scale to measure attitudes toward blind people may yield similar scores when administered to the same group of respondents over a period of time (it has a high degree of reliability), but it fails to predict the behavior of the respondents in the presence of blind people (low degree of validity). On the other hand, a valid scale must possess a high degree of reliability. That is, a scale cannot measure any concept unless it does so consistently and accurately. Reliability is, therefore, said to be necessary but not a sufficient condition for validity (Mehrens and Lehmann, 1978).

In addition to the reliability of the scale, the validity of an attitude scale is affected by the respondent's knowledge of or insight into his or her attitudes and belief system, and the respondent's willingness to admit to and share with the researcher his or her inner world when responding to the attitude scale (Nunnally, 1978). The concern regarding the respondent's insight into his or her attitudes is not considered to be a major limitation if the scale items are worded in a clear, concise, and straightforward manner, and if the attitude referent is clearly specified (Gottlieb and Siperstein, 1976). The final concern, namely the respondent's willingness to share his or her private world of attitudes with a stranger, is a potential limitation and will be considered in the section on response styles in Chapter 8.

TYPES OF VALIDITY

Similar to our discussion of reliability in the preceeding chapter, several types of validity will be discussed. In its publication entitled *Standards for Educational and Psychological Tests and Manuals,* the American Psychological Association (1974) organized validity into three general classes: (a) content validity, (b) criterion-related validity (including both concurrent and predictive validity), and (c) construct validity. (Another type of validity sometimes mentioned is face validity. When a test appears to measure what it claims to measure, the test is then said to have face validity. Face validity is usually considered to be a low level form of content validity.)

Content Validity

Content validity refers to the extent to which the scale items may be considered to be an adequate, appropriate, complete, and representative sample of the hypothetical domain that is being measured (i.e., attitudes toward people who are physically disabled). Content validity is, therefore, established through the researcher's logical and judgmental analysis of the content of the scale. Rather than being a data-based process, this is a subjective process which is based, to a large extent, on the professional opinion and background of the researcher. There is no agreed-upon numerical expression of the content validity of a scale. Instead, it is determined by systematically inspecting, analyzing, and judging the specific items as to how representative they are of the domain under consideration.

The development of a table of specifications may be used as a facilitative device to better organize the sample items. The use of such an organizing table, however, is more appropriate when constructing an achievement, aptitude, or similar cognitive domain instrument. For example, a test concerning a country's history may be conceived along two dimensions: chronological period and contextual aspects (e.g., political, social, economic). A matrix presenting the sigificant elements of these two dimensions is created and a certain number of items are written which presumably represent each of the elements of the matrix. In this way, the researcher is assisted in preparing items which adequately sample both dimensions of the country's history. Due to the abstractness of some of the concepts in the realm of attitude measurement (e.g., religiosity, educational philosophy), this procedure is not often practical (Carmines and Zeller, 1979).

In general, content validity procedures, when applied to the construction of attitude scales, include these practices: (a) a specific and precise definition of the referent (e.g., type of disability group, level of severity or visibility, context of interaction); (b) a thorough review of related literature (theoretical, clinical, and empirical sources); (c) development and derivation of an initial item pool drawn from the literature sources; (d) consultation of experts in reviewing and critiquing item content, representativeness, accuracy, relevance, and thoroughness, and in assessing the adequacy of the scoring key; and (e) collecting and analyzing pilot study data to eliminate inappropriate and psychometrically poor items.

Because there are a number of equally justifiable ways to operationalize the definition of the attitude referent, and since there are no agreed-upon objective criteria for determining when a particular attitude measure has attained adequate content validity, additional procedures are required to completely establish the validity of an attitude scale. One or more of the data-based validity procedures to be discussed next must be followed.

Criterion-Related Validity

Criterion-related validity refers to the extent to which a scale demonstrates an association with some independent and external measure or criterion. In other words, the respondent's score on the scale is used to predict his or her behavior, status, or performance on a predetermined criterion. The criterion-related validity estimate is typically expressed as the degree of correspondence (e.g., a correlation coefficient) between the respondent's scale score (i.e., the predictor) and his or her behavior (i.e., the criterion).

A distinction is made between two kinds of criterion-related validity, namely concurrent validity and predictive validity. If the data on the criterion measure for all the respondents are already available, or if both the scale data and criterion data are collected at the same time (or roughly so), then concurrent validity is assessed by correlating the data on these two measures. If, on the other hand, the comparison will be made of present scale data with future behavioral data, the procedure is known as predictive validity. Mehrens and Lehmann (1970) argue that when differentiating between the two time periods involved in data collection (present-to-present vs. present-to-future), we are dealing with a procedural distinction. A second distinction between the two kinds of criterion-related validity is viewed by these authors as being logical. This differentiation relates to the purpose of the testing. In concurrent validation, the researcher attempts to substitute the scores generated by the new scale for a less efficient but available method of obtaining criterion data. In predictive validation, the researcher is concerned with the usefulness of the scale scores in predicting the respondent's future behavior.

Concurrent Validity. Perhaps the most widely used concurrent validation procedure is the so-called known groups procedure (Betz and Weiss, 1976; Brinberg and Kidder, 1982). In this procedure, the attitudes of groups of individuals known to differ in their endorsement of the attitude referent are compared to each other using the attitude scale. For example, a scale to measure attitudes toward racial integration should be able to differentiate between members of the local chapters of the NAACP and the KKK. In attempting to validate a scale measuring attitudes toward people who are disabled, such known groups are more difficult to specify. One possible approach is to compare the statement endorsements of different groups of professionals. For example, the scores of recently trained human service providers (e.g., rehabilitation counselors or social workers) should reflect a more favorable attitude than the scores of professionals not employed in human-service professions (e.g., accountants or scientists). A related procedure is to compare the endorsements of family members of disabled individuals with those of individuals with no known disabled family members. Presumably, family members of disabled individuals should exhibit a more favorable attitude toward members of that specific disability group than people chosen at random from the general population who have no disabled family members. The statistical procedures typically used in this validation procedure include multiple regression analysis (see Antonak, 1981b, for an example), and discriminant function analysis (see Schmelkin, 1981, for an example).

An alternative to the known groups concurrent validation method involves the identification of a previously published scale measuring the same attitude and comparing the scores of the respondents on these two scales administered at the same time. This method, however, has two drawbacks. First, if the previously published scale measuring the same attitude is valid, then the researcher would have selected it for his or her research. Second, if the researcher is undertaking the costly and time-consuming process of constructing an attitude scale to replace an already existing scale, then he or she should have examined and rejected the originally published scale as an invalid measures of the attitude in question, rather than correlate and compare the newly developed scale to it. This concurrent validation procedure is defensible, however, when the researcher hopes to construct an attitude scale which achieves the same aims as the original scale does, but in a more efficient manner (Messick, 1980). For example, the new scale may be shorter and less time-consuming to administer, score, and interpret. If the new scale succeeds in reaching this goal, it may then substitute for the original, more cumbersome, scale due to its greater usefulness, practicality, and utility.

A somewhat related concurrent validation method uses a scale which measures an ostensibly different, though related, attitude or personality domain. For example, the researcher may compare the scores of respondents on a scale of attitudes toward disabled people with scores on scales measuring attitude or personality characteristics hypothesized to be associated with attitudes toward disabled people. These characteristics may include: (a) authoritarianism [for example, using the Adorno, Frenkel-Brunswik, Levinson, and Sanford's (1964) F(Facism)-Scale], (b) ethnocentrism [for instance, using the Adorno et al. (1964) E-Scale], (c) dogmatism, (d) manifest anxiety (both state and trait anxiety), (e) self-concept and ego strength, (f) body image and self-satisfaction, (g) tolerance of ambiguity, and (h) aggressiveness. In general, however, these procedures are more appropriate for studying the construct validity of the scale, to be discussed shortly.

For further discussion of these concurrent validation methods, the reader is referred to Cloerkes (1981), English (1971), and Livneh (1982a). For more specific examples of methods to collect data bearing on the criterion-related validity of a scale to measure attitudes toward disabled people (the ATDP Scales), the reader is referred to Yuker and Block (1986), and Yuker et al. (1966).

Predictive Validity. The second type of criterion-related validity is predictive validity, which involves the comparison of present data obtained from an attitude scale (i.e., the predictor) with future behavioral data (i.e., the criterion) obtained from the same group of respondents. For example, the attitude scores of entering college freshmen can be used to predict their future occupational choices. These entry level attitudes would then be compared with actual occupations after graduation. Attitudes of employers can be used to predict the hiring practices of their companies. Attitude scores of rehabilitation worker trainees toward a variety of physically, mentally, and emotionally disabling conditions can be used to recommend internship sites and to suggest career alternatives in the field of rehabilitation.

Several authors (e.g., Ajzen and Fishbein, 1980; Nunnally, 1978; Triandis et al., 1984) caution the researcher that while self-reported attitudes are not always a good predictor of future behavior, they may be very good predictors of verbalized attitudes. Nunnally (1978) argues further that it is reasonable to be interested in verbalized attitudes, but the researcher should not make the (often false) claim that these attitudes are the cause of future behavior.

Construct Validity

The third class of validation procedures, referred to as construct validation, involve the assessment of the extent to which the scale measures the theoretical construct or trait it intends to measure. In other words, if a scale possesses construct validity, respondents' scores will vary in accordance with the theory or hypotheses underlying the particular attitude construct (i.e., respondents who are presumed to exhibit more favorable attitudes toward people who are disabled will actually score higher—be more accepting—on the scale in question).

Construct validation should, therefore, be conceived within a theoretical context and be concerned with the degree to which several measures, all consistent with theoretically-derived hypotheses about the measured construct, relate (or do not relate) to each other (Carmines and Zeller, 1979; Nunnally, 1978). Furthermore, because these theoretical constructs are proposed as correlates or explanations of broad classes of human behavior, construct validation procedures should involve the accumulation of data concerning the construct under consideration (e.g., the attitude referent) from a variety of sources using a variety of measurement indicators. Such a multi-source multi-indicator approach to the study of attitudes would include self-reported data (e.g., paper-and-pencil attitude scales), peer-reported data (e.g., sociometric ratings), observations by professionals or trained judges (e.g., behavioral ratings), and projective data (e.g., Rorschach, TAT or Draw-A-Person test results). Due to its inclusiveness, several authors (e.g., Guion, 1977; Messick, 1980) view construct validity as the unifying concept for all forms of validity.

Construct validation is a continuous process (Allen and Yen, 1979; Bolton, 1979) which includes four phases.

1. A theoretical phase, which involves a logical examination of the theory-derived constructs and the relationship between several of these constructs. For example, a relationship is presumed to exist between poor self-concept, low body satisfaction, and rejection of individuals who are physically disabled.
2. An hypothesis-testing phase, which involves the advancement of certain hypotheses regarding the behavior of persons possessing high and low levels of the theory-derived construct. For example, individuals with poor self-concept and low body satisfaction will tend to reject the presence of individuals who are physically disabled.
3. An empirical phase, where data are obtained to test the relationship between the measures of the two (or more) constructs. For example, correlating the scores of a group of respondents on a self-concept scale [such as the Tennessee Self-Concept Scale (Fitts, 1965)], a body-satisfaction scale [such as the Body Cathexis Scale (Secord and Jourard, 1953)], and a scale measuring attitudes toward disabled people [such as the ATDP Scale (Yuker et al., 1966)].
4. An inference-drawing phase, in which the researcher interprets the data collected and arrives at a conclusion as to whether or not the theory explains or is supported by the data obtained.

Three construct validation procedures are typically used by psychometricians. These procedures are based on the demonstration of empirical relationships among a variety of measures, and include (a) the multitrait-multimethod approach, consisting of both convergent and divergent discriminant validity types; (b) the factor analytic method; and (c) the experimental method.

Multitrait-Multimethod Validity. Construct validation requires both confirmatory and disconfirmatory strategies (Messick, 1980). The multitrait-multimethod approach (Campbell and Fiske, 1959) allows the researcher to do just that by investigating two complimentary types of validity: convergent and divergent validity. *Convergent* (or *confirmatory*) validity refers to evidence of the relatedness of the measure under consideration to other measures of the same construct (e.g., data obtained from other sources using other measures which are related to the construct). For example, if the construct to be measured is attitudes toward disabled individuals, then convergent validity should be obtained from measures of concepts such as ethnocentrism, authoritarianism, self-concept, anxiety, aggressiveness, and so on. *Discriminant* (or *disconfirmatory*) validity, on the other hand, refers to evidence of the lack of relatedness of the measure in question with measures of irrelevant constructs or traits. For instance, a scale to measure attitudes toward disabled individuals would not be expected to correlate (positively or negatively) with measures of sexual behavior or political affiliation.

In order to use the multitrait-multimethod validity approach, Campbell and Fiske (1959) suggested the construction of a multitrait-multimethod validity matrix with reliability coefficients along the main diagonal and correlation coefficients as off-diagonal entries. The values of the reliability coefficients are expected to be the largest. The values of the entries relating measures of the same construct or trait are expected to be smaller, but yet substantial, and the values of the coefficients of unrelated constructs are expected to have the smallest values.

The multitrait-multimethod validity strategy has been used in areas such as clinicians' judgments (Goldberg and Werts, 1966), assessment of institutional functioning (Centra, 1971), managerial job performance (Lawler, 1976), affective states and traits (Zuckerman, Persky, Eckman, and Hopkins, 1967), and psychological defense mechanisms (Vickers and Hervig, 1981), to name just a few. The use of multitrait-multimethod validation procedures in attitude research has also gained in popularity. Maher, Watt, and Campbell (1960), for example, used two projective methods and two structured attitude scales to investigate attitudes of prison inmates toward home and parents, and toward law and justice. Hicks (1967) sought to compare direct and indirect methods of attitude measurement toward three stimulus referents (Negroes, the Peace Corps, and the field of journalism) with the use of three attitude measures. A Likert scale and a semantic differential scale were the direct methods, while the objective judgment of statement favorability was the indirect method. Finally, Jaccard, Weber, and Lundmark (1975) compared the relative validities of four measurement procedures (Likert's method, Thurstone's method, Guilford's self-rating method, and the semantic differential) in assessing the attitudes of respondents toward cigarette smoking and capital punishment.

Factor Analytic Validity. Factor analysis of the data obtained from the scale in question is often used as a preferred method in construct validation. Nunnally (1978) viewed factor analysis as being at the heart of the measurement of psychological constructs. Factor analysis is essentially a group of mathematical procedures used for finding clusters of variables by analyzing the interrelationships among them. Each derived cluster of variables, denoted as a factor, is defined by that group of variables whose members (e.g., scale items) correlate higher among themselves than they correlate with variables of other unrelated clusters. If an attitude scale was constructed as a homogeneous measure, then the factoring of the scale's inter-item correlation matrix should yield a single, or main, factor which accounts for the majority of the variance observed in the data. Factor analysis of both the scores obtained on the attitude scale and scores obtained on related measures of the same attitude construct is a procedure (referred to as factorial congruence analysis) often recommended to provide supporting evidence of the scale's validity (Sontag and Pedhazur, 1972). An example of this procedure is the study of the construct validity of the SADP reported by Antonak (1985a).

Details about the use of factor analysis with attitude scale data are presented in Chapter 8. A number of factor analytic studies have been carried out to examine the internal cohesiveness of several of the scales measuring attitudes toward disabled people (e.g., the ATDP, DFS-G, OMI, SADP). The results of these factor analytic studies will be discussed in the chapters of Part III concerned with scales for the measurement of attitudes.

Experimental Validity. The third method of construct validation involves an experimental manipulation of the construct being measured. Scores of respondents on a scale measuring the construct in question should change following an experimental intervention designed to alter the expression of the construct. For example, self-reports of respondents following an intervention directed at improving their attitudes toward a particular referent group should reflect this change in favorableness from pre-intervention reports. Such apparent attitude improvements may be short-lived, however, and not necessarily linked to permanent changes in the respondents' subsequent behaviors.

The Validation Process

The three methods of validating a scale which have been presented and discussed (i.e., content, criterion-related, and construct validity) are only independent conceptually. A complete validation of a scale would normally require information about all three types of validity. Furthermore, as previously indicated, validation of a scale is a comprehensive and continuous process which seeks to progressively redefine and upgrade the accuracy and usefulness of the measure. It is, generally, the intended use of the scale rather than its nature or structure that determines what kind of supporting evidence of validity is required.

FACTORS AFFECTING VALIDITY

Several factors may affect the validity estimates of a scale in addition to the actual association which exists between respondents' scores on the scale and their scores on other measures. These factors which influence the data-based validity estimates may be conveniently placed into the following five categories.

Reliability of the Predictor and Criterion

The more consistently the predictor measures the construct, the less error variance will be present in the sample data, the higher its reliability coefficient will be, and, therefore, the higher its validity coefficient will be. The same can be said for any criterion measure. Taken together, the magnitude of the validity estimate (e.g., the correlation between the predictor and the criterion) is limited by the reliabilities of both measures. As more error is present in these measures, the correlation between scores on these two measures will be lower. [For a more thorough discussion of the mathematical relationship between reliability and validity, the reader is referred to Anastasi (1982) or Mehrens and Lehmann (1978).]

Heterogeneity of the Sample

The more heterogeneous the sample of individuals with respect to the construct measured by both the predictor and the criterion measures, the higher will be the resultant validity estimate. This is similar to the point made in discussing reliability coefficients in the preceeding chapter where sample heterogeneity was found to result in a higher reliability estimate. Scores of individuals known to hold extremely favorable attitudes toward a specific disability group, however, may not be highly correlated with their actual behavior when interacting with members of that group. This is not due to a discrepancy between their professed attitudes and actual behavior, but rather because of the high degree of homogeneity and, therefore, reduced variance, inherent in the data from both measured variables.

Characteristics of the Sample

Characteristics of the group of respondents on whom a scale is validated (e.g., sex, age, educational level, occupation, personality), other than their heterogeneity on the construct being measured, will influence the criterion-related validity estimate of a scale. A scale may have high validity in predicting the criterion measure with one sample of respondents yet have low validity with another sample. The more similar the respondents in a subsequent investigation are to the respondents in the validation sample, the more confidence the researcher will have that the value of the validity estimate will generalize to the new data. It is essential, therefore, for the scale constructor to specify the characteristics of the group on which the validity coefficient was calculated, and for the researcher to be certain that the characteristics of the research sample match the characteristics of the validation sample.

Length of the Scale

Similar to reliability, the validity of a scale varies with the scale's length. Under most conditions, the longer the scale (i.e., the more items it contains), the larger will be the sample variance, and, consequently, the larger will be the validity estimate.

Criterion Contamination

Finally, the validity of the criterion may affect how the scores on a particular measure are being determined. In other words, criterion scores as measures of a particular variable may, if known to the respondent, partially determine (contaminate) his or her responses to that measure. For example, prior knowledge of students' grade point averages may affect the instructor's grade assignments in a particular course. Although less pervasive in attitude measurement (see Chapter 5), knowledge of an experimentally observed subject's score on a particular attitude scale may strongly influence ratings of his or her behavior by an observer (e.g., checking for the presence of specific behavioral acts presumably manifested when interacting with members of a particular referent group).

SUMMARY AND PRELUDE

Concern for the validity of a scale is concern for the capability of the scale to achieve its desired measurement aims. We began our consideration of validity with a definition of the concept and a taxonomy of types of validity. Three classes of validity estimates were presented and discussed: content, criterion-related, and construct validity. We concluded the chapter with a consideration of five factors known to affect the validity of a scale.

In the next chapter, we will examine in detail the psychometric characteristics of the most widely used method to measure attitudes toward people who are disabled: that is, rating scales. This examination should assist researchers to critically review available scales, as well as to carry out the complex and time-consuming process of creating a new attitude measure.

Chapter 8

PSYCHOMETRIC CHARACTERISTICS OF ATTITUDE SCALES

IT IS APPROPRIATE at this point to return to the question which was asked in Chapter 2 – Which measurement method to select to investigate attitudes toward people who are disabled? The answer given there was to select the method which allowed the most adequate operational definition of the researcher's theoretical assumptions concerning attitudes toward disabled people. That is, the researcher should select the method which will provide the data needed to answer the research question within the parameters of the research situation. The majority of attitude research questions have been operationalized with direct measurement methods, and the most common scaling method selected by researchers has been the probabilistic summated rating scale. In Nunnally's (1978) view, this is not unusual. Summated rating scales use an appealing and mathematically reasonable measurement model, can be adapted to answer many different research questions, and, if well-developed, can provide meaningful and reliable research data.

This chapter will present guidelines for the creation and psychometric analysis of summated rating scales. This presentation has two purposes: (a) the researcher who is seeking a previously constructed attitude rating scale can follow these guidelines in reviewing available scales, and (b) the researcher who is unable to locate a previously constructed rating scale can follow these guidelines in the process of constructing a new rating scale. The novice researcher and students are cautioned that of these two alternatives, the former is by far the most reasonable. The process of constructing a summated rating scale, although it appears to be relatively easy, is a task requiring considerable time, resources, and commitment. To begin with, the researcher needs a large pool of respondents. As will be seen in the following sections, for the construction of a 25-item scale this number will be roughly 700 respondents of various demographic and experiential characteristics. In addition, the researcher needs considerable research support (e.g., secretarial and printing services, computer software resources, research associates), essentially unlimited computer access, and two years or more of time to invest in the process. The process includes not only the initial development and testing of the instrument, but also the essential investigations of the scale's reliability, utility, dimensionality, and validity.

Although we will focus on summated rating scales, many of the psychometric characteristics to be discussed in this chapter apply equally to other attitude measurement methods. The detailed item and scale analyses to be discussed will require that the researcher has available a computer of considerable memory capacity as well as general purpose item and scale analysis programs. Many of the necessary algorithms are available on standard statistical software packages. Other analyses to be discussed are available only on special purpose software on mainframe computer systems (Antonak, 1979b, 1980a; Antonak, Bart, and Lele, 1979), but could easily be modified for microcomputer systems.

In the following presentation, the goal will be to construct a 25 item summated rating scale to measure attitudes toward disabled people. The instructions presented on the final scale will ask respondents to indicate their endorsement of each item on a six-point scale (i.e., no 0-point, or neutral response, is permitted), ranging from −3, to signify "I disagree very much," to +3, to signify "I agree very much." A sum of the respondent's item responses plus a constant of 75 (that is, 3*25) will provide a measure of his or her global attitude toward disabled people. Scores will range from 0 to 150, with a higher score indicating a more favorable attitude.

ITEM PREPARATION

The researcher begins the scale construction process with a definition of the attitude referent which will be the subject of the attitude scale. This definition can be accomplished by reviewing the research literature on attitudes toward the referent, examining previously published scales and measurement instruments, and conducting interviews with experts in the relevant professional field as well as with disabled individuals. Initially, this definition should be comprehensive and broad to permit latitude in the preparation of items. In later stages of the scale construction process, the definition can be narrowed and the scale focused on one or a small number of specific components (dimensions) of the definition of the referent.

Items are then written, at first without critical review of content, intensity, or valence (degrees of favorability or unfavorability). Wang's (1932) 15 "practical rules for writing attitude statements" apply as well today as they did more than 50 years ago. Once the researcher has seemingly exhausted the store of items, the total set is critically reviewed to eliminate those which are redundant, clarify those which are confusing, and revise those which are poorly worded. The researcher may enlist the aid of one or more experts in this review process. These steps are repeated, in sequence, until the researcher obtains an initial pool of 100 to 150 items. This total is roughly four to six times the desired number of items to be presented on the final version of the scale.

The definition of the terminal points of the item response continuum should not be so extreme that the respondent is unlikely to select them (e.g., "Absolutely disagree"). That is, all the possible responses should be selectable in order to assure an adequate dispersion of the item responses for a sample of respondents. The number of item response alternatives to provide is the decision of the researcher. As a general rule of thumb, the number of categories should be even, and between four and ten. Providing an odd number of alternatives is usually not recommended (Anastasi, 1982; Nunnally, 1970, 1978). The middle point on the continuum is not a true neutral point, no matter what the anchor may say, and does not represent "no attitude." Even if it did, the resultant data are useless to the researcher who is interested in attitudes and not non-attitudes. For most purposes, six response alternatives will be reasonable.

A modified version of Edward's (1957a) scale discrimination process is then recommended. The initial pool of 100 to 150 items is presented to a set of experts in the field (six to ten experts are sufficient in most cases) who are asked to read each item and then rate it on a six-point scale representing the extent to which the item expresses a favorable or unfavorable attitude toward the referent. That is, they are not asked to express *their* endorsement of the items, but rather their view of the valence and intensity of each item. In addition, the experts are asked to comment on any item which they view as ambiguous, poorly worded, double-barrelled, or confusing. The researcher then analyzes the responses of the experts and retains those items which are viewed as unambiguous and which are rated as moderate to extreme expressions of the attitude construct. A reasonable criterion for moderate to extreme response is that the item mean must be in the upper 50th percentile of the distribution, with all the experts' values above (or below, if it is a negatively worded item) the midpoint of the response continuum. Neutral items are not useful since they will not generate the variance necessary to study respondents' attitudes.

Half the remaining items (approximately 50 to 75) are then reworded so that an agree response indicates a favorable attitude, while the other half are worded so that a disagree response indicates a favorable attitude. The newly worded items are then randomly arranged on a composite scale which will be used in the subsequent pilot studies.

PILOT STUDIES

For the first pilot study, a sample of respondents roughly equal to five times the number of items is necessary (i.e., 250 to 375 in our case). The respondents should resemble as much as possible the population with which the final scale will be used. That is, if the researcher intends to use the scale to measure the attitudes of parents of mentally retarded children toward eugenic methods of prevention, it would not be acceptable to use as the pilot study sample a group of undergraduates in an introductory psychology course, even if they are readily available and are required to participate in experiments.

The pilot version of the scale should resemble the final version in every aspect, except length. This includes item layout, response format, and instructions. The format of the scale and the instructions provided should be carefully considered and prepared. Previously published scales should be reviewed. [Consult Shaw and Wright (1967) or the scales presented in Chapters 9 to 13 of this book.] Experts may also be consulted in the preparation of the scale's format. Any additional questions should appear on the pilot version as well. This would include questions designed to obtain demographic information (e.g., sex, age) and experiential information (e.g., training in the subject, contact with people who are disabled) about the respondents. The researcher should be careful to only collect information which contributes data necessary to answer the research question. Just because data can be readily obtained does not mean that they should be collected. Many times data are lost when a respondent refuses to complete a scale because of these intrusive questions (e.g., asking the age or sex of the respondent, or whether he or she has a college degree).

The data from this pilot study are then coded, entered into the computer, and analyzed. The goal is to reduce the number of items in order to create a shorter, more efficient scale with sound psychometric characteristics. This process is an iterative one. That is, certain items are deleted and the process is repeated on the reduced scale using the same pilot study data. (The criteria for inclusion will be presented in the following section.) Three or four iterations of the process should yield a set of approximately 30 to 35 items.

Once again, half of the final set of items are worded positively and half are worded negatively and these reworded items are arranged randomly on a second composite scale in the appropriate (and perhaps revised) format. This second scale is then administered in a second pilot study to a second sample of respondents, once again roughly equal to five times the number of items (i.e., 150 to 175 in our case) and resembling the final population. The final version of the attitude scale is dervied from detailed item, scale, and factor analyses of these data.

ITEM ANALYSES

Response Distributions

The first step in the item analysis process is to calculate the mean, standard deviation, skewness, and kurtosis for each item, as well as the product-moment correlation coefficients between each item and the total scale score (i.e., a discrimination index), and between all possible item pairs (i.e., a homogeneity index). Each item should also be scored dichotomously by collapsing (in our case) the three "agree" response options into one category and the three "disagree" response options into a second category. The dichotomous items are then scored as correct or incorrect (in the direction of a positive attitude) according to the experts' favorability key obtained in the item preparation step.

Difficulty and Discrimination

The item difficulty (i.e., percentage of respondents getting the item correct), and standard deviation are calculated, as well as the point-biserial correlation coefficient between each dichotomously scored item and the total scale score. This is done in two ways—the first calculation includes the item in the total scale score, and the second calculation excludes the item from the total scale score. The former index is often spuriously high, especially with scales of 25 or fewer items, because the item score is part of the total scale score. Both of these indices are calculated and tested for significance for each item separately for those who got the item correct and those who got the item incorrect. It should be noted that correct on an attitude scale is not the same as correct on an achievement, aptitude, or intelligence scale. In the case of attitude scales, correct should be understood to mean commonness (or popularity or typicalness) of a belief.

Tables of these continuous and dichotomous indices are constructed and the statistics examined in order to select those items which should be deleted. The decision is based on a composite of several of the indices. The item dispersion should indicate reasonable variability and not an extremely skewed or compact range of responses. The absolute value of item-to-scale correlations should be significant for both the correct item response and the incorrect response. (The signs of these coefficients will depend upon whether the item is a positively worded item or a negatively worded item.)

The item-to-scale correlations can be ranked independently for the positive and negative items, and an equal number of those with the highest values can be retained for the final scale. If the item-exclusive point-biserial discrimination index is significant, then the item-inclusive index will be as well. If the exclusive index is not significant and the inclusive index is, then the researcher should carefully examine other indices (e.g., the dispersion characteristics or difficulty index) to decide whether to retain the item.

Prior to the general availability of computer programs to perform these detailed item analyses, the 27 percent rule first proposed by Kelley (1939), was commonly used to select items. In this method, the percentages of correct item responses of only those respondents in the upper and lower 27 percent of the total scale score distribution were computed. One difficulty with this method is that it underestimates the item's discrimination as the values approach 100 percent and overestimates the values as they approach zero percent, by as much as 12 percent (D'Agostino and Cureton, 1976; Guilford and Fruchter, 1978). Second, a great deal of information is lost when 46 percent of the scores are discarded. The 27 percent rule should customarily not be followed. Rather, the procedures proposed in this section are recommended because it is now a simple matter with high speed computers to calculate the various indices and correlations for each item using all the respondent data.

Baker (1985) and other psychometricians have proposed a set of item analysis procedures based on a so-called item characteristic curve. This curve is derived from a model expressing the probability that a respondent with a particular attitude will respond to an item in the keyed (i.e., correct) direction. The item difficulty and discrimination indices are then taken to represent certain characteristics of this probability curve. While these indices are useful for the analysis of scale items, they have not been widely adopted because of the sophistication of the mathematics involved in their calculation. The recent availability of microcomputer statistical programs to perform the necessary calculations (e.g., Baker, 1985) suggests that these indices may become more widely used by researchers.

SCALE ANALYSIS

Distribution of Scores

The total scale score for each respondent is determined and the mean and dispersion characteristics of the scale scores are calculated. These dispersion characteristics (the standard deviation, skewness, and kurtosis) are used to test the normality of the distribution of scale scores. As noted in Chapter 2, the scale scores are not truly interval level data. The same score for several different respondents can be obtained from completely different arrays of item responses. Consequently, the scores of two respondents may be compared to determine which respondent expresses a more favorable attitude toward the referent, but the underlying attitude difference cannot be determined from the scores (Oppenheimer, 1966). To put it another way, a respondent with a score of 36 manifests a more favorable attitude toward the referent than a respondent with a score of 35, but he or she is not 1 more favorable.

If the assumption of normality of the distribution of scores is tenable, and the item dispersion and discrimination characteristics are reasonable, the researcher can generally proceed as if the data were interval level. Conclusions concerning the scores of groups of respondents can be reasonably stated, but the researcher should avoid statements about the score of an individual respondent.

Dimensionality

The researcher may set out to construct an attitude scale to measure more than one dimension of attitude toward the referent. In this case, all of the item and scale analyses outlined in the preceding section are necessary, including reliability and validity analyses, for each subscale. The researcher who did not set out to construct a measure with subscales may discover, however, as a result of a factor or cluster analyses of the respondents' data, that there is more than one dimension which the attitude scale appears to measure. In that case, the researcher may eliminate or add items to the scale in an effort to create a more homogeneous scale. An iterative procedure to improve the scale's reliability (i.e., homogeneity or internal consistency) is the relevant procedure to follow. Items are added or deleted, and the reliability recalculated, until the desirable level of homogeneity is obtained. Alternatively, the researcher may decide to retain all of the factors which emerge from the factor analysis, perhaps by adding additional items which presumably measure the unforeseen factors. If the researcher proposes or decides that the attitude scale is composed of subscales, then a specificity analysis is necessary.

Specificity

Horst (1966) defined specificity as the extent to which one of a set of tests measures a factor or trait not measured by any of the other tests in the set. In general, if among a battery of tests, or a set of subscales in our case, each subscale is only slightly correlated with all of the other subscales of the set, but moderately to strongly correlated with the total scale, and if the items on each subscale are highly correlated with the other items on the subscale, but not with items on the other subscales, then the subscales are said to be specific. A variety of statistical measures are available for specificity analysis.

To begin with, each of the subtests must be reliable before it can be specific. Therefore, the reliability values should be high. Second, the items within each subscale should be highly correlated. Third, the correlation of each item with the subscale of which it is a part should be high, but the correlations of each item with the subscales on which it is not scored should be low. Fourth, the inter-subscale correlations should be low (ideally they should be near zero), but the correlations of each subscale with the total scale should be moderate to high. Horst (1966) provides a general formula to estimate the specificity of a subscale as a function of the multiple correlation of the subscale with other subscales in a multiple set. Finally, a second-order factor analysis, using the scores on the subscales as dependent variables, should yield a single factor which accounts for the majority of variance in the factor (subscale) scores.

Latent Structure Analysis

To validate the subscales' content conceptualization, a statistical technique described by Hartke (1979), derived from latent partition analysis (Wiley, 1967), can be used. In this technique, a panel of experts is asked to sort the items of the scale into ad hoc content categories. If the content categories of items can be shown to be consistent across judges, and if the categories, and the items which comprise them, can be shown to be similar to the item clusters derived from the factor or cluster analyses, then this evidence supports a conclusion that the attitude scale is construct valid.

To identify groups of items, a matrix of proportions of joint agreement for the judges' categorizations of the items (the category approximation matrix) is analyzed using an iterative principal factors method. Dissimilar to factor analysis in which the resultant factor titles are coined by the researcher alone, titles for the derived categories of items are distilled from a review of the titles written by the judges as part of the sorting task. The resultant categories are compared to the results of previous factor analyses of respondent data. An example of this procedure is contained in the report of the construct validation of the SADP (Antonak, 1985a).

RESPONSE STYLES

It is an accepted practice that the developer of a scale to measure some dimension of personality must report the extent to which respondents' scores on the scale are influenced by non-relevant respondent personality traits and response determinants (Edwards, 1957a). Social psychologists and psychometricians have called for similar analyses with scales purporting to measure attitudes (Goldstein, 1960; Taylor, 1961). Four response styles, three of which were introduced in Chapter 5, are particularly relevant to attitude rating scales.

Acquiescence Response Style

Acquiescent responding is typified by yeasayers and naysayers (Couch and Keniston, 1960). One means to prevent this response set is to key half the number of items so that a yes, or positive, response is the favorable attitude and half the number of items so that a no, or negative, response is the favorable attitude. These items are then randomly arranged on the final attitude scale.

Social Desirability Response Style

Socially desirable responding is defined as the tendency of the respondent to endorse only those items on an attitude scale which he or she considers to represent the socially appropriate or socially sanctioned response (Edwards, 1957b). To claim construct validity, an attitude scale must demonstrate that it measures more than just socially desirable responding to a set of attitude statements. Although contemporary researchers are developing new scales to assess social desirability (e.g., Schuessler, Hittle, and Cardascia, 1978), the Crowne and Marlowe (1960) Social Desirability Scale (SDS) continues to be the most widely used instrument.

Responses to the attitude scale are collected from a sample of respondents, and immediately afterwards the respondents are asked to complete the Crowne-

Marlowe scale. Following the procedures outlined by Marlowe and Crowne (1961), the subjects' scores on the SDS are dichotomized at the mean and the subjects are divided into Hi-SDS and Lo-SDS groups. The variance of the attitude scale scores for the Hi-SDS group is then compared to the variance of the scores for the Lo-SDS group and tested for significance. If the difference is not significant, then it can be concluded that the attitude scale is not merely a measure of socially desirable responding to a set of attitude statements. Stated differently, the attitude scale scores are not influenced by the subject's desire to adhere to socially desirable expectations.

Extreme Position Response Tendency

To determine if the respondents tend to select the extreme response options (i.e., -3 or $+3$ for our hypothetical scale), a midpoint-deviation score is calculated following procedures outlined by Nunnally (1978). This score is the sum across all items of the differences between the midpoint of the item response continuum (0 in our case) and the alternative selected by the respondent. The correlation of this score with the total scale score for the sample of respondents is squared and this value is divided by the product of the reliabilities of each of these two scores. This index of extreme position response tendency is called the shared common variance. Values near .90 are considered ideal for attitude rating scales.

Faking

On a summated rating attitude scale, the intention of the items is apparent to the respondent. Consequently, the respondent may deliberately distort his or her responses to present a favorable impression ("fake good") or an unfavorable impression ("fake bad"). In some cases, the respondent may respond in both ways at random in order to sabotage the research. Fakeability of a scale is defined to be the extent to which scores on the scale are distorted under conditions encouraging respondents to alter their original response. The researcher asks a sample of respondents to complete the scale honestly and then to complete the scale in a false way. For example, the respondents may be asked to present a socially favorable response, or a response which would be typical of some group of people (e.g., as disabled people would respond). The two (or more) sets of scores for the respondents are then calculated and compared to determine the extent to which the scores can be faked. The detailed information of the fakeability of the ATDP Scale which is provided by Yuker (1986) will assist the researcher who is investigating this response style.

NORMATIVE DATA

If the results of analyses of data from the attitude scale support the conclusion that it is reliable, valid, and specific, then the researcher may proceed to present

Table 8.1

SADP Centile Norms for the Sex, Age, and Education Groups

	SADP Score										
	Sex		Age Group				Education Group				
Centile	Male	Female	1	2	3	4	1	2	3	4	Comb
99	142	143	137	140	142	138	138	139	142	143	141
95	136	139	134	137	141	137	137	137	139	139	138
90	135	136	131	135	140	134	131	135	137	136	136
85	132	134	129	134	138	127	128	134	135	135	134
80	131	133	126	132	136	126	125	132	133	134	132
75	129	132	120	131	135	124	120	131	132	133	131
70	127	130	119	130	134	122	119	130	130	131	129
65	126	128	118	129	133	121	117	128	128	130	127
60	124	126	114	127	131	120	114	125	126	129	125
55	121	124	112	124	130	119	112	124	125	127	124
50	118	122	109	123	127	123	109	123	123	125	122
45	115	120	108	122	126	110	107	122	121	124	119
40	111	119	106	120	125	104	105	119	119	123	117
35	108	116	104	118	122	103	104	118	118	121	114
30	104	113	102	116	118	101	100	116	114	117	111
25	99	110	99	113	114	95	97	113	111	114	108
20	94	107	93	109	111	93	92	111	108	112	105
15	92	104	90	105	107	92	88	109	103	105	100
10	87	100	86	98	105	87	84	106	96	96	92
5	81	86	77	85	94	69	77	103	85	90	84
1	62	71	46	71	68	63	46	100	70	66	69
N	140	345	107	231	112	35	114	35	209	127	485
Mean	113	119	109	120	124	111	108	123	120	122	118
SD	19	16	18	15	16	19	18	11	16	16	17

Notes. All values are rounded to the nearest whole number.

Reprinted with permission, from Antonak, R. F. (1985b). <u>Construct validation and psychometric analysis of the Scale of Attitudes Toward Disabled Persons</u> (Technical Report No. 2). Durham, NH: University of New Hampshire, Education Department.

normative data for the scale. Livneh (1982a) has called for norms to be constructed for attitude instruments which reflect different respondent characteristics. In order to interpret a respondent's raw score, it is converted to a standard score which is compared with the scores obtained from other respondents who can be categorized into various groups.

As an example, the data from large samples of respondents to our hypothetical scale can be used to construct separate norms for different respondent variables, such as sex, age, and educational level. For the age variable, the respondents can be organized into age groups, such as 13 to 18 years, 19 to 34 years, 35 to 50 years, and ages 51 years and up. Similarly, the educational level variable can be organized into education groups: grades 9 to 12, grades 13 to 16 (college years), grades 17 to 18 (graduate school), and grades 19 to 21 (post-graduate school). Norms can then be calculated (see Guilford and Fruchter, 1978) presenting information on the relative standing of a respondent in comparison to others of similar and different ages and educational levels. Other researchers using the scale can contribute their data and the researcher who developed the scale can periodically incorporate these data into revised centile norms.

Researchers are cautioned to avoid the use of norms derived from only a single and small data set. Analyses of data from large samples of respondents of widely differing characteristics are necessary before norms can safely be used to interpret individual respondent scores. As an example, the preliminary centile norms for the SADP are presented in Table 8.1.

SUMMARY AND PRELUDE

Summated rating scales, based on a probabilistic scaling technique, continue to be the most widely used of the direct measurement methods in investigations of attitudes toward people who are disabled. The researcher who is seeking a previously constructed attitude scale to use in an investigation should only consider a scale if its author has paid careful attention to the psychometric characteristics presented in this chapter. Moreover, the scale's author must also present detailed information on reliability and validity, as discussed in Chapters 6 and 7, respectively.

Recognizing that this is a time-consuming task which many researchers will be unwilling to undertake, we will present in the five chapters of the next section of this book the results of our analyses of a set of scales published in the last three decades which purport to measure attitudes toward people who are disabled. Based upon our reviews of more than 60 scales, we will discuss a total of 22 scales, organized into five categories. We consider these scales to be psychometrically adequate, or at least capable of becoming psychometrically adequate if their authors undertake the reasonable amount of work necessary to publish a suitable revision.

Part III

SCALES FOR THE MEASUREMENT OF ATTITUDES

SILLER (1984) expressed optimism in the conclusion of his review of trends in research concerning the measurement of attitudes toward people who are physically disabled, noting that "studies are becoming increasingly sophisticated and more appropriate to the complexity of the subject . . . It is to be hoped that systematic programs of research directed toward specific problems of need will be accomplished by attention to basic theoretical and measurement concerns" (p. 201). He did, however, state that "there is justification for strong criticism of much of the past research literature on a variety of grounds" (p. 201). Among these grounds are vague definitions of the referent "disabled," the failure of researchers to conceptualize attitudes as multidimensional, and "the absence of adequate technical information to assess the measuring instruments" (p. 185). It is to this last concern that the five chapters in Part III will be specifically directed.

In Chapters 3, 4, and 5 we presented a taxonomy of direct and indirect methods for the measurement of attitudes. In Chapters 6, 7, and 8 we presented detailed guidelines for the psychometric adequacy of rating scales. The chapters in this part will present reviews of 22 previously published scales for the measurement of attitudes toward people who are disabled which possess at least minimal psychometric adequacy. The reviews will follow generally the format used by Shaw and Wright (1967). A brief description of the scale and its development will be followed by information on the scale's response mode, administration, and scoring. Available reliability and validity data will be presented, and the summary will conclude with general comments about the usefulness of the scale.

The scales to be reviewed have been divided into five categories. In Chapter 9 we will present specific technical information on six scales all of which attempt to measure general attitudes toward people who are disabled. In Chapter 10 we will review four scales all of which attempt to measure attitudes toward people with a physical disability. In Chapter 11 we will review three scales all of which attempt to measure attitudes toward psychiatrically disabled people. In Chapter 12 we will review four scales all of which attempt to measure attitudes toward people who are mentally retarded. Finally, in Chapter 13, we will review five scales all of which attempt to measure the extent to which respondents endorse premises concerning societal responsibilities to people who are disabled.

Chapter 9

GENERAL ATTITUDES TOWARD PEOPLE WITH DISABILITIES

ACCEPTANCE SCALE (A-SCALE)

Description

THE ACCEPTANCE SCALE was developed by Voeltz (1980) to measure the attitudes of non-handicapped children toward handicapped peers integrated into regular classroom settings. It was intended that this instrument provide the data needed to evaluate one aspect of the effectiveness of educational integration efforts. The design of the original version of the scale and the selection of items were guided by previously published general personality scales, such as the E (ethnocentrism) scale (Adorno et al., 1964) and the C (conservatism) scale (Wilson and Patterson, 1968). No specific information on item selection is provided.

Beginning in 1977, the state of Hawaii began to integrate severely and multiply handicapped children into regular educational settings in neighborhood public schools to replace institutional services. This program provided Voeltz with "the impetus and opportunity" for the development of the A-Scale. A prototype attitude instrument was administered to more than 2,500 public school children in grades 2 through 7 in Hawaii in the fall of 1978. Subjects were divided by schools with varying levels of integration of handicapped peers.

The A-Scale has been modified since this early research, and currently consists of four versions: Lower Elementary Level (Grades 1-2); Upper Elementary Level (Grades 3-6); Secondary Level, A-Version; and Secondary Level, B-Version. The author suggests that the lower elementary version may also be usable with Kindergarten children "given sufficient preparation." The two secondary level versions have been used with youth in grades 7 to 9, although the author states that the scale should be usable with students in grades 10 to 12 as well. Secondary version A is to be used "whenever reading level might be a problem," while version B is for students with at least a fourth grade reading ability.

Response Format

The Lower Elementary Level of the A-Scale consists of 22 items. Of these, the first two are screening items to ensure that the respondent comprehends the task and response requirements ("veridicality check" items), five are social-desirability items concerning the student's general feelings of self and friendship (items #9, 13, 15, 19, and 20), and the remaining 15 concern differences among children or acceptance of handicaps and handicapped children. Three response options are provided for each item: Yes, to signify "I agree," No, to signify "I disagree," and Maybe, to signify "I'm not sure." A total of nine items were randomly worded positively and the other six were worded negatively to prevent acquiescence response style.

The Upper Elementary Level version of the scale consists of 34 items: two are veridicality check items (#1 and 13), two are general friendship items (#10 and 21), and the remaining 30 are acceptance items. Of these 30 items, two are worded positively. The Secondary Level versions consists of 37 items: three are veridicality check items (#3, 8, and 36), two are general friendship items (#9 and 26), and the other 32 are acceptance items. Of these 32 items, 19 are worded positively.

Administration and Scoring

The scale is designed to be administered in large groups (e.g., by classroom). The items on the two elementary versions are read aloud by the administrator and the children are instructed to mark their response on an individual answer sheet one at a time. The pages for the lower level are color coded, while the pages for the upper level are printed back to back. The response instructions are repeated to the group every three or four items. Administration of the scale to groups of approximately 25 children takes 15 to 20 minutes.

The directions and items for version A of the secondary level scale are also read aloud, and administration takes approximately 20 minutes. The directions for version B are also read aloud, but the student completes the scale in silence. This version takes approximately 15 minutes to administer.

Each accepting response is scored with an index of 2, each nonaccepting responses is scored with an index of 0, and each undecided response is scored with an index of 1. The range of scores on each of the four versions of the scale is: Lower Elementary, 0 to 30; Upper Elementary, 0 to 60; Secondary A or B, 0 to 64. In each case, a high score reflects a more accepting attitude.

Reliability

Difficulty and discrimination indices were provided for each item of the original version of the scale (Voeltz, 1980). A Spearman-Brown corrected split-half reliability index of + .82 was reported, as well as an alpha coefficient of + .77. A test-retest stability coefficient of + .68 was obtained by retesting a sample of 101 children on two occasions separated by three weeks. No reliability data on the current four version of the scale have been published to date.

Validity

Three groups of children in the original validation sample were identified: a group with no handicapped children in their school, a group with severely multiply handicapped children enrolled in their school for approximately one semester, and a group with severely multiply handicapped children enrolled in their school for approximately one year. In addition, a randomly selected sample of "special friends" from a larger group of volunteers in the latter (high contact) group in grades four through six was identified. These children participated in a special program designed to increase the integration of handicapped children through carefully structured contact among handicapped and non-handicapped children. The mean A-Scale scores for the special friends sample was significantly more positive than that for the entire sample. In addition, a correlation of + .46 between A-Scale scores and actual attendance in the special friends program was interpreted by Voeltz (1982) as support for the predictive validity of the scale.

Construct validation of the original version of the scale involved the factor analysis of both the pretest (Voeltz, 1980) and post test (Voeltz, 1982) item responses and subsequent analyses of factor score differences due to sex, grade, and degree of contact with handicapped peers. Four factors emerged from the analysis of the pretest data and five factors emerged from the analysis of the post test data. Two of the pretest and three of the post test factors were highly specific with few items loading on them. In general, girls in the higher grades in the high contact schools expressed the most favorable attitudes toward their handicapped peers.

No validity information on the current four versions of the A Scale have been published to date. The author provided directions on how to score the A Scale at the upper elementary and secondary levels into "dimensions" (presumably subscales derived from factor analyses), but does not provide any information on the validity and specificity of these subscales.

Comments

This scale holds promise as an attitude scale specifically constructed to measure the attitudes of children toward their handicapped peers. More work needs to be done, including additional validity analyses and refinement of the scale's dimensionality. Several of the items on the elementary level versions seem problematic, and the three-option response mode is questionable (the author could not determine what "Maybe" meant to the young children). In addition, an analysis of the linguistic complexity of the items on the scale would be appropriate to establish the lower age limit of utility of the scale. The availability of the current four versions may permit the use of the scale at all grade levels if the author can provide additional information of the validity and reliability of each version. In addition, investigations of the scales' susceptibilities to socially desirable responding and faking are necessary.

Towfighy-Hooshyar and Zingle (1984) modified the A-Scale after a pilot study by replacing certain items to help students in grades two, four, and six to understand them, and by adding two new items. It is unclear which items were modified and why. This revised scale was administered to 240 non-handicapped children and the resultant data factor analyzed. A coefficient alpha reliability of + .76 was reported for the modified scale. This study illustrates the type of psychometric work which may yield the needed refinements of this promising attitude scale.

Exhibit 9-1

Acceptance Scale

(Lower Elementary Level)

---

1. At school, we eat lunch in the cafeteria.
2. Santa Claus wears a blue suit.
3. I could be good friends with a kid who can't talk yet.
4. I don't play with kids who look different.
5. I sometimes pick on other kids.
6. I would like to push a handicapped kid in a wheelchair.
7. I have a friend who is retarded.
8. I don't like to play with a kid who is different.
9. I say hello to kids who are retarded.
10. I like to play with the special ed kids.
11. I only play with one or two best friends.
12. I am sometimes mean to other kids.
13. I have a friend who is in a wheelchair.
14. It's not nice to call someone "mental."
15. It is hard for me to make new friends.
16. I wouldn't spend my recess with a handicapped kid.
17. I have a best friend.
18. I would like to be friends with a handicapped kid.
19. I have helped someone in a wheelchair.
20. I sometimes call other kids names like "dummy."
21. I like being the way I am.
22. I sometimes play with kids from other rooms at recess.

 Detailed instructions for administration are available from the author. Instructions and items are read aloud to the children.

Exhibit 9-2

Acceptance Scale

(Upper Elementary Level)

---

1. We usually have school lunch at nine o'clock in the morning.
2. I have a friend who uses a wheelchair at school.
3. My school should try to figure out a way for kids in wheelchairs to go on field trips with us.
4. If I had a retarded brother or sister, I wouldn't tell anyone.
5. I have talked with some mentally retarded students at my school.
6. If I found out that someone I play with is mentally retarded, I would still keep on playing with him.
7. I have talked to some students who use wheelchairs.
8. I don't think it's nice to call a special ed kid "mental."
9. I'm not friends with any of the kids who use wheelchairs.
10. It's hard for me to make new friends.
11. I don't like to be close to a kid who looks or acts different.
12. I think that a kid who is deaf or blind could be in my room.
13. If someone gave me two flower leis and I gave one away, I would have one left.
14. I don't think it's OK to call one of your friends "mental."
15. I don't want a child from the special ed class to sit next to me on the bus or on a field trip.
16. I think that the severely handicapped kids should have lunch with my class in the cafeteria.
17. If a mentally retarded child wanted to play with me and my friends at the park, that would be OK.
18. During recess, I never play with any special ed kids who are retarded.
19. I think I could be good friends with a special ed student.
20. If one of my good friends called a special ed kid "mental," I would tell my friend not to say that.
21. I play with kids from different clasrooms at recess.

Exhibit 9-2 (Continued)

---

22. I wish I could make friends with a mentally retarded student.

23. I have made friends with a mentally retarded student.

24. I don't say hello to kids who are retarded.

25. You shouldn't call someone "dummy" just because he made a mistake.

26. I have played on the playground with some mentally retarded students.

27. I have helped some students in wheelchairs.

28. If a kid can't do something or does something wrong, he will probably be called a "dummy" by other kids.

29. Children who are retarded could come into my room at school for activities.

30. I don't want to be friends with a severely handicapped child.

31. Sometimes, I wish I could play with some mentally retarded students like other kids.

32. If someone told me about a new TV show about handicaps, I would watch it if I could.

33. I would like my class to go to camp the same week that a class of handicapped kids was there.

34. If a mentally retarded child wanted to play with me at the park, that would be nice.

 Detailed instructions for administration are available from the author. Instructions and items are read aloud to the children. The term in item #13 should be altered to local usage.

Exhibit 9-3

Acceptance Scale

(Secondary Level, Version B)

On the next four pages, you will find a list of sentences. You should read each sentence one at a time and after reading the sentence, decide if you:

AGREE: If you agree, this means that the sentence is true for you. It is a sentence that you could say, so you should circle the word AGREE

DISAGREE: If you disagree, this means that the sentence is not true for you. It is a sentence that you could not say, so you should circle the word DISAGREE

UNDECIDED: If you are not sure how you feel about the sentence, you can say you are undecided, so you should circle the word UNDECIDED

There are not really any right or wrong answers to most of the sentences on this survey. We are only interested in what you think. How you answer the sentence depends on your feelings.

REMEMBER. THE ANSWER IS UP TO YOU! SINCE THERE ARE NO REAL "RIGHT" OR "WRONG" ANSWERS WHEN THE SENTENCE IS ABOUT YOUR FEELINGS, YOUR ANSWERS WILL BE DIFFERENT FROM SOMEONE ELSE'S!

---

1. My school should plan for students in wheelchairs to accompany the other students on field trips with regular classes.

   AGREE DISAGREE UNDECIDED

2. I don't have any friends who are mentally retarded or handicapped.

   AGREE DISAGREE UNDECIDED

3. If someone gave me nine flower leis and I gave three away, I would have six left.

   AGREE DISAGREE UNDECIDED

4. If my sister or brother were retarded, I wouldn't talk about it to anyone.

   AGREE DISAGREE UNDECIDED

Exhibit 9-3 (Continued)

---

5. I have talked to students who use wheelchairs.

AGREE DISAGREE UNDECIDED

6. If I found out that someone I hang around with is mentally retarded, I would still be his friend.

AGREE DISAGREE UNDECIDED

7. I have talked with some mentally retarded students at school.

AGREE DISAGREE UNDECIDED

8. We usually have school lunch at 9 a.m.

AGREE DISAGREE UNDECIDED

9. I like the idea of having a variety of friends.

AGREE DISAGREE UNDECIDED

10. There is no reason for me to spend time with anyone who is handicapped.

AGREE DISAGREE UNDECIDED

11. I'm not friends with any of the students who use wheelchairs.

AGREE DISAGREE UNDECIDED

12. It's not nice to call a special education student "mental."

AGREE DISAGREE UNDECIDED

13. I think that a student who is deaf or blind could be in my class.

AGREE DISAGREE UNDECIDED

14. I don't have a friend who has to use a wheelchair.

AGREE DISAGREE UNDECIDED

15. I wouldn't want a special education student to sit next to me on the bus or on a field trip.

AGREE DISAGREE UNDECIDED

16. I believe that the severely handicapped students should have lunch with the other students in the cafeteria.

AGREE DISAGREE UNDECIDED

17. If a mentally retarded student wanted to be with me and my friends at the park, that would be OK.

AGREE DISAGREE UNDECIDED

Exhibit 9-3 (Continued)

---

18. I have never held a conversation with a person who is paralyzed or couldn't walk.

    AGREE DISAGREE UNDECIDED

19. During breaks at school, I never associate with any special ed students who are retarded.

    AGREE DISAGREE UNDECIDED

20. I believe that I could become close friends with a special ed student.

    AGREE DISAGREE UNDECIDED

21. If one of my good friends called a special ed student "mental," I would tell my friend to watch his mouth.

    AGREE DISAGREE UNDECIDED

22. I have helped some students who are in wheelchairs.

    AGREE DISAGREE UNDECIDED

23. I wish I could become friends with a mentally retarded person.

    AGREE DISAGREE UNDECIDED

24. I have become friends with a mentally retarded student.

    AGREE DISAGREE UNDECIDED

25. I don't greet "hello" to students who are retarded.

    AGREE DISAGREE UNDECIDED

26. It's difficult for me to make new friends.

    AGREE DISAGREE UNDECIDED

27. You shouldn't call a person "dummy" just because he made a mistake.

    AGREE DISAGREE UNDECIDED

28. I have associated with some mentally retarded students during my freetimes at school.

    AGREE DISAGREE UNDECIDED

29. I would prefer not to be around students who look or act different.

    AGREE DISAGREE UNDECIDED

Exhibit 9-3 (Continued)

---

30. It's OK to call one of your friends "mental."

    AGREE DISAGREE UNDECIDED

31. If a student can't perform a task or does it incorrectly, he'll probably be called a "dummy" by other kids.

    AGREE DISAGREE UNDECIDED

32. Students who are retarded should not come into my class for activities at school.

    AGREE DISAGREE UNDECIDED

33. Sometimes I wish I could hang around with some mentally retarded students like the other kids.

    AGREE DISAGREE UNDECIDED

34. If someone told me about a new TV program about handicaps, I would watch it if I could.

    AGREE DISAGREE UNDECIDED

35. I would like my class to participate with a special ed class in different activities--like camp, field trips, etc.

    AGREE DISAGREE UNDECIDED

36. It doesn't snow on the island of Oahu in Hawaii.

    AGREE DISAGREE UNDECIDED

37. If a mentally retarded student wanted to be with me at the park, that would be OK.

    AGREE DISAGREE UNDECIDED

 Detailed instructions for administration are available from the author. The terms in items #3 and 36 should be altered to local usage.

ATTITUDE TOWARD DISABLED PERSONS SCALE (ATDP)

Description

The ATDP scale is, without a doubt, the best known and most widely used of the scales purporting to measure attitudes toward disabled people in general. This self-report scale was originally published in 1960 as a 20-item summated rating scale named the ATDP-Form O (Yuker et al., 1960). Two equivalent 30-item forms, A and B, were subsequently developed and published in 1962 (Yuker et al., 1966). The items on the scale represent statements suggesting differences (or, when rejected, similarities) between disabled and non-disabled people. The items depict two types of statements—characteristics of disabled individuals (e.g., personal, intellectual, emotional, social) and treatment modalities (e.g., educational, vocational, social integration). The scale purports to measure both the attitudes of non-disabled people toward physically disabled people (on an acceptance-rejection continuum) and attitudes of disabled people toward themselves. In the latter case, self-directed attitudes are perceived as a measure of self-acceptance, or rejection of being disabled. The authors argue that the three forms are unidimensional and measure a generalized attitude (i.e., positive vs. negative attitude) toward physically disabled individuals as a group.

Response Format

Respondents express their agreement or disagreement with each item on a six-point scale ranging from −3 ("I disagree very much"), −2 ("I disagree pretty much"), −1 ("I disagree a little"), +1 ("I agree a little"), +2 ("I agree pretty much"), to +3 ("I agree very much"). No neutral response can be given. Respondents may either enter their numerical response in the space provided to the left of each item (Form O) or circle their response to each item on a specifically designed answer sheet (Forms A and B).

Administration and Scoring

The ATDP scales may be administered in either an individual or a group format. Instructions to respondents are provided at the top of the page. Scoring of the ATDP scales requires careful consideration of the signs of the responses. Because approximately half the items, on each scale form, are worded positively while the remaining items are worded negatively, the first step is to alter the signs of the positively-worded items. At the completion of this task, all responses are summed, the sign of this sum is then reversed, and a constant is added to eliminate any possible negative value. This set of operations provides scores which range from 0 to 120 (Form O) or from 0 to 180 (Forms A and B), with a high score indicating a positive attitude in each case. Each ATDP scale takes approximately ten minutes to administer.

Reliability

The original monographs published by the Human Resources Center provide extensive data on the development and psychometric characteristics of the three ATDP scale forms. A subsequent series of monographs (Block, 1974; Yuker and Block, 1986; Yuker et al., 1966, 1970) presents detailed item, scale, reliability, and validity information for the scales, as well as summaries of a large number of studies which have used the ATDP scales. As was briefly outlined in Chapter 6, several reliability estimates are provided for the different forms. Estimates of the stability (i.e., test-retest) of Form O range from +.66 to +.89. The number of estimates of the stability of Forms A and B is smaller with only a single estimate for Form A (+.79) and two estimates for Form B (+.71 and +.83). Time intervals range from two weeks to 18 months. Estimates of alternate-forms (equivalence) reliability range from +.57 (O to B) to +.83 (A to B), while internal (split-half) reliability estimates range from +.75 to +.85 for Form O, from +.73 to +.89 for Form A, and from +.72 to +.87 for Form B. Finally, stability-equivalence reliability estimates range from +.41 to +.83, with time intervals ranging from two weeks to five months.

Validity

The authors (Yuker et al., 1966, 1970) reported that an extensive literature review of statements describing disabled persons was undertaken. This was followed by having several psychologists review and assess the extracted items as to their relevance for use in the scale (content validation). Item analyses were then conducted to assure item discrimination between high-scoring and low-scoring groups for each form. In order to establish criterion-related and construct validation of the ATDP scales, scores on the scales were correlated with a variety of demographic and personality measures. In general, no relationship was found between age of respondents and acceptance, or rejection, of physically disabled people. When respondents' gender was correlated with the ATDP Scale scores, sex differences were found. Females demonstrated greater acceptance of physical disability than did males. Educational level appears to be positively related to acceptance of the physically disabled person.

When personality variables of respondents were associated with the ATDP Scale scores, the following characteristics were usually positively correlated with acceptance of physically disabled people: low aggressiveness and hostility, intraception (i.e., self-insight and other-insight), positive self-concept, ego-strength, and low anxiety level. No evidence of association with measures of intelligence or interest (avocational or vocational) was found. ATDP Scale scores were also correlated with scores on measures of attitudes toward members of other groups, such as old people, alcoholics, mentally ill people, and a variety of ethnic groups, in addition to scores on other measures of attitudes toward disabled people. Most of these studies reported positive relationships between ATDP Scale scores and the foregoing measures. In addition, correlations were reported between ATDP Scale scores and measures of authoritarianism, ethnocentrism, dogmatism, Machiavellianism, and intellectualism. Somewhat conflicting results were obtained from these studies, although some support was lent to the hypotheses of association between authoritarian, ethnocentric, Machiavellian, and pragmatic individuals and rejection of physically disabled people.

A final group of studies attempted to correlate respondents' experiential and behavioral variables with attitudes toward disabled people. Studies of the extent of personal contact with disabled people suggested that, in general, increased contact with disabled individuals is associated with more favorable attitudes. This is especially true with regard to close personal contact in educational, social, and vocational (rather than medical) settings. The effects of specific educational experiences (e.g., academic courses) on increasing favorable attitudes toward disabled people were only mildly successful.

Studies regarding the susceptibility of the ATDP Scale to faking, social desirability, and acquiescence response style have yielded mixed conclusions. The authors (Yuker et al., 1970) present limited data in support of their claim that the ATDP-Form O is not fakeable. However, more recent studies (Cannon and Szuhay, 1986; Scott and Rohrbach, 1977; Vargo and Semple, 1984) found that the ATDP Scale may be susceptible to faking. A summary of some of these mixed findings may be found in Yuker (1986). The ATDP Scale was also subjected to investigation of the influence of respondents' social desirability responding on its scores. Yuker et al. (1970) provide some data which indicate that the ATDP-Form O is not significantly correlated with either the Edwards (1957b) Social Desirability Scale or with the Crowne-Marlowe (1960) Social Desirability Scale, and conclude that the ATDP Scale measures something other than socially desirable responding. No data concerning social desirability were provided for Forms A and B. Other investigators concluded from their studies that scores on the ATDP Scale are influenced by social desirability [Siller et al., 1967 (Form O); Feinberg, 1967 (Form A); Moses, Rubin, and Turner, n.d. (Form B)] and high social pressure [Horenstein, 1978 (Form B)]. Finally, it seems that acquiescence response style does not exert a significant influence on ATDP Scale scores. That is, low correlations were demonstrated (Siller, 1963; Siller and Chipman, 1963) between the ATDP-Form O and Couch and Keniston's (1960) Acquiescence Scale, Fulkerson's (1958) Acquiescence Response Scale, or the MMPI F-Scale.

Factor analytic studies of the ATDP Scale have suggested that Forms A and O are not structurally unidimensional (i.e., not factorially pure). In other words, little empirical data support the presumed favorable-unfavorable attitudinal dimension which the authors argued constituted the underlying structure of the scale. In earlier factorial studies of the ATDP Scale, Siller and Chipman (1964) reported extracting two independent factors (Form O), while Jaques and Linkowski's study (reported in Yuker et al., 1966) yielded nine factors (Form A). More recently Antonak (1979a, 1980c; Form O) and Livneh (1982a, 1983; Form A) concluded, similarly, that the two forms may contain anywhere from two to four independent factors. Hafer, Wright, and Godley (1983), although arguing for the basic unidimensionality of Form B, nevertheless admitted to the possible presence of a multifactorial solution. Finally, based upon the results of their study which used a factorial research design, Sloat and Frankel (1972) seriously questioned the unidimensionality of the ATDP-Form A. Their findings demonstrated the susceptibility of the scale scores to variance contributed by components such as types of disabilities portrayed, situations, content items, and interactions among these components and respondents' gender.

Comments

The ATDP Scale has been the subject of, or been used in, an enormous amount of empirical research. Although research conducted on the three forms strongly suggests that the scale demonstrates a considerable degree of internal and external reliability, it lacks unequivocal evidence of its validity. Furthermore, recent examinations of the psychometric properties of the ATDP-Form O (Antonak, 1979a, 1980c, 1981b) suggested that this particular form should be used with extreme caution because of poor item characteristics, extreme position response tendency, and factorial ambiguity. This 25-year-old scale contains items which are inappropriate in light of recent changes in the provision of educational and rehabilitative services and contemporary societal views of people who are disabled. Investigations of the dimensionality of Forms A and B suggest that the unidimensional structure hypothesized by the authors may also be somewhat inappropriate (Hafer, Wright, and Godley, 1983; Livneh, 1982a, 1983). Empirical research on related psychometric properties of Forms A and B has not been reported recently.

A number of researchers have modified the ATDP Scale by replacing the word disabled with one or more different words (e.g., handicapped, cancer, deaf), and suggest that the resultant scale is a sound measure of attitudes toward that group. Unless the researchers who undertake such revisions provide complete and detailed psychometric data, such as that recommended in Chapter 8, these scales and the research results derived from their use should be ignored. The modification of the ATDP to create the Attitudes Toward Handicapped Individuals (ATHI) scale (Lazar, Gensley, and Orpet, 1971) may be an exception. Some limited data appear to be available concerning the psychometric characteristics of the ATHI (Lazar, Stodden, and Sullivan, 1976).

Exhibit 9-4

Attitude Toward Disabled Persons Scale

Form-O

Directions

Mark each statement in the left margin according to how much you agree or disagree with it. Please mark every one. Write +1, +2, +3; or -1, -2, -3; depending on how you feel in each case.

Key

+3: I agree very much	-1: I disagree a little
+2: I agree pretty much	-2: I disagree pretty much
+1: I agree a little	-3: I disagree very much

___ 1 Parents of disabled children should be less strict than other parents.

___ 2 Physically disabled persons are just as intelligent as non-disabled ones.

___ 3 Disabled people are usually easier to get along with than other people.

___ 4 Most disabled people feel sorry for themselves.

___ 5 Disabled people are the same as anyone else.

___ 6 There shouldn't be special schools for disabled children.

___ 7 It would be best for disabled persons to live and work in special communities.

___ 8 It is up to the government to take care of disabled persons.

___ 9 Most disabled people worry a great deal.

___ 10 Disabled people should not be expected to meet the same standards as non-disabled people.

___ 11 Disabled people are as happy as non-disabled ones.

___ 12 Severely disabled people are no harder to get along with than those with minor disabilities.

___ 13 It is almost impossible for a disabled person to lead a normal life.

___ 14 You should not expect too much from disabled people.

Exhibit 9-4 (Continued)

___ 15 Disabled people tend to keep to themselves much of the time.

___ 16 Disabled people are more easily upset than non-disabled people.

___ 17 Disabled persons cannot have a normal social life.

___ 18 Most disabled people feel that they are not as good as other people.

___ 19 You have to be careful what you say when you are with disabled people.

___ 20 Disabled people are often grouchy.

Reprinted with permission of the authors; from Yuker, H. E., Block, J. R., & Campbell, W. J. (1960). A scale to measure attitudes toward disabled persons (Human Resources Study No. 5). Albertson, NY: Human Resources Center.

Exhibit 9-5

Attitude Toward Disabled Persons Scale

Form-A

Directions

Mark each statement in the left margin according to how much you agree or disagree with it. Please mark every one. Write +1, +2, +3; or -1, -2, -3; depending on how you feel in each case.

Key

+3: I agree very much	-1: I disagree a little
+2: I agree pretty much	-2: I disagree pretty much
+1: I agree a little	-3: I disagree very much

___ 1 Disabled people are often unfriendly.

___ 2 Disabled people should not have to compete for jobs with physically normal persons.

___ 3 Disabled people are more emotional than other people.

___ 4 Most disabled persons are more self-conscious than other people.

___ 5 We should expect just as much from disabled as from non-disabled persons.

___ 6 Disabled workers cannot be as successful as other workers.

___ 7 Disabled people usually do not make much of a contribution to society.

___ 8 Most non-disabled people would not want to marry anyone who is physically disabled.

___ 9 Disabled people show as much enthusiasm, as other people.

___ 10 Disabled persons are usually more sensitive than other people.

___ 11 Severely disabled people are usually untidy.

___ 12 Most disabled people feel that they are as good as other people.

___ 13 The driving test given to a disabled person should be more severe than the one given to the non-disabled.

___ 14 Disabled people are usually sociable.

Exhibit 9-5 (Continued)

___ 15 Disabled persons usually are not as conscientious as physically normal persons.

___ 16 Severely disabled persons probably worry more about their health than those who have minor disabilities.

___ 17 Most disabled persons are not dissatisfied with themselves.

___ 18 There are more misfits among disabled persons than among non-disabled persons.

___ 19 Most disabled persons do not get discouraged easily.

___ 20 Most disabled persons resent physically normal people.

___ 21 Disabled children should compete with physically normal children.

___ 22 Most disabled persons can take care of themselves.

___ 23 It would be best if disabled persons would live and work with non-disabled persons.

___ 24 Most severely disabled people are just as ambitious as physically normal persons.

___ 25 Disabled people are just as self-confident as other people.

___ 26 Most disabled persons want more affection and praise than other people.

___ 27 Physically disabled persons are often less intelligent than non-disabled ones.

___ 28 Most disabled people are different from non-disabled people.

___ 29 Disabled persons don't want any more sympathy than other people.

___ 30 The way disabled people act is irritating.

Exhibit 9-6

Attitude Toward Disabled Persons Scale

Form-B

Directions

Mark each statement in the left margin according to how much you agree or disagree with it. Please mark every one. Write +1, +2, +3; or -1, -2, -3; depending on how you feel in each case.

Key

+3: I agree very much	-1: I disagree a little
+2: I agree pretty much	-2: I disagree pretty much
+1: I agree a little	-3: I disagree very much

___ 1 Disabled people are usually friendly.

___ 2 People who are disabled should not have to pay income tax.

___ 3 Disabled people are no more emotional than other people.

___ 4 Disabled people can have a normal social life.

___ 5 Most physically disabled persons have a chip on their shoulder.

___ 6 Disabled workers can be as successful as other workers.

___ 7 Very few disabled persons are ashamed of their disabilities.

___ 8 Most people feel uncomfortable when they associate with disabled people.

___ 9 Disabled people show less enthusiasm than non-disabled people.

___ 10 Disabled persons do not become upset any more easily than non-disabled people.

___ 11 Disabled people are often less aggressive than normal people.

___ 12 Most disabled persons get married and have children.

___ 13 Most disabled persons do not worry anymore than anyone else.

___ 14 Employers should not be allowed to fire disabled employees.

___ 15 Disabled people are not as happy as non-disabled ones.

Exhibit 9-6 (Continued)

___ 16 Severely disabled people are harder to get along with than are those with minor disabilities.

___ 17 Most disabled people expect special treatment.

___ 18 Disabled persons should not expect to lead normal lives.

___ 19 Most disabled persons tend to get discouraged easily.

___ 20 The worst thing that could happen to a person would be for him to be very severely injured.

___ 21 Disabled children should not have to compete with non-disabled children.

___ 22 Most disabled people do not feel sorry for themselves.

___ 23 Most disabled people prefer to work with other disabled people.

___ 24 Most severely disabled people are not as ambitious as physically normal persons.

___ 25 Disabled people are not as self-confident as physically normal persons.

___ 26 Most disabled persons don't want more affection and praise than other people.

___ 27 It would be best if a physically disabled person would marry another disabled person.

___ 28 Most disabled people do not need special attention.

___ 29 Disabled persons want sympathy more than other people.

___ 30 Most physically disabled persons have different personalities than normal persons.

Reprinted with permission of the authors; from Yuker, H. E., Block, J. R., & Campbell, W. J. (1962). Disability types and behavior (Human Resources Study No. 6). Albertson, NY: Human Resources Center.

DISABILITY FACTOR SCALES (DFS)

Description

The Disability Factor Scales were constructed to overcome what the authors (Siller, Ferguson, Vann, and Holland, 1967) perceived to be three basic faults inherent in previously developed measures of attitudes toward disabled people (e.g., the ATDP Scale and the Attitude to Blindness Scale). These perceived weaknesses were: (a) the failure of previously published scales to consider the multidimensionality of attitudes toward disabled individuals, (b) the ambiguity associated with the use of the term "disability" (in the ATDP scale) as a general trans-referent class which often conveys vagueness and arouses negativeness, and (c) the specificity of some attitudinal scales which only measure reactions toward a particular disabling condition (i.e., the Attitude to Blindness Scale).

Consequently, Siller and his colleagues developed an array of self-report summated rating scales to measure attitudes toward specific disabilities and across disabilities. The disabilities selected, which were to sample different degrees of both functionality and visibility of impairment, included: amputation, blindness, and cosmetic conditions (Siller, Chipman, Ferguson, and Vann, 1967; Siller, Ferguson, Vann, and Holland, 1967), deafness (Ferguson, 1970), obesity (Vann, 1970), and cancer (Siller and Braden, 1976). In addition, Siller (1969, 1970) has proposed a general, trans-disability scale. Each Disability Factor Scale was derived from scale development and factor analytic investigations, and each is scored on a number of separate dimensions. For example, the General form of the scale (DFS-G, Siller, 1969, 1970) is a 69-item scale composed of statements depicting a variety of reactions, assumed attributes, and advocated policies toward several types of physical disabilities (i.e., amputation, blindness, heart trouble, deafness, epilepsy, cancer, paralysis, scarring, and hunchback). The seven factorially-defined attitude dimensions include: Interaction Strain (nine items), Rejection of Intimacy (11 items), Generalized Rejection (12 items), Authoritarian Virtuousness (ten items), Inferred Emotional Consequences (eight items), Distressed Identification (12 items), and Imputed Functional Limitations (seven items) (Siller, 1976, 1984). The DFS-Amputation (DFS-A) is composed of the same seven dimensions totalling 101 items, and the DFS-Blindness (DFS-B) is also composed of these seven dimensions totalling 105 items. The DFS-Cosmetic Conditions (DFS-C) is somewhat different, including six dimensions totaling 80 items. The remaining three scales appear only in unpublished manuscripts. These scales and their final number of items and number of factor-analytic derived dimensions are: DFS-Deafness (DFS-D, 104 items, eight dimensions), DFS-Obesity (DFS-O, 86 items, eight dimensions), and DFS-Cancer (DFS-K, 118 items, seven dimensions; also known as the Opinions About Cancer Scale).

Response Format

In expressing their level of agreement or disagreement with each of the statements, respondents select one of six possible choices, ranging from 1 ("Strongly agree"), through 2 ("Agree"), 3 ("Not sure but tend to agree"), 4 ("Not sure but tend to disagree"), 5 ("Disagree"), to 6 ("Strongly disagree"). No neutral responses are permissible. Respondents enter their numerical choice of response in the space provided to the left of each item.

Administration and Scoring

The Disability Factor Scales can be administered individually or in a group setting. Instructions to respondents are printed on a cover sheet. Scoring of the DFS requires attention to the reversal of the signs of the responses to several items. However, this is confined to all seven of the Imputed Functional Limitations subscale items, and to three of the Interaction Strain and one of the Rejection of Intimacy subscales' items. Scores for each subscale range from a minimum of $n \times 1$ to a maximum of $n \times 6$, where n signifies the number of items on the subscale. For example, the Interaction Strain subscale ($n = 9$) scores range from 9 to 54. A high score on each subscale indicates a positive attitude. Each DFS takes 15 to 20 minutes for administration, depending upon the length of the particular scale administered.

Reliability

Several unpublished monographs by Siller and his colleagues, reproduced by the New York University School of Education, provide data on the construction and psychometric properties of the DFS-A, DFS-B, DFS-C, and DFS-G. Limited data are available on the DFS-D, DFS-O, and DFS-K.

Estimates of stability (i.e., test-retest) for the original three scales (DFS-A, B, and C) are summarized in the Siller, et al. (1967) monograph. The test-retest reliability coefficients range from +.76 to +.92 for the seven DFS-A subscales (two week interval), from +.69 to +.88 for the seven DFS-B subscales (two week and three month intervals), and from +.61 to +.89 for the six DFS-C subscales (two week and three month intervals). No data are provided on the test-retest reliability coefficients of the DFS-G, or any of the remaining scales. Internal consistency reliability coefficients (Cronbach's alpha) for the original scales range from +.80 to +.92 for the DFS-A, from +.80 to +.91 for the DFS-B, and from +.62 to +.89 for the DFS-C. Internal consistency coefficients for the DFS-D subscale (Ferguson, 1970) range from +.74 to +.91 for seven of the subscales, but only +.47 for the Denial of Severity subscale. For the DFS-K, internal consistency coefficients range from +.52 (Nonstigmatization subscale) to +.91 (overall Rejection subscale). No internal consistency reliability coefficients are reported for the DFS-O, although factor loadings for each subscale may be found in Vann (1970). Finally, internal consistency coefficients for the DFS-G (Siller, 1969, 1970) range from + .73 (Imputed Functional Limitations subscale) to + .87 (Distressed Identification subscale).

Validity

Siller and his collaborators reported that in order to identify salient dimensions of reactions toward disabled people, four general categories of attitudes were conceived. They included assumed attributes of people having specific disabilities, personal reactions toward such disabled people, normative assumptions regarding reactions of other able-bodied people, and policy orientations. Within these four categories, a large number of specific reactions were suggested based on both clinical and research experience in addition to data yielded by an extensive literature review. An initial item pool was constructed to tap each of the dimensions. The disability universe was sampled and three disability types (amputation, blindness, and cosmetic condition) were selected for the original scales, representing differing points on the functionality and visibility of impairment dimensions. These three disability-specific initial item pools, with additional related personal, attitudinal, and other items, were then administered by the authors to various subject groups. The matrices of item intercorrelations were factor analyzed, resulting in reductions of the item pools. The revised and reduced questionnaires were then administered to a wide range of respondent groups. A second series of factor analytic procedures resulted in the final forms of the three original Disability Factor Scales (DFS-A, DFS-B, and DFS-C).

Factorial validity was established by computing the correlation between the sum of a set of item scores and the factor they share in common for each of the three original scales. These factor validity coefficients ranged from + .64 (Amputation—Imputed Functional Limitations) to + .93 (Blindness—Authoritarian Virtuousness). Construct validity was further established by demonstrating not only the stability of the attitudinal factors over a successive series of analyses with various groups of respondents, but also by showing their recurrence across different types of disabilities.

Two external sources of construct validation were also used. Scores on the DFS questionnaires were correlated with demographic variables (i.e., sex, age, education, and contact with disabled people). As expected, males, high school students, and individuals with minimal contact, scored lower than females, college students, and people with extensive contact with disabled people. Finally, some limited additional evidence was provided regarding the lack of association between DFS scores and scores on what the authors perceived to be a variety of irrelevant preference, vocational, intellectual, interest, and personality measures.

Criterion-related validation, in the form of concurrent validity correlations between each of the 20 DFS (A, B, and C) subscales and the ATDP Scale for two groups of college students, is reported (Siller, Ferguson, Vann, and Holland, 1967). Scores on five of the seven subscales of both the DFS-A and DFS-B correlated moderately, but significantly, with the total score on the ATDP Scale. Only two of the six DFS-C subscales, however, demonstrated significant correlations with the ATDP Scale. Some further correlational evidence between the DFS-General form and the ATDP Scale may be found in Elsberry (1975). Finally, using the known-groups procedure, the authors hypothesized that student trainees in a field offering direct services to disabled individuals (i.e., physical therapy) would demonstrate more favorable attitudes than respondents from the general population. This hypothesis was indeed supported by their findings (Siller, Ferguson, Vann, and Holland, 1967).

Similar validation procedures are reported for the General form of the DFS (Siller, 1969, 1970). Factor analysis of this scale's original items intercorrelation matrix have led to the retention of seven of the eight extracted factors (the eighth factor, Denial of Severity, was later dropped due to poor item representation).

Comments

The Disability Factor Scales appear to possess adequate reliability and validity. Support for the attitudinal structure of the DFS-G was reported by Livneh (1985a, 1985c) using both factor and cluster analytic procedures. Six of the seven factors were found to be replicated. Only the Imputed Functional Limitation factor, which contains a small number of items all associated with epilepsy, appears to lack psychometric soundness. Additional evidence relating the DFS-G second order factorial structure may be found in Kohler and Graves (1973), and in Livneh (1985b).

The major problem for researchers wishing to use the DFS is that the scales are contained mainly in unpublished monographs and research reports. Although subsequent analyses were conducted by Siller and his colleagues and students at New York University, they primarily appear in the forms of doctoral dissertations and verbal presentations at professional meetings. Also lacking, at present, is evidence as to the scales' susceptibility to the influences of social desirability, fakeability, and acquiescence response style. Until these scales have been further examined by other researchers and additional psychometric data have been published, they should be used mainly for experimental and research purposes for the investigation of the multidimensionality of attitudes toward disabled people.

Exhibit 9-7

Disability Factor Scale--General

Instructions

On the following pages you will find statements of ideas and attitudes about disabled people. There are many different opinions about this subject. People agree with some of these statements and disagree with others. We would like to know what you think about each one. There are no right or wrong answers; we are interested only in your opinions. Please make a choice for every statement.

At the right of each statement are six choices as follows:

1 Strongly Agree	2 Agree	3 Not sure but tend to agree	4 Not sure but tend to disagree	5 Disagree	6 Strongly disagree

Please put a circle around the choice that come closest to how you feel about the statement. For example, if you Strongly agree with a statement, circle (1); if you are Not sure but tend to disagree, circle (4). It is very important that you answer every item.

---

1 Strongly Agree	2 Agree	3 Not sure but tend to agree	4 Not sure but tend to disagree	5 Disagree	6 Strongly disagree

1. I feel uneasy when I'm near someone missing an arm or leg. 1 2 3 4 5 6
2. I would never adopt a child who is paralyzed. 1 2 3 4 5 6
3. People with cancer ought to be kept apart from the normal community. 1 2 3 4 5 6
4. Blind people have unusually good memories. 1 2 3 4 5 6
5. Deaf people are usually suspicious. 1 2 3 4 5 6
6. Sometimes I worry about getting heart trouble myself. 1 2 3 4 5 6
7. I think if I became blind I could make a pretty good adjustmnt. 1 2 3 4 5 6
8. Hunchbacks are as capable as anyone else. 1 2 3 4 5 6
9. I would be unhappy if a friend of mine thought of marrying a person who has epilepsy. 1 2 3 4 5 6
10. There should be laws against marriage between two amputees. 1 2 3 4 5 6

Exhibit 9-7 (Continued)

1	2	3	4	5	6
Strongly Agree	Agree	Not sure but tend to agree	Not sure but tend to disagree	Disagree	Strongly disagree

11. People who are paralyzed tend to develop special intellectual gifts.	1	2	3	4	5	6
12. People with cancer are often angry at the world.	1	2	3	4	5	6
13. Sonetimes I am afraid of getting badly scarred.	1	2	3	4	5	6
14. I would feel nervous with a blind person because a lot of the time I wouldn't know the right thing to do.	1	2	3	4	5	6
15. People with epilepsy can do most things as well as anyone else.	1	2	3	4	5	6
16. I would be unhappy if a friend of mine thought of marrying a person with a bad heart.	1	2	3	4	5	6
17. It would be better for deaf people if they didn't try to talk.	1	2	3	4	5	6
18. When I see a blind person, I try to imagine what it is like to be blind.	1	2	3	4	5	6
19. Most people who are paralyzed feel bitter.	1	2	3	4	5	6
20. I would never vote for a person for President if he had bad scars on his face.	1	2	3	4	5	6
21. If I were missing an arm or leg I would feel like hiding and avoiding people.	1	2	3	4	5	6
22. People with epilepsy are probably closer to the really important things in life.	1	2	3	4	5	6
23. I would never adopt a child who is blind.	1	2	3	4	5	6
24. Paralyzed people are best off staying among themselves.	1	2	3	4	5	6
25. Finding out that someone has cancer make me worry about getting it myself.	1	2	3	4	5	6
26. If I were a hunchback I would feel like hiding and avoiding people.	1	2	3	4	5	6
27. A child who has epilepsy can, with proper drugs, function as well as a normal child.	1	2	3	4	5	6
28. Deafness often improves a person's character.	1	2	3	4	5	6

Exhibit 9-7 (Continued)

	1 Strongly Agree	2 Agree	3 Not sure but tend to agree	4 Not sure but tend to disagree	5 Disagree	6 Strongly disagree
29. People with heart trouble feel sorry for themselves.	1	2	3	4	5	6
30. I would be upset if a child of mine dated a person with bad facial scars.	1	2	3	4	5	6
31. It's probably silly, bit I can't help connecting amputation with bad character.	1	2	3	4	5	6
32. Many people with heart trouble use their condition to take advantage of others.	1	2	3	4	5	6
33. Meeting a deaf person makes me worry about unpleasant things that could happen to me.	1	2	3	4	5	6
34. I would rather be dead than paralyzed.	1	2	3	4	5	6
35. Blind people and normal people can't really understand each other.	1	2	3	4	5	6
36. A person missing an arm or leg can function well with an artificial limb.	1	2	3	4	5	6
37. Children with heart trouble are usually more friendly than other children.	1	2	3	4	5	6
38. Even if I fall in love with a person who has cancer, I don't think I would marry him or her.	1	2	3	4	5	6
39. I feel that a person with a hunchback must have done something to deserve it.	1	2	3	4	5	6
40. Blind people tend to be irritable.	1	2	3	4	5	6
41. If I lost an arm or leg, I think I would make a good adjustment.	1	2	3	4	5	6
42. I get nervous about my own health when I hear about someone who has cancer.	1	2	3	4	5	6
43. People with epilepsy are just as intelligent as normal people.	1	2	3	4	5	6
44. When I know a child is deaf, I feel especially warm toward him.	1	2	3	4	5	6
45. I don't think I could fall in love with a person who is a hunchback.	1	2	3	4	5	6

Exhibit 9-7 (Continued)

---

1 Strongly Agree	2 Agree	3 Not sure but tend to agree	4 Not sure but tend to disagree	5 Disagree	6 Strongly disagree

Item						
46. Because a blind person can't see me, he could never really know me.	1	2	3	4	5	6
47. Meeting someone with heart trouble makes me worry about something wrong with me.	1	2	3	4	5	6
48. If I introduced a paralyzed person to my friends, I think they would feel uneasy.	1	2	3	4	5	6
49. Because of their condition, people with cancer are probably closer to the important things in life.	1	2	3	4	5	6
50. Seeing a blind person makes me realize how easily I could lose my sight.	1	2	3	4	5	6
51. I wouldn't let myself fall in love with a person who is missing a limb.	1	2	3	4	5	6
52. Deaf people are best off staying among themselves.	1	2	3	4	5	6
53. Blind people get a truer first impression of others than most people do.	1	2	3	4	5	6
54. When I meet a person with epilepsy I try to imagine what it is like.	1	2	3	4	5	6
55. I think if I became paralyzed I would make a pretty god adjustment.	1	2	3	4	5	6
56 With today's drugs, epilepsy is not a serious condition.	1	2	3	4	5	6
57. When I see an amputee I can't help thinking how it must feel to have a stump.	1	2	3	4	5	6
58. I would date a blind person as readily as I would anyone else.	1	2	3	4	5	6
59. There must be something the matter with someone who marries a person with heart trouble.	1	2	3	4	5	6
60. A person who is paralyzed can understand people better than someone who isn't.	1	2	3	4	5	6
61. I am sometimes afraid of losing an arm or leg.	1	2	3	4	5	6
62. Even if I fall in love with someone who is deaf, I don't think I would marry him or her.	1	2	3	4	5	6

Exhibit 9-7 (Continued)

1 Strongly Agree	2 Agree	3 Not sure but tend to agree	4 Not sure but tend to disagree	5 Disagree	6 Strongly disagree

Item						
63. People with bad facial scars are often resentful.	1	2	3	4	5	6
64. Paralyzed people ought to be kept apart from the normal community.	1	2	3	4	5	6
65. I don't think of a person with epilepsy as being disabled.	1	2	3	4	5	6
66. I would rather have no children than a child who is a hunchback.	1	2	3	4	5	6
67. Amputees tend to develop special intellectual gifts.	1	2	3	4	5	6
68. I am sometimes afraid that I will become paralyzed.	1	2	3	4	5	6
69. Most amputees are angry at the world.	1	2	3	4	5	6

Reprinted with permission of the author; from Siller, J. (1969). The general form of the Disability Factor Scales. Unpublished manuscript, New York University, School of Education, New York.

DISABILITY SOCIAL DISTANCE SCALE (DSDS)

Description

The Disability Social Distance Scale was developed by Tringo (1970) as part of his doctoral dissertation at the University of Connecticut (Tringo, 1968) comparing attitudes and prejudice toward specific disability groups. The scale is based on the original social distance scale as developed by Bogardus (1925b, 1933). Using the method of equal-appearing intervals, nine scale items were selected to represent the range of social distancing of the nondisabled respondent to 21 disability groups. The disabled individuals and disability groups include: physical disabilities (e.g., amputee, cerebral palsy), sensory disabilities (e.g., blindness, deafness), mental disabilities (e.g., mental retardation), psychiatric disabilities (e.g., mental illness), and socio-behavioral disabilities (e.g., alcoholism, ex-convict).

Response Format

In expressing their attitudes, respondents are asked to indicate their degree of acceptance or felt closeness toward each disability on a 1 to 9 scale. The nine levels of social proximity are as follows: (1) Would marry, (2) Would accept as a close kin by marriage, (3) Would have as a next door neighbor, (4) Would accept as a casual friend, (5) Would accept as a fellow employee, (6) Would keep away from, (7) Would keep in an institution, (8) Would send out of my country, and (9) Would put to death.

Administration and Scoring

The DSDS was originally administered as a group measure. It does, however, allow for individual administration. Instructions to respondents are read while they look over the form (the instructions may be found in Tringo, 1970, p. 297). Respondents' scores, reflecting their degree of acceptance toward each of the 21 disability groups, are then converted to their equivalent scale values determined by the method of successive intervals (see Tringo, 1970, p. 297). In addition, the respondents' scores (i.e., equivalent scale values) may be averaged across all 21 items (i.e., scores on all disability groups scales) to yield an overall score. Higher scores indicate a more negative attitude toward each disability group, or alternatively a wish to maintain more social distance from members of this group. Conversely, lower scores reflect willingness to accept closer relationships with people belonging to that particular group. The DSDS takes approximately five minutes to administer.

Reliability

The author does not report test-retest reliability estimates. As far as internal reliability is concerned, data are provided to support the existence of a consistent hierarchy of preference (i.e., relative positioning or ranking) toward the 21 disability groups, as noted by their mean social distance scores. This highly consistent ranking of preference toward disability groups was evident (ranging in size from $r = +.95$ to $r = +.98$) for all groups of respondents differing in gender, age, and educational level compositions.

Validity

Content validity of the DSDS was established through a sequence of steps. First, 21-item statements were selected that reflected a wide range of social distance proximities. These ranged from "Would accept as an intimate friend" and "Would marry" on one pole, to "Would be better off dead" and "Would put to death" on the other pole of the perceived social distance scale. Second, these items were submitted to a panel of judges (faculty members and graduate students) to establish their scaling values. No reference was made, at this point, to any specific disability groups. Nine items on the original 21-item list were selected from the responses of the 66 judges, based on their representativeness of all points on the social distance continuum and their high degree of inter-judge agreement. Finally, a list of 21 disability groups was constructed to represent the major disability types in the United States.

The construct validity of the scale was assessed in different ways. As previously noted, the instrument's internal consistency in rank-ordering the 21 disability groups across different samples of respondents may be conceived as also supporting the construct of hierarchical preference toward a variety of disability groups. Second, as was hypothesized by Tringo (1968), based on previous empirical findings of other investigators, the males' mean score was higher than that of the females (i.e., females are more accepting than males). Also, as predicted, higher educational level was associated with lower mean scores, or more accepting attitudes toward disability groups. Finally, an intercorrelation matrix among all 22 disability variables (21 disability groups and an overall social distance score) contained all positive correlations, ranging in size from $+.12$ to $+.77$. Tringo (1970) argued that this finding supported some generalized, and possibly common, attitudinal components toward people with disabilities.

Comments

Although the DSDS's internal reliability and validity data seem reasonable, no subsequent investigations of its psychometric characteristics have been located. Further studies of the scale should include investigations of its temporal stability, especially considering that approximately 20 years have elapsed since its construction. Also, hierarchy of disability groups preference should be studied in the general population rather than solely among high school and college students, thereby expanding the representations of differential age groups.

Finally, future researchers should consider altering the original list of 21 disability groups in two ways. First, several presently uncommon disability groups may be deleted (e.g., tuberculosis) or replaced with other types of disabilities (e.g., muscular dystrophy or multiple sclerosis). Second, a standardized terminology format should be implemented. Inasmuch as the present DSDS confounds the use of both disability nouns (e.g., alcoholism) and disabled individuals (e.g., amputees), it may create a certain amount of confusion among respondents (i.e., lack of clarity as to what is expected to be rated—disabled people or abstract disability categories). Standardization of the DSDS disability variables is, therefore, in order.

Exhibit 9-8

Disability Social Distance Scale

Directions

There are many degrees of understanding that may exist between persons. Nine of these relationships are listed below in order of closeness, with number 1 describing the closest relationship and number 9 the most distant relationship.

1	2	3	4	5	6	7	8	9
Would marry	Would accept as a close kin by marriage	Would have as a next door neighbor	Would accept as a casual friend	Would accept as a fellow employee	Would keep away from	Would keep in an insti-tution	Would send out of my country	Would put to death

---

Which item on the above scale best describes the closest relationship you feel toward each disability group listed below? Next to each disability place the number of the item on the scale that describes the closest relationship you would be willing to have with a person with such a disability.

____ Alcoholism
____ Amputee
____ Asthritis
____ Asthma
____ Blindness
____ Cancer
____ Cerebral palsy
____ Deafness
____ Diabetes
____ Dwarf
____ Epilepsy
____ Ex-convict
____ Heart disease
____ Hunchback
____ Mental illness
____ Mental retardation
____ Old age
____ Paraplegic
____ Stroke
____ Tuberculosis
____ Ulcer

Reprinted from Tringo, J. L. (1970). The hierarchy of preference toward disability groups. Journal of Special Education, 4, 295-306.

RUCKER-GABLE EDUCATIONAL PROGRAMMING SCALE (RGEPS)

Description

Rucker and Gable (1974) developed the RGEPS with attitude operationalized as the degree of social distance which teachers and others wished to maintain between themselves and handicapped students. The impetus for the development of the scale was to evaluate the success of the educational policy of mainstreaming through the investigation of the knowledge and attitudes of those professionals responsible for the implementation of the policy. The scale has been used to evaluate the effectiveness of training on the attitudes of teachers (Shaw and Gillung, 1975), and to study the attitudes of teachers and administrators in various school settings (Cline, 1981; McCauley, Morris, and Cooper, 1978; Pfeiffer and Naglieri, 1984).

Response Format

The scale presents 30 brief descriptions of students with mild, moderate, or severe mental retardation, learning disabilities, or emotional disturbance. The respondent is asked to read each description and, given ideal conditions and understanding that placements are not permanent, to select an educational environment which the respondent considers to be the most appropriate for that child from among seven which are presented. The alternatives and their values are: Regular Classroom (7), Consultation (6), Consultation and Direct Service (5), Resource Room (4), Part-Time Special Class (3), Full-Time Special Class (2), and NOT (that is, a non-educational residential school or hospital setting, value of 1). This novel response format makes the RGEPS unique among the attitude rating measures presented in this chapter.

Administration and Scoring

The respondent's total score is the mean placement index for all 30 children portrayed, and is described as a measure of the respondent's willingness to adopt a policy which places the highest value on the integration of handicapped children into the mainstream of the educational system. Subscale scores may also be calculated for each of the three handicapping conditions (ten items each) and for each of the three severity levels: mild, moderate, and severe, with eight, 16, and six items, respectively. The authors suggest that in addition to the attitude scores obtained in this manner, each respondent's selections can be scored as a knowledge test when his or her decisions are compared to those of a group of 65 experts. Similar to the six subscales of the attitude score, six subscales for the knowledge score can be computed.

Reliability

The scale's development is well documented by the authors (Rucker and Gable,

1974) who report coefficient alpha and split-half values ranging from +.81 to +.99. The reliability indices obtained in subsequent investigation have been variable. Graham and Henry (1981) reported a coefficient alpha value of +.80 and a two-week stability coefficient of +.60. Henry and Graham (1983) reported a Spearman-Brown corrected reliability value of +.80, alpha coefficients of +.84 and +.88, and an equivalence-stability coefficient of +.27 over two weeks. Graham and Deaton (1983) reported a coefficient alpha value of +.83 and alpha values for the attitudes subscales ranging from +.69 to +.76.

Validity

Studies of the construct validity and factorial structure of the RGEPS have also been variable (Graham and Deaton, 1983; Graham and Henry, 1981, 1982; Henry and Graham, 1980, 1983). Graham and Deaton (1983), for example, in a principal factors analysis of the data from 205 graduate students, retained four factors after the elimination of seven items for psychometric reasons. These factors accounted for only 42 percent of the variance. These researchers concluded that the evidence of this study, when combined with the results of their previous studies, did not support the existence of the attitude constructs postulated by Rucker and Gable (1974). No studies of the scale's concurrent or predictive validity have been located. Graham and Henry (1981) did, however, report significantly more positive mean RGEPS scores for a group of respondents who attended a special education lecture than for groups of respondents who attended either a general education lecture or no lecture.

Comments

The RGEPS attempts to measure an important construct, and is unique in the item response format it presents to the respondent. The failure of research to support the existence of the scale's hypothesized component constructs suggests that the subscales should not be used in any but experimental research. The intervening 12 years since the publication of the RGEPS have included the passage of significant legislation and the implementation of integration policies nationwide. It would be appropriate for the authors of the RGEPS to reconsider the content of their scale, and to undertake more detailed investigations of the scale's validity. Until then, data obtained from the use of the scale should be cautiously interpreted.

SCALE OF ATTITUDES TOWARD DISABLED PERSONS (SADP)

Description

Research by Antonak (1979a, 1980c, 1981b) and by others (e.g., Siller and Chipman, 1964) questioned the reliability and validity of the ATDP Form-O of Yuker and his associates (Yuker, et al., 1960). Antonak (1980c) suggested that a more contemporary, easy-to-use, and psychometrically sound instrument was needed by researchers investigating attitudes toward disabled people as a group. The SADP was developed by Antonak (1981a, 1982) to provide an alternative to the ATDP Form-O for the investigation of questions concerning the formation, correlates, and modification of these attitudes.

The specification of the scale's item content was derived from reviews of the research literature on attitudes toward disabled and exceptional people, from examination of previously published scales, and from analyses of open-ended interviews with experts in the fields of special education and rehabilitation. An initial pool of 176 items was edited to yield sets of 86 and then 76 items. These 76 items were then evaluated by a panel of ten experts to identify ambiguities and eliminate redundant items, and to determine the value of each item on a six-point scale, ranging from −3, to signify "Very unfavorable," to +3, to signify "Very favorable."

A set of 64 items were retained and randomly arranged onto a composite scale. The responses of 228 individuals were obtained and a series of item, scale, and factor analyses were undertaken to reduce the number of items and create a more efficient scale with adequate general factor variance and internal consistency, and sound psychometric characteristics. This iterative process yielded sets of 51, 38, and finally 30 items. These 30 items were then arranged on a second composite scale and the responses of a new sample of 225 individuals were obtained. Similar scale reduction analyses yielded the final 24-item version of the SADP. Subject scores were recalculated and complete item, scale, and factor analyses were performed (Antonak, 1981a).

Additional analyses of SADP data collected from 1981 to 1983 from new samples of respondents were conducted by Antonak (1985a, 1985b) to confirm and clarify the reliability, validity, and utility of the scale. These samples included high school students, undergraduate and graduate majors in human services, nonmatriculated professionals in courses for continuing educational purposes, and participants at workshops and conferences in several New England states. The SADP has been translated into Chinese for use in a cross-cultural validation study by Chan, Hua, Ju, and Lam (1984).

Response Format

The SADP, a 24-item summated rating scale, requires the respondent to rate each statement on a six-point scale, ranging from − 3, to signify "I disagree very much," through + 3, to signify "I agree very much." No neutral response option is provided. Directions to the respondent are printed on the questionnaire form together with a response key. A separate response form was used by the author so that the questionnaire could be used again, but the scale may be easily modified to incorporate the response sheet with the questionnaire to create a single page instrument.

Administration and Scoring

The scale was designed to be administered to groups, but may also be used with individuals either directly or by mail. Respondents are encouraged to respond to every item on the scale. It is suggested that protocols omitting responses to four or more items should not be scored. Protocols with omitted items are scored with the omitted responses assigned a value of zero. Half of the items are worded so that an agree response (i.e., + 3, + 2, or + 1) represents a favorable attitude, and half of the items are worded so that a disagree response (i.e., − 3, − 2, or − 1) represents a favorable attitude. The SADP is scored by first reversing the sign of the response (from + to −, or from − to +) for those items which are worded negatively (items #1, 3, 4, 7, 8, 9, 10, 14, 17, 18, 19, and 22). The sum of the responses to the 24 items is then calculated and a constant of 72 is added to the total. This last step eliminates negative scores. Resultant scores can range from 0 to 144, with a higher score indicating a favorable attitude toward disabled people.

Reliability

The results of reliability analyses yielded Spearman-Brown corrected reliability coefficients ranging from + .81 to + .85, and alpha coefficients ranging from + .88 to + .91. Three subscales of length 11, seven, and six items were derived from a principal factors analysis. The factors corresponding to these subscales accounted for 76 percent of the variance in the SADP scores. The first factor was labeled Optimism-Human Rights, the second factor was labeled Behavioral Misconceptions, and the third factor was labeled Pessimism-Hopelessness. The values of the psychometric indices are acceptable for subscales of these lengths. In particular, the reliability coefficients range from + .55 to + .73 and the coefficient alpha homogeneity indices range from + .77 to + .87. Investigations of the subscale data provided modest support for the specificity of the three subscales, with specificity coefficients ranging from + .42 to + .71.

Validity

Preliminary investigation of the validity of the SADP included analyses of the relationship between the scores on the SADP and other attitude scales. Scores on an 18-item reduced version of the ATDP Form-O were found to correlate moderately ($r = + .54$) with SADP scores, and with scores on each of the three SADP subscales ($r = +.47$, $+.33$, and $+.31$, respectively). A principal factors analysis of the pooled ATDP Form-O and SADP items yielded five oblique factors with ATDP Form-O items defining two of the factors and SADP items defining the other three factors. A single second-order factor, obtained from a factor analysis of the five first-order factors, was interpreted as a general factor representing global attitudes toward people who are disabled. Taken together, these results were considered preliminary evidence of the convergent validity of the SADP.

A study by Chan et al. (1984) reported the results of a multidimensional scaling analysis of SADP data collected in Chinese from 80 students in Hong Kong, Singapore, and Taiwan. A two-dimensional solution, accounting for 88 percent of the variance, was accepted with the first dimension labeled Optimism/Human Rights, and the second dimension labelled Pessimism/Behavioral Misperceptions. The second factor was interpreted to be a combination of the two negative factors reported by Antonak (1982). Chan et al. (1984) concluded that the factorial structure was compatible across the two cultures.

Support for the criterion-related validity of the SADP was found using the known-groups technique. Multiple regression analyses of the relationship between the scale scores and the respondent demographic and experiential variables showed that SADP scores were partially attributed to differences in the subjects' characteristics. While the construction of SADP norms has begun (Antonak, 1985b), the researcher is cautioned to exercise care in the use of the norms until analyses of data from large samples of subjects of widely differing characteristics are reported.

Analyses of SADP and SDS (Crowne and Marlowe, 1960) data lead to the conclusion that the SADP is not merely a measure of socially desirable responding to a set of attitude statements. To validate the SADP subscales' content conceptualization, 25 judges' categorizations of the items were analyzed using a statistical technique described by Hartke (1979), derived from latent partition analysis (Wiley, 1967). The analyses of the data showed the consistency of the judges' categorizations of the 24 items and the homogeneity of the items within the categories. The similarity of the item assignments in this analysis to the item assignments in the earlier factor analysis suggested that the SADP may measure three domains of attitudes toward people who are disabled, titled Civil and Legal Rights: Equity and Equality, Anti-Normalization and Discrimination in Habilitation Programs, and Destructive Stereotypes of Personality and Social Characteristics. The first domain may also consist of three dimensions: Equality of Employment Opportunity, Community Participation Equity, and Integration in Society. No predictive validity analyses of the SADP have been reported as yet.

Comments

The SADP appears to be a psychometrically sound and reliable instrument. Reports of investigations of the scale's validity are encouraging, but they are not completely adequate as yet. Analyses of data from large randomly selected samples of respondents who differ in known ways on demographic and experiential characteristics are needed. In addition, the factorial structure must be clarified before subscale scores can be calculated and used.

The convenience of the SADP, together with the available data on its validity, reliability, and structure, support the usefulness of the scale by researchers and practitioners in rehabilitation and related fields. The former group will find the SADP useful for investigations of the formation, structure, and correlates of attitudes toward disabled people. The latter group will find the SADP useful in applied settings, such as measuring the effectiveness of professional training programs and attitude change programs.

Exhibit 9-9

Scale of Attitudes Toward Disabled Persons

Directions

The statements presented below express opinions or ideas about people who are disabled. There are many differences of opinion; Many people agree and many people disagree with each statement. We would like to know your opinion about them. Put an "X" through the appropriate number, from -3 to +3, which best corresponds with how you feel about the statement. There are no right or wrong answers. You should work as quickly as you can, but don't rush. There is no time limit. Please respond to every statement.

Key

-3: I disagree very much	+1: I agree a little
-2: I disagree pretty much	+2: I agree pretty much
-1: I disagree a little	+3: I agree very much

1	Disabled children should not be provided with a free public education.	-3	-2	-1	+1	+2	+3
2	Disabled people are not more accident prone than other people.	-3	-2	-1	+1	+2	+3
3	A disabled individual is not capable of making moral decisions.	-3	-2	-1	+1	+2	+3
4	Disabled people should be prevented from having children.	-3	-2	-1	+1	+2	+3
5	Disabled people should be allowed to live where and how they choose.	-3	-2	-1	+1	+2	+3
6	Adequate housing for disabled people is neither too expensive nor too difficult to build.	-3	-2	-1	+1	+2	+3
		-3	-2	-1	+1	+2	+3
7	Rehabilitation programs for disabled people are too expensive to operate.	-3	-2	-1	+1	+2	+3
8	Disabled people are in many ways like children.	-3	-2	-1	+1	+2	+3
9	Disabled people need only the proper environment and opportunity to develop and express criminal tendencies.	-3	-2	-1	+1	+2	+3
10	Disabled adults should be involuntarily committed to an institution following arrest.	-3	-2	-1	+1	+2	+3
11	Most disabled people are willing to work.	-3	-2	-1	+1	+2	+3
12	Disabled individuals are able to adjust to a life outside an institutional setting.	-3	-2	-1	+1	+2	+3

Exhibit 9-9 (Continued)

13	Disabled people should not be prohibited from obtaining a driver's license.	-3	-2	-1	+1	+2	+3
14	Disabled people should live with others of similar disability.	-3	-2	-1	+1	+2	+3
15	Zoning ordinances should not discriminate against disabled people by prohibiting group homes in residential districts.	-3	-2	-1	+1	+2	+3
16	The opportunity for gainful employment should be provided to disabled people.	-3	-2	-1	+1	+2	+3
17	Disabled children in regular classrooms have an adverse effect on other children.	-3	-2	-1	+1	+2	+3
18	Simple repetitive work is appropriate for disabled people.	-3	-2	-1	+1	+2	+3
19	Disabled people show a deviant personality profile.	-3	-2	-1	+1	+2	+3
20	Equal employment opportunities should be available to disabled individuals.	-3	-2	-1	+1	+2	+3
21	Laws to prevent employers from discriminating against disabled people should be passed.	-3	-2	-1	+1	+2	+3
22	Disabled people engage in bizarre and deviant sexual activity.	-3	-2	-1	+1	+2	+3
23	Disabled workers should receive at least the minimum wage established for their jobs.	-3	-2	-1	+1	+2	+3
24	Disabled individuals can be expected to fit into competitive society.	-3	-2	-1	+1	+2	+3

Reprinted with permission of the author; from Antonak, R. F. (1981). Development and psychometric analysis of the Scale of Attitudes Toward Disabled Persons (Technical Report No.1). Durham, NH: University of New Hampshire, Education Department.

Chapter 10

ATTITUDES TOWARD PHYSICAL DISABILITY GROUPS

ATTITUDES TO BLINDNESS SCALE (AB)

Description

THE Attitudes to Blindness scale was developed by Cowen, Underberg, and Verrillo (1958) as a brief and reliable measure of verbalized attitudes toward blind people. A total of 97 propositions, which appeared to be related to the attitudes demonstrated by sighted people toward blindness and blind people, were extracted from earlier studies. Of this initial pool, 30 items were selected for the final self-report, summated rating AB Scale. The authors argue that the scale is unidimensional with scores reflecting varied degrees of favorableness toward blindness and blind people.

Response Format

Respondents to the scale express their endorsement of each of the scale's items on a four-point rating scale from strongly disagree (D = 1 point), mildly disagree (d = 2 points), mildly agree (a = 3 points), to strongly agree (A = 4 points). Respondents indicate their opinion by circling one of the four options (i.e., A, a, d, D). No neutral responses may be given.

Administration and Scoring

The AB Scale may be administered in both individual and group settings. Instructions to respondents are listed at the top of the page. The four response alternatives are converted to a numerical scale with weights of 4, 3, 2, and 1. A set of 20 items are negatively phrased while the remaining ten items are worded positively. The responses to the positive items are reversed (i.e., 4 = 1 and 3 = 2) before summing across all items to yield the final attitude scale score. Scores on the AB Scale can range from 30 to 120, with higher scores reflecting a more negative attitude toward blind people. The AB Scale takes approximately five minutes for administration.

Reliability

No temporal stability coefficients are provided. The authors report only a single internal consistency reliability estimate, namely, a Spearman-Brown corrected split-half reliability coefficient of + .91.

Validity

Content validity for the AB Scale was established through the use of previously constructed scales measuring some aspects of attitudes toward blindness (Cowen, Underberg, and Verrillo, 1958). The initial pool of 97 propositions was assembled from existing measures and reviewed by a panel of five professionals working with blind people. These professionals judged each proposition as to how indicative it was of positive or negative attitudes toward blind people. Based on the judges' responses, 56 items were selected and then given to a combined sample of 101 respondents enrolled in adult education courses at the University of Rochester. An item analysis, conducted on all 56 items, resulted in retaining the 30 items with the highest item-to-scale correlations (ranging from + .44 to + .75).

The authors hypothesized, based on earlier psychoanalytic writings, that male subjects would exhibit more negative attitudes toward blindness than female subjects. This result did not materialize from the analysis of their data, although the results were in the expected direction. It is not clear if the failure of the AB Scale to reflect these hypothesized gender differences is due to its structure or the ambiguity surrounding that particular theory (i.e., man's castration anxiety is symbolically related to the fear of the loss of one's eyesight and, therefore, to the rejection of individuals who act as reminders of it—blind people).

Partial construct validation estimates were provided by correlating the AB Scale with three California scales. The AB Scale correlated + .36 with the Anti-Minority Scale, + .33 with the Anti-Negro Scale, and + .45 with the Attitude to Authority Scale. Correlating the AB Scale with the same three scales for a smaller cross validation sample resulted in coefficients of similar magnitude. The authors interpret these moderate but significant correlations as suggesting a common attitudinal factor toward other racial and religious minority groups. A recent experimental study (Skrtic, Clark, and White, 1982) discovered, however, that the mean AB score of a group of 22 members of the professional staff at a residential center for the visually handicapped was not significantly different from the mean AB score of either a group of 34 regular education undergraduate majors or a group of 53 undergraduates electing to take an introductory special education course. No other construct or criterion-related validation studies have been located.

Comments

The AB Scale may have adequate internal stability. No test-retest reliability estimates, however, have been reported. As to the scale's criterion-related and construct (i.e., factorial) validity, insufficient evidence is provided. No support has been established for the scale's immunity to subjects' response styles and social desirability tendencies. It seems, therefore, that data on the AB Scale's reliability and validity are sorely needed in conjunction with reanalyses of this 30-year-old scale's content (i.e., item validity).

Exhibit 10-1

Attitude to Blindness Scale

Directions:

Read each of the statements below and then rate them as follows:

A	a	d	D
Strongly Agree	Mildly Agree	Mildly Disagree	Strongly Disagree

Indicate your opinion by drawing a circle around the "A" if you strongly agree, around the "a" if you mildly agree, around the "d" if you mildly disagree, and around the "D" if you strongly disagree.

There are no right or wrong answers, so answer according to your own opinion. It is very important to the study that all questions be answered. Many of the statements will seem alike but all are necessary to show slight differences of opinion.

1	A blind person might as well accept the fact that blindness makes people pretty helpless.	A	a	d	D
2	On the whole, blind children seem to be less intelligent than sighted children.	A	a	d	D
3	Blind people are used to failing in most of the things they do.	A	a	d	D
4	A blind person should not have to meet the same demands as others.	A	a	d	D
5	Blind people are conatnatly worried about the future.	A	a	d	D
6	Blindness has little or no effect upon intelligence.	A	a	d	D
7	A blind person is not afraid to express his feelings.	A	a	d	D
8	A blind person can never really be happy.	A	a	d	D
9	Most blind people are dissatisfied with themselves.	A	a	d	D
10	A blind person can't afford to talk back to people.	A	a	d	D
11	One can live in a competitive society and still compete successfully without sight.	A	a	d	D

Exhibit 10-1 (Continued)

12	It makes me feel a little guilty to know than I can see and others cannot.	A	a	d	D
13	You should not expect too much from a blind person.	A	a	d	D
14	Most blind people feel that they are worthless.	A	a	d	D
15	It is possible to know the beauty of the world without sight.	A	a	d	D
16	My attitude towards a blind person would be based more upon his personality than upon the fact that he is blind.	A	a	d	D
17	Blind people do not have as much initiative as sighted people.	A	a	d	D
18	It is very difficult to make a blind person change his mind once he has decided on something.	A	a	d	D
19	It must be bitterly degrading for a blind person to depend so much upon others.	A	a	d	D
20	Many blind people are economically independent.	A	a	d	D
21	Blind people are more easily upset than sighted people.	A	a	d	D
22	Most blind people think and act alike.	A	a	d	D
23	It's difficult to understand the blind because they keep so much to themselves.	A	a	d	D
24	There are things worse than being blind.	A	a	d	D
25	Acceptance of blindness is the same thing as acceptance of anything else in life.	A	a	d	D
26	The blind adult is not quite as mature or "grown-up" as the sighted adult.	A	a	d	D
27	Blindness does not change the person anymore than any other physical handicap.	A	a	d	D
28	The blind have as many interests as the sighted have.	A	a	d	D

Exhibit 10-1 (Continued)

29	I feel that blindness is as hard to bear as complete paralysis.	A	a	d	D
30	A blind person is constantly worried about what might happen to him.	A	a	d	D

Reprinted with permission of the authors; from Cowen, E. L., Underberg, R. P., & Verillo, R. T. (1958). The development and testing of an attitude to blindness scale. The Journal of Social Psychology, 48, 297-304.

ATTITUDES TO DEAFNESS SCALE (AD)

Description

The Attitudes to Deafness (AD) Scale was constructed by Cowen, Bobrove, Rockway, and Stevenson (1967) by rewording the 30 items of the original Attitudes to Blindness Scale (Cowen et al., 1958) by substituting the terms deafness or deaf person for the terms blindness or blind person. An additional 20 items were written based on attitudinal statements regarding deaf people located in the literature. A set of 25 items were later selected for the final self-report summated rating AD Scale. The authors argue that the scale is unidimensional and its scores purport to measure the degree of acceptance, or rejection, held by the respondent toward deafness and deaf people.

Response Format

Respondents to the scale express their endorsement of each of the scale's items on a four-point rating scale from strongly disagree (D = 1 point), mildly disagree (d = 2 points), mildly agree (a = 3 points), to strongly agree (A = 4 points). Respondents indicate their opinion by circling one of the four options (i.e., A, a, d, D). No neutral responses may be given.

Administration and Scoring

The AD Scale may be administered in both individual and group settings. Instructions to respondents are listed at the top of the page. The four response alternatives are converted to a numerical scale with weights of 4, 3, 2, and 1. A set of 21 items are negatively phrased (i.e., agreement with these items denotes a negative attitude toward deaf people), while the remaining four items are worded positively (i.e., agreement denotes a positive attitude toward deaf people). The responses to the positive items are reversed (e.g., 4 = 1 and 3 = 2) before summing across all items to yield the final attitude scale score. The final attitude scale score can range from 25 to 100, with higher scores reflecting a more negative attitude toward deaf people. The AD Scale takes approximately five minutes to be administered.

Reliability

No test-retest reliability estimates are disclosed. The authors report the results of a single internal reliability study, yielding a Spearman-Brown corrected split-half reliability coefficient of + .83.

Validity

Content validation of the AD Scale was attempted by (a) using 30 items drawn from the previously developed AB Scale and replacing the attitude referent, (b) adding 20 items extracted from a literature survey of attitudes toward deafness and deaf people, and (c) having a panel of five clinically trained judges review the additional items as to their attitudinal dispositions (i.e., whether the statements reflect a positive or a negative attitude toward deaf people). The combined total of 50 items was finally administered to a sample of 100 students enrolled in an introductory psychology class. An item analysis performed on all 50 items resulted in retaining the 25 items with the highest item-to-scale correlations (ranging from + .43 to + .83). The 25-item AD Scale was subsequently cross-validated on a independent sample of 160 introductory psychology students, with somewhat lower, but generally similar, correlation coefficients.

The authors also report the results of a construct-validation study, in which scores on the AD Scale were correlated with a series of relevant attitude and personality measures, including abbreviated versions of the Anti-Minority, Anti-Negro, and Authoritariansim scales from the California Scales. In addition, the Crowne-Marlowe Social Desirability Scale (Crowne and Marlowe, 1960) was administered to assess the effect of social desirability response tendencies on respondents' scores. Finally, Rotter's Locus of Evaluation Scale (Rotter, Seeman, and Liverant, 1962), and the Buss-Durkee Hostility Scale (Buss and Durkee, 1957) were also administered to the sample with the hypotheses that generalized hostility and externalization of blame (or responsibility) for occurred events were related to negative attitudes toward deaf people. Correlations with the California Scales of + .36. (Authoritarianism), + .50 (Anti-Minority), and + .50 (Anti-Negro) led the authors to conclude that the AD Scale's construct validity had been demonstrated. Furthermore, they infer that attitudes toward disabling conditions in general, exhibit a common factor shared with attitudes toward minority groups. The absence of a relationship between the AD Scale and the Social Desirability Scale ($r = +.01$) attests to the former's robustness against the influence of socially desirable responding. The correlations between the AD Scale and the remaining two scales used in this study, measuring hostility and locus of evaluation were non-significant, suggesting that the AD Scale had adequate divergent validity.

The authors also report the results of a predictive validity study. Respondents were asked to participate in interviews with two confederates, one of whom was of normal hearing and the other was ostensibly hearing impaired. A sample of 48 respondents was drawn from the initial sample—half were the extreme high and half the extreme low AD Scale scoring groups. These subjects were asked to rate the personal characteristics of the two confederates following the interviews using a semantic differential scale. The results demonstrated that the respondents with the least favorable attitudes toward deafness (i.e., high scorers on the AD scale) also rated the hearing impaired interviewee significantly less favorably on the semantic differential scale. On the other hand, those who held the most favorable attitudes toward deaf people (i.e., low scorers on the AD Scale) also exhibited the most favorable response on the semantic differential scale.

Comments

The AD Scale may possess acceptable internal stability. No test-retest reliability estimates are provided, so judgment as to its temporal stability cannot be made. Also, no data are reported on the scale's factorial or criterion-related validity. Finally, the scale seems to possess an adequate degree of immunity to social desirability tendencies. In sum, additional data on the reliability and validity of the AD scale with other and more diverse groups of respondents are needed, as is an updated investigation of the scale's content validity.

Exhibit 10-2

Attitudes to Deafness Scale

Directions:

Read each of the statements below and then rate them as follows:

A	a	d	D
Strongly Agree	Mildly Agree	Mildly Disagree	Strongly Disagree

Indicate your opinion by drawing a circle around the "A" if you strongly agree, around the "a" if you mildly agree, around the "d" if you mildly disagree, and around the "D" if you strongly disagree.

There are no right or wrong answers, so answer according to your own opinion. It is very important to the study that all questions be answered. Many of the statements will seem alike but all are necessary to show slight differences of opinion.

1	The deaf generally have a less mature personality than the hearing.	A	a	d	D
2	In general, deaf people are more neurotic than those who hear.	A	a	d	D
3	It is impossile to get "close" to a deaf person.	A	a	d	D
4	Deaf people somehow seem sadder and more wrapped up in themselves than hearing people.	A	a	d	D
5	The deaf do not seem to be bothered by ordinary life events any more than hearing people.	A	a	d	D
6	Because of his need to be pitied, it is particularly important that the deaf person have someone very tolerant to whom he can talk.	A	a	d	D
7	Deaf people also seem to have more than the usual number of other physical complaints.	A	a	d	D
8	Deaf people show personality characteristics which frequently make them seem odd.	A	a	d	D
9	A person who is deaf is as apt to be born a leader as anyone else.	A	a	d	D
10	Deaf people seem to be overly polite and to lack spontaneity.	A	a	d	D

Exhibit 10-2 (Continued)

11	Most deaf people feel that they are worthless.	A	a	d	D
12	Most deaf people are dissatisfied with themselves.	A	a	d	D
13	The deaf have as many interests as the hearing have.	A	a	d	D
14	The deaf adult is not quite as mature or "grown-up" as the hearing adult	A	a	d	D
15	It is difficult to understand the deaf because they keep so much to themselves.	A	a	d	D
16	It must be bitterly degrading for a deaf person to depend so much on others.	A	a	d	D
17	On the whole, deaf children seem to be less intelligent than hearing children.	A	a	d	D
18	I feel that deafness is as hard to bear as complete paralysis.	A	a	d	D
19	A deaf person can't afford to talk back to people.	A	a	d	D
20	You should not expect too much from a deaf person.	A	a	d	D
21	A deaf person is constantly worried about what might happen to him.	A	a	d	D
22	A deaf person is not afraid to express his feelings.	A	a	d	D
23	Deaf people are more easily upset than people who can hear.	A	a	d	D
24	The deaf are prone to have many more fears about the world than the hearing.	A	a	d	D
25	The deaf are usually on their guard with people.	A	a	d	D

Reprinted with permission of the authors; from Cowen, E. L., Bobrove, P. H., Rockway, A. M., & Stevenson, J. (1967). Development and evaluation of an attitude to deafness scale. Journal of Personality and Social Psychology, 6, 183-191.

A SCALE OF KNOWLEDGE AND ATTITUDES TOWARD EPILEPSY AND PEOPLE WITH EPILEPSY (ATPE)

Description

Most contemporary professionals in education, medicine, and rehabilitation agree that epilepsy is a community, as well as a personal, problem. That is, the person with epilepsy will be a burden on the social and financial resources of the community when he or she is prevented from participating as a productive member. Because of myths, misunderstandings, and negative attitudes, people with epilepsy are rejected and stigmatized by society, and, consequently, denied essential rights and life opportunities. Data from the public, from employers, and from professionals must be collected and analyzed to design and determine the effectiveness of programs to break stereotypes, to eliminate barriers to integration, and to increase knowledge of this neurological impairment. The ATPE was developed by Antonak and Rankin (1981, 1982) to provide these data by measuring both attitudes toward, and knowledge of, epilepsy and people with epilepsy.

The definition of the scale's item content was accomplished by reviewing previously published research literature and scales of attitudes toward disabled people, and by analyzing open-ended interviews with experts in the fields of neurology, special education, and rehabilitation counseling. An initial pool of 106 items was revised to yield 76 items which were given to a panel of ten experts to evaluate. Each expert was asked to rate the favorableness of the items on a six-point scale. In addition, the experts were asked to differentiate between those items which expressed an attitude toward epilepsy or people with epilepsy, those items which represented knowledge of epilepsy, or those items which reflected both attitudes and knowledge. A set of 26 attitude items and 14 knowledge items were retained following analyses of the experts' responses.

These items were randomly reworded so that half expressed a favorable attitude or correct statement and half expressed an unfavorable attitude or incorrect statement, and randomly arranged on a summated rating scale which was given to 253 new respondents. Detailed item, scale, and factor analyses led to the final version of the ATPE.

Response Format

The ATPE is a 32-item summated rating scale of which 25 items are scored as an attitude measure, and 13 items are scored as a knowledge measure. (A total of six items are scored as both attitude and knowledge measures.) Respondents are asked to indicate their agreement with each statement on a six-point scale ranging from −3, to signify "I disagree very much," to +3, to signify "I agree very much." No neutral response option is provided. Directions to the respondent are printed on the questionnaire form together with a response key. The original version of the scale included a separate response form, but the scale could be easily modified to include the directions, the items, and the response options on two sides of one page.

Administration and Scoring

The scale was designed to be administered to groups, but may also be used individually and mailed to respondents. Respondents are encouraged to respond to every item on the scale. Protocols with omitted items are scored with the omitted responses assigned a value of zero. To obtain the attitude score, the negative item responses (items #3, 7, 9, 10, 12, 14, 15, 17, 19, 22, 28, 30, and 31) are first reversed (i.e., from + to −, or from − to +). The respondent's score is the sum of the individual item responses plus a constant of 75. Attitude scores range from 0 to 150 with a high score indicating a favorable attitude.

The three agree response options to the 13 knowledge items (#3, 4, 5, 9, 11, 15, 18, 20, 24, 25, 26, 29, and 32) are collapsed into one category (True) and the three disagree response options are collapsed into a second category (False). The responses are scored dichotomously according to the key derived from the experts' responses (F, T, F, F, T, F, T, T, F, F, T, T, and T). Knowledge scores ranged from 0 to 13, with a higher score representing correct responses to more items.

Reliability

The Spearman-Brown corrected reliability coefficient for the attitude scale was reported to be +.81; the alpha homogeneity coefficient was +.87. The Kuder-Richardson reliability coefficient for the knowledge scale was +.69, and the alpha homogeneity coefficient was +.97. A factor analysis of the ATPE attitude item correlation matrix yielded three factors which accounted for 68 percent of the variance in the data. These three factors were rotated to a terminal solution using a varimax criterion.

The first factor, accounting for 70 percent of the common variance, was labeled Prejudicial Stereotypes, and included six items characterizing the person with epilepsy as insane, dangerous, and a threat to others. The second factor accounted for 16 percent of the common variance and was labeled Behavioral Misconceptions. The six items loading on this factor suggest that people with epilepsy are accident prone, do not make good parents or spouses, are prone to criminal behavior, and prefer to live in isolated colonies. The last factor accounted for the remaining common variance and was labeled Behavioral Optimism. The six items loading on this factor state positive views of the educability, employability, personal skills, and social adaptability of people with epilepsy. Seven of the attitude items failed to exceed the cutoff value of .35 for unequivocal assignment to one of the three factors.

Validity

Multiple regression analyses of ATPE scores with the respondents' age, sex, educational level, and professional specialization as dependent variables supported the criterion-related validity of both the attitude and the knowledge portions of the scale. Females had a significantly higher mean attitude score than males, but no sex difference in the knowledge mean scores was found. In general, the best predictor of both attitude score and knowledge score was educational level—more favorable attitudes and accurate knowledge were found among the most highly educated respondents in the sample. In addition, professionals trained in one of the human service professions were found to have the most favorable attitudes and accurate knowledge. The redundancy-corrected correlation between the attitude and knowledge scores was found to be .80.

Comments

Additional analyses of ATPE data from different samples of respondents in different circumstances and settings are needed before the scale's validity and utility can be finally accepted. Investigations of the influence of socially desirable responding, and further analyses of the attitude item factorial structure, are also needed. The scale appears to be a psychometrically sound measure which should prove useful in research designed to narrow the gap between contemporary medical and psychological knowledge about epilepsy and people with epilepsy, and the knowledge and attitudes of professionals and the general public.

Exhibit 10-3

Scale of Knowledge and Attitudes Toward

Epilepsy and People with Epilepsy

Directions

The statements presented below express opinions or ideas about people with epilepsy. There are many differences of opinion; many people agree and many people disagree with each statement. We would like to know your opinion about them. Put an "X" through the appropriate number, from -3 to +3, which best corresponds with how you feel about the statement. There are no right or wrong answers. You should work as quickly as you can, but don't rush. There is no time limit. Please respond to every statement.

Key

-3: I disagree very much	+1: I agree a little
-2: I disagree pretty much	+2: I agree pretty much
-1: I disagree a little	+3: I agree very much

1	Schools should be prepared to accept children with epilepsy into regular classrooms.	-3	-2	-1	+1	+2	+3
2	People with epilepsy possess the same rights, civil or otherwise, as all people.	-3	-2	-1	+1	+2	+3
3	Epilepsy is a manifestation of insanity.	-3	-2	-1	+1	+2	+3
4	People with epilepsy can safely operate machinery	-3	-2	-1	+1	+2	+3
5	The individual with epilepsy does not possess a normal life expectancy.	-3	-2	-1	+1	+2	+3
6	Insurance companies should not deny insurance on the basis of an individual's having epilepsy.	-3	-2	-1	+1	+2	+3
7	The individual with epilepsy should be prevented from having children.	-3	-2	-1	+1	+2	+3
8	Children with epilepsy should attend regular public school classes.	-3	-2	-1	+1	+2	+3
9	People with epilepsy should be prohibited from driving.	-3	-2	-1	+1	+2	+3
10	The onset of epileptic seizures in an adult is sufficient grounds for a divorce.	-3	-2	-1	+1	+2	+3
11	Individuals with epilepsy are not necessarily mentally retarded.	-3	-2	-1	+1	+2	+3

Exhibit 10-3 (Continued)

12	People with epilepsy are a danger to the public.	-3	-2	-1	+1	+2	+3
13	Individuals with epilepsy can hold a job in the community after adequate vocational training.	-3	-2	-1	+1	+2	+3
14	Children need to be protected from classmates who have epilepsy.	-3	-2	-1	+1	+2	+3
15	Individuals with epilepsy are accident-prone.	-3	-2	-1	+1	+2	+3
16	The responsibility for educating children with epilepsy rests with the community.	-3	-2	-1	+1	+2	+3
17	Parents should not expect of children with epilepsy what they expect of other children in the family.	-3	-2	-1	+1	+2	+3
18	People with epilepsy can safely participate in strenuous activities.	-3	-2	-1	+1	+2	+3
19	People with epilepsy are more likely to develop and express criminal tendencies then are other people.	-3	-2	-1	+1	+2	+3
20	People with epilepsy can marry and have children.	-3	-2	-1	+1	+2	+3
21	Laws citing epilepsy as a basis for the annulment of adoption should be repealed.	-3	-2	-1	+1	+2	+3
22	People with epilepsy prefer to live in colonies with others of similar characteristics.	-3	-2	-1	+1	+2	+3
23	Equal employment opportunities should be available to individuals with epilepsy.	-3	-2	-1	+1	+2	+3
24	Epilepsy is a degenerative condition.	-3	-2	-1	+1	+2	+3
25	The offspring of two individuals with epilepsy will have epilepsy.	-3	-2	-1	+1	+2	+3
26	People with epilepsy can participate in any activity they choose.	-3	-2	-1	+1	+2	+3
27	When their seizures are controlled by medication, people with epilepsy are just like anyone else.	-3	-2	-1	+1	+2	+3

Exhibit 10-3 (Continued)

28	Families of children with epilepsy should not be provided supportive social services.	-3	-2	-1	+1	+2	+3
29	Epilepsy is not contagious.	-3	-2	-1	+1	+2	+3
30	Children with epilepsy in regular classrooms have an adverse effect on the other children.	-3	-2	-1	+1	+2	+3
31	People with epilepsy are incapable of making moral judgments.	-3	-2	-1	+1	+2	+3
32	Individuals with epilepsy can cope with a 40-hour work week.	-3	-2	-1	+1	+2	+3

Reprinted with permission of the authors; from Antonak, R. F., & Rankin, P. R. (1981). Measurement and analysis of knowledge and attitudes toward epilepsy (Technical Report No. 1). Durham, NH: University of New Hampshire. Education Department.

DISABILITY SOCIAL RELATIONSHIP SCALE (DSRS)

Description

The DSR Scale was developed by Grand, Bernier, and Strohmer (1982) as a multidimensional measure of the influence of social-situation factors on the attitudes of non-disabled people toward disabled people, and variations in the influence of these factors on attitudes toward four different disability groups. A review of previous scales and the research literature led to the creation of a large pool of items expressing situation-specific attitudes. These items were reviewed by a panel of experts for clarity and redundancy, and a set of 31 items was retained for a series of pilot studies.

The prototype version of the scale expressed attitudes toward the social relations of work, dating, and marriage. Each set of items was repeated for the four disability groups: cerebral palsy, epilepsy, arm amputation, and blindness. A total of 191 subjects from among the faculty and staff at a large Northeastern university responded to this version of the scale, and these data were analyzed with a detailed set of item and scale analyses.

A total of 18 items were retained for the final version of the DSR Scale based on item analysis results. Six items concern aspects of work, six concern dating, and six concern marriage. They are repeated (at random) for each of the four disability groups. Items were presented in a random order on each scale. In a subsequent investigation (Strohmer, Grand, and Purcell, 1984), the DSR Scale was given to a sample of 214 individuals from the staff and faculty of the State University of New York at Albany. The 84 females and 130 males ranged in age from 19 to 73 years and ranged in educational level from less than high school to post-doctoral levels.

Response Format

The respondent is instructed to answer True ("Whether you feel it is MOSTLY TRUE") or false ("Whether you feel it is MOSTLY FALSE") to each item. No neutral response alternative is allowed.

Administration and Scoring

The DSR Scale booklet consists of a cover page of instructions and four pages of 18 items for each of the disability groups. While subjects are asked to respond to all the items, items may be omitted if the respondent finds them "intrusive." Each disability group is defined briefly at the top of the appropriate page. Responses are recorded by circling either T or F on the pages of the booklet.

Half of the items in each of the social situations were randomly reversed in wording so that a false response is the accepting response. Each item is scored as 1 ("accepting") or 0 ("non-accepting") according to a key developed from a panel of experts, and a total score for each social situation is obtained (range 0 to 6), as well as for each disability group (range 0 to 18). A global score expressing attitude toward disabled people in general is the sum of the disability subscale scores (range 0 to 72).

Reliability

The authors (Grand et al., 1982) presented detailed item, subscale, and scale analysis data. Internal consistency (K-R 20) reliability coefficients for the subscales ranged from +.86 to +.95. While test-retest reliability values for the pilot versions of the scale are reported, similar values are not presented for the final versions of these scales. No reliability data are presented in the Strohmer et al. (1984) study.

Validity

Analyses of differences in the disability subscale scores by social situation (Grand et al., 1982) led the authors to conclude that the scale is a valid measure of the multidimensional structure of attitudes toward disabled people. The mean dating and marriage subscale scores did not differ, although both were significantly less than the mean of the work scores. The mean score for the cerebral palsy scale was significantly less than the mean for the blindness scale, both of which were less than the means for the amputation and epilepsy scales, which did not differ significantly from each other. The mean pairwise correlation between the disability scales was +.57; the mean pairwise correlation between the social situations was +.77.

Analyses of the data from the Strohmer et al. (1984) study showed the same order of the three subscale means, with the Work subscale and Dating subscale means both significantly greater than the Marriage subscale mean, but not significantly different from each other. The four disability subscale means were all significantly different and ordered, from highest to lowest, as follows: cerebral palsy, blind, amputee, and epilepsy. Multiple regression analyses of the relationships between the scale scores and the respondents' demographic characteristics showed that 23 percent of the variance in the total DSR Scale scores was accounted for by the variables of age, contact with disabled people, and educational level. These three variables also contributed, in various ways, to the prediction of scores on the disability and social-situation subscales.

Comments

The DSR Scale represents an attempt to construct an attitude scale which incorporates situation-specific factors into the measurement of attitudes toward four disability groups. The scale appears to have adequate reliability. Additional analyses of the construct validity of the scale's proposed factorial structure are needed, however, as are investigations of the scale's susceptibility to acquiescence and socially desirable responding. The three social-situation and four disability subscales may not be as homogeneous nor as specific as the authors imply. The results of the Grand et al. (1982) report of the lack of difference in the means for the marriage and dating scales, and a similar lack of difference in the work and dating subscale means reported by Strohmer et al. (1984) suggests that these three subscales may not represent different factors. Additional construct and predictive validity analyses of the DSR Scale are needed.

The authors indicate that they are developing additional social-situation subscales, and are continuing their investigation of the validity of the DSR Scale. Researchers should be cautious, however, in the use and interpretation of this scale and its subscales until the results of these additional analyses are reported.

Exhibit 10-4

Disability Social Relationship Scale

Instructions

The following questionnaire concerns your feelings about relationships with people representing four different disabilities (blindness, cerebral palsy, epilepsy, and an arm amputation).

It is realized that you are being asked to comment on rather personal feelings and that is some instances you may be reluctant to disclose certain attitudes, but please bear in mind that only through accurate knowledge of your true feelings can we become aware of those areas that require further study and development. However, if you find certain questions intrusive, feel free not to answer them.

Marking Your Answer -- For each of the statements on the following pages, please indicate whether you feel it is MOSTLY TRUE or MOSTLY FALSE by circling T or F following each statement.

CEREBRAL PALSY QUESIONS

Definition of Cerebral Palsy: Cerebral palsy is a condition caused by damage to the nervous system, usually at birth, and results in difficulties in muscle control affecting walking and speech.

1	If I were to date a person with cerebral palsy, I would be willing to have a sexual relationship.	T	F
2	If I were to date a person with C.P., I would be willing to have a friendship, but nothing more.	T	F
3	If I were to date a person with C.P., I would find sex or physical contact with the person embarrassing.	T	F
4	If I were to work with a person with C.P., I would not be surprised if he or she fell behind in their work.	T	F
5	Marriage to a person with C.P. would be more difficult than marriage to an able-bodied person because the disabled person would be too dependent on me.	T	F
6	If I were to date a person with C.P., I would feel embarrassed if I had to help the person eat in public.	T	F
7	Marriage to a person with C.P. would be a problem because this person would not be able to earn an adequate income.	T	F
8	If I were to work with a person with C.P., I would expect that he or she would require extra help and attention which would disrupt normal activity.	T	F
9	Marriage to a person with C.P. is something I'd consider.	T	F

Exhibit 10-4 (Continued)

10	If I were to work with a person with C.P., I would prefer it not be a close relationship.	T	F
11	Marriage to a person with C.P. would be difficult because this person would not be able to take full responsibility as a parent.	T	F
12	If I were to work with a person with C.P., I would be particularly careful in choosing my words when speaking to him or her.	T	F
13	If I were to date a person with C.P., I would be uncomfortable because people would stare.	T	F
14	If I were to date a person with C.P., I would worry about what other people would think.	T	F
15	If I were to work with a person with C.P., it would be O.K. as long as I didn't have to socialize or hang out with him or her.	T	F
16	Marriage to a person with C.P. would be difficult because I'd feel uncomfortable about making love to a person with this disability.	T	F
17	Marriage to a person with C.P. would be worth a try if I loved the person.	T	F
18	If I were to work with a person with C.P., I would be uncomfortable eating lunch with him or her.	T	F

Exhibit 10-4 (Continued)

EPILEPSY QUESIONS

Definition of Epilepsy: Epilepsy usually occurs between infancy and yong adulthood. It is an impairment in the nervous system producing periodic losses of consciousness during which convulsions may occur.

1	Marriage to an epileptic would be a problem because this person would not be able to earn an adequate income.	T	F
2	If I were to work with an epileptic person, it would be O.K. as long as I didn't have to socialize or hang out with him or her.	T	F
3	If I were to work with an epileptic person, I would not be surprised if he or she fell behind in their work.	T	F
4	Marriage to an epileptic would be difficult because I'd feel uncomfortable about making love to a person with this disability.	T	F
5	If I were to date an epileptic, I would be willing to have a friendship, but nothing more.	T	F
6	Marriage to an epileptic is something I'd consider.	T	F
7	If I were to date an epileptic, I would be willing to have a sexual relationship.	T	F
8	If I were to work with an epileptic person, I would expect that he or she would require extra help and attention which would disrupt normal activity.	T	F
9	If I were to date an epileptic, I would feel embarrassed if I had to help the person eat in public.	T	F
10	If I were to date an epileptic, I would worry about what other people would think.	T	F
11	Marriage to an epileptic would be difficult because this person would not be able to take full responsibility as a parent.	T	F
12	If I were to date an epileptic, I would be uncomfortable because people would stare.	T	F
13	Marriage to an epileptic would be more difficult than marriage to an able-bodied person because the disabled person would be too dependent on me.	T	F
14	If I were to work with an epileptic person, I would be particularly careful in choosing my words when speaking to him or her.	T	F

Exhibit 10-4 (Continued)

15	If I were to work with an epileptic person, I would be uncomfortable eating lunch with him or her.	T	F
16	If I were to work with an epileptic person, I would prefer it not be a close relationship.	T	F
17	If I were to date an epileptic, I would find sex or physical contact with the person embarrassing.	T	F
18	Marriage to an epileptic would be worth a try if I loved the person.	T	F

Exhibit 10-4 (Continued)

AMPUTEE QUESIONS

Definition of Amputation: Amputation is a loss of a limb (arm or leg).

1	If I were to work with an amputee, I would be uncomfortable eating lunch with him or her.	T	F
2	Marriage to an amputee would be more difficult than marriage to an able-bodied person because the disabled person would be too dependent on me.	T	F
3	If I were to work with an amputee, I would prefer it not be a close relationship.	T	F
4	If I were to date an amputee, I would be uncomfortable because people would stare.	T	F
5	If I were to work with an amputee, it would be O.K. as long as I didn't have to socialize or hang out with him or her.	T	F
6	If I were to work with an amputee, I would not be surprised if he or she fell behind in their work.	T	F
7	Marriage to an amputee is something I'd consider.	T	F
8	Marriage to an amputee would be difficult because this person would not be able to take full responsibility as a parent.	T	F
9	Marriage to an amputee would be difficult because I'd feel uncomfortable about making love to a person with this disability.	T	F
10	If I were to work with an amputee, I would be particularly careful in choosing my words when speaking to him or her.	T	F
11	If I were to work with an amputee, I would expect that he or she wold require extra help and attention which would disrupt normal activity.	T	F
12	If I were to date an amputee, I would be willing to have a friendship, but nothing more.	T	F
13	If I were to date an amputee, I would feel embarrassed if I had to help the person eat in public.	T	F
14	If I were to date an amputee, I would worry about what other people would think.	T	F

Exhibit 10-4 (Continued)

15	If I were to date an amputee, I would be willing to have a sexual relationship.	T	F
16	Marriage to an amputee would be a problem because this person would not be able to earn an adequate income.	T	F
17	Marriage to an amputee would be worth a try if I loved the person.	T	F
18	If I were to date an amputee, I would find sex or physical contact with the person embarrassing.	T	F

Exhibit 10-4 (Continued)

BLINDNESS QUESIONS

Definition of Blindness: Blind or visually handicapped individuals may have been born with a visual impairment or may have lost their sight (completely or partially) at any time during their lives.

1	If I were to work with a blind person, I would prefer it not be a close relationship.	T	F
2	If I were to work with a blind person, I would expect that he or she would require extra help and attention which would disrupt normal activity.	T	F
3	If I were to work with a blind person, I would not be surprised if he or she fell behind in their work.	T	F
4	Marriage to a blind person would be difficult because this person would not be able to take full responsibility as a parent.	T	F
5	If I were to date a blind person, I would worry about what other people would think.	T	F
6	If I were to date a blind person, I would feel embarrassed if I had to help the person eat in public.	T	F
7	Marriage to a blind person would be difficult because I'd feel uncomfortable about making love to a person with this disability.	T	F
8	If I were to date a blind person, I would be willing to have a friendship, but nothing more.	T	F
9	If I were to work with a blind person, I would be uncomfortable eating lunch with him or her.	T	F
10	Marriage to a blind person would be more difficult than marriage to an able-bodied person because the disabled person would be too dependent on me.	T	F
11	If I were to date a blind person, I would find sex or physical contact with the person embarrassing.	T	F
12	Marriage to a blind person would be worth a try if I loved the person.	T	F
13	Marriage to a blind person would be a problem because this person would not be able to earn an adequate income.	T	F
14	If I were to work with a blind person, it would be O.K. as long as I didn't have to socialize or hang out with him or her.	T	F

Exhibit 10-4 (Continued)

15	Marriage to a blind person is something I'd consider.	T	F
16	If I were to date a blind person, I would be willing to have a sexual relationship.	T	F
17	If I were to date a blind person, I would be uncomfortable because people would stare.	T	F
18	If I were to work with a blind person, I would be particularly careful in choosing my words when speaking to him or her.	T	F

 From Grand, S. A., Bernier, J. E., & Strohmer, D. C. (1982). Attitudes toward disabled persons as a function of social context and specific disability. Rehabilitation Psychology, 27, 165-173.

Chapter 11

ATTITUDES TOWARD PSYCHIATRIC DISABILITY GROUPS

CUSTODIAL MENTAL ILLNESS IDEOLOGY SCALE (CMI)

Description

THE Custodial Mental Illness Ideology Scale was constructed by Gilbert and Levinson (1956) as a measure by which to place respondents on a continuum of attitudes toward mental illness ranging from *custodialism* (the belief in the traditional medical model of the chronic mental hospital which provides a highly controlled setting for detention of inmates) to *humanism* (the belief in the individuality and human needs of patients and the view of the hospital as a therapeutic community). The scale consists of a total of 20 statements which were derived from extensive interviews and observations of hospital life.

Response Format

Respondents to the scale indicate their degree of agreement or disagreement with each statement on a six-point scale, ranging from + 3, to signify "I agree very much," to − 3, to signify "I disagree very much." No neutral responses are permitted.

Administration and Scoring

The CMI Scale was intended as a group scale, but may be administered individually. Instructions to respondents are provided at the top of the page. Responses to each item are converted to a scale ranging from 1 to 7 (i.e., − 3 = 1, − 2 = 2, − 1 = 3, omit = 4, + 1 = 5, + 2 = 6, and + 3 = 7). Seventeen of the scale's items are worded as custodial, while the remaining three (#4, 9, and 12) are phrased as humanistic in format (to prevent a possible acquiescence response style). The responses to these three items are reversed (e.g., − 3 = + 3, − 2 = + 2, and − 1 = + 1) before the item score is added to the total score. Using the authors' scoring system, the range of total scores is 20 to 140.

The highest score on the CMI Scale indicates an extreme custodial attitude and traditional belief about mental illness. That is, that mentally ill people are irrational, insensitive to others, unpredictable, dangerous, are unlikely to recover, and need to be kept on secure wards of a closed hospital. The lowest score indicates an extreme humanistic orientation or liberal view of mental illness. That is, that people who are mentally ill are capable of rational and responsible behavior, that they need not be placed in restrictive hospital settings, and that they are likely to recover with treatment. If the total score is divided by 20, the mean score per item is obtained. The authors suggest that this value should be multiplied by ten to yield a range of scores from 10 to 70, with a midpoint of 40. The CMI Scale takes approximately five minutes to administer.

Reliability

Gilbert and Levinson (1956) reported a Spearman-Brown corrected reliability estimate of + .85. The sample was composed of 335 staff members in three Massachusetts mental hospitals. Test-retest reliability estimates on several small groups of these mental hospital personnel were reported to be in the mid + .80's. No mention is made of the size of these groups or the time intervals used. No other reliability estimates were reported by the authors.

Validity

The 20 items on the CMI Scale cover various facets of the beliefs concerning the causes and nature of mental illness, hospital conditions, patient-staff relationships, and so on. These items were derived from extensive interviews and observations of daily hospital living conditions. Content validity, then, appears to be adequate.

Construct validation involved the known-groups procedure. The CMI Scale scores of ten hospital administrators and a group of professional staff members at a social rehabilitation hospital unit—individuals known for their advocacy of humanistic policies—were compared to the CMI Scale scores of a group of attendants and nurses at other mental hospitals. As predicted, the scores of the former group were significantly lower than the scores of the latter group (i.e., the former group expressed a more humanistic ideology). Also, as predicted by the authors, the scale was found to correlate significantly with both the California F Scale (a measure of authoritarianism), and the Traditional Family Ideology (TFI) Scale (a measure of autocratic beliefs concerning family relations). The correlations between the scale scores of a small group of personnel at the three separate hospitals ranged from + .67 to + .76 for the CMI and F Scales, and from + .50 to + .77 for the CMI and TFI Scales. The authors concluded that views regarding mental illness and hospital policies are embedded within a broader, but similar, ideological and psychodynamic belief system.

The authors also report a high rank-order correlation (+ .92) between CMI

Scale scores and the degree of custodialism in policy requirements in the three hospitals comprising the sample. In other words, individuals who worked in hospital units having the most custodial policy requirements demonstrated the most custodial model beliefs (as measured by the CMI Scale) and the most authoritarian personalities (as measured by the F Scale).

In a later study, Clark and Binks (1966) gave the CMI Scale to 56 workers, who differed by age and educational level, at a large mental health facility. Their analyses of the data revealed that those respondents who were the youngest and more highly educated expressed more humanistic (liberal) attitudes than the older and less well-educated respondents, as predicted by the authors.

Comments

Although the CMI Scale is the earliest scale to measure attitudes toward psychiatrically disabled people, only one reference to it could be located in the literature over the past 30 years. The scale appears to possess an adequate degree of reliability. While the content validation of the scale seems to be reasonable for the time of its construction, it should be viewed as inadequate by present-day researchers. Recent liberal policies toward emotionally impaired people, such as the creation of community mental health centers and the adoption of policies of deinstitutionalization and community integration of former mental hospital patients, require that the content of the items of the scale be carefully reviewed and possibly substantially revised. There is a lack of data on the scale's factorial validity, criterion-related validity, and immunity to response set and socially desirable response tendencies. Unless these additional validity and psychometric studies are undertaken, the CMI Scale should be viewed as an historically interesting, although outdated and possibly psychometrically unsound, measurement instrument designed to investigate attitudes toward psychiatrically disabled people.

Exhibit 11-1

Custodial Mental Illness Ideology Scale

Directions:

Mark each statement in the left margin according to how much you agree or disagree with it. Please mark every one. Write in +1, +2, +3; or -1, -2, -3; depending on how you feel in each case.

+1: I AGREE A LITLE -1: I DISAGREE A LITTLE
+2: I AGREE PRETTY MUCH -2: I DISAGREE PRETTY MUCH
+3: I AGREE VERY MUCH -3: I DISAGREE VERY MUCH

___ 1. Only persons with considerable psychiatric training should be allowed to form close relationships with patients.

___ 2. It is best to prevent the more distrurbed patients from mixing with those who are less sick.

___ 3. As soon as a person shows signs of mental disturbance he should be hospitalized.

___ 4. Mental illness is an illness like any other.

___ 5. Close association with mentally ill people is liable to make even a normal person break down.

___ 6. We can make some improvements, but by and large the conditions of mental hospital wards are about as good as they can be considering the disturbed patient living there.

___ 7. We should be sympathetic with mental patients, but we cannot expect to understand their odd behavior.

___ 8. One of the main causes in menal illness is lack of moral strength.

___ 9. When a patient is discharged from a hospital, he can be expected to carry out his responsibilities as a citizen.

___ 10. Abnormal people are ruled by their emotions; noraml people by their reason.

___ 11. A mental patient is in no position to make decision about even everyday living problems.

___ 12. Patients are often kept in the hospital long after they are well enough to get along in the community.

___ 13. There is something about mentally ill people that makes it easy to tell them from normal people.

Exhibit 11-1 (Continued)

___ 14. Few, if any, patients are capable of real friendliness.

___ 15. There is hardly a mental patient who isn't liable to attack you unless you take extreme precautions.

___ 16. Patients who fail to recover have only themselves to blame; in most cases they have just not tried hard enough.

___ 17. "Once a schizophrenic, always a schizophrenic."

___ 18. Patients need the same kind of control and discipline as an untrained child.

___ 19. With few exceptions, most patients haven't the ability to tell right from wrong.

___ 20. In experimenting with new methods of ward treatment, hospitals must consider, first and foremost, the safety of patients and personnel.

Reprinted with permission of the authors; from Gilbert, D. C., & Levinson, D. J. (1956). Ideology, personality, and institutional policy in the mental hospital. Journal of Abnormal and Social Psychology, 53, 263-271.

MENTAL HEALTH INFORMATION QUESTIONNAIRE (MHIQ)

Description

Nunnally (1961) constructed the MHIQ to investigate what the public "knows and thinks" about mental health. An initial pool of 3,000 opinion items concerning the causes, symptoms, prognosis, incidence, and social significance of mental health was collected from interviews of relatives of residents of mental hospitals, professional publications, popular print media, and public-information pamphlets. This set of items was reduced to yield 240 items which were presented on a questionnaire with a seven-point response format to a collection of 349 people in Illinois. One-half the items were selected at random to be written so that an agree response represented a favorable opinion, and the other half were written so that a disagree response represented a favorable opinion. This was done to minimize the effects of acquiescent response style.

A total of 60 items were immediately discarded because of extreme response tendencies (i.e., lack of variance in the response data). Factor analyses of the remaining data yielded ten factors which accounted for the majority of the common factor variance of the data. A second set of 50 items was retained based upon factor loadings, and the sample data was rescored. In addition, the new questionnaire was presented to representative samples of the populations of Knoxville, Tennessee, and Eugene, Oregon. The questionnaire was also presented to a mail sample of 150 psychologists across the United States.

Factor analyses of these, and other, data over more than two years of research led to the final 60-item version of the MHIQ. Several of the original items were modified in trivial ways, others were modified in more substantial ways, and ten new items were written to measure specific dimensions of information concerning mental health.

Response Format

Each statement on the questionnaire is followed by a seven-point rating scale: from "Completely disagree" (1), to "Mostly disagree," "Disagree more than agree," "Neutral" (4), "Agree more than disagree," "Mostly agree," to "Completely agree" (7).

Administration and Scoring

The 60 items are presented in a booklet with instructions printed on the first page. The respondent is urged to respond to all items, and not to "spend more than a few seconds marking each statement."

Reliability

Item means and standard deviations for the various samples are presented by the author, together with factor loadings. No reliability information is reported by Nunnally (1961), and no other study has been located in which the reliability of the MHIQ was reported.

Validity

Differences in MHIQ scores among various sample groups supported the validity of the scale. For example, people with more years of formal schooling, and people who were younger, were found to have more correct information. The results of the factor analyses of the data obtained from the general public samples led Nunnally to conclude that information and beliefs of the public toward mental health were not well-structured at that time. Few of the item loadings exceeded + .40, and the ten factors extracted accounted for less than 25 percent of the total item variance. Plots of the mean factor scores for the general public and the experts showed significant differences, especially concerning treatment prognosis and sexual issues.

Comments

A subset of the original 60-item version of the MHIQ was modified by Hood (1973) to create three subscales: Mental Illness, Suicide, and Homosexual. Mean test-retest reliability coefficients for the three subscales from data collected from 122 students in an introductory psychology course was + .73. It is, however, unclear how the modifications of the original MHIQ items were accomplished, and no analysis of the validity of these new subscales was provided.

The lack of any information on the reliability of the MHIQ implies that the scale cannot be used in research investigating attitudes toward people who are mentally ill. Because the questionnaire is more than 25 years old, it is suggested that a complete set of psychometric analyses of the MHIQ be conducted with appropriate revisions of item content reflecting contemporary views in the field of mental health. The reputation of the author of the MHIQ as a researcher and psychometrician suggests that the questionnaire is sound and worthy of this work. The small number of useful attitude instruments in this important research domain also supports this conclusion.

Exhibit 11-2

Mental Health Information Questionnaire

Instructions:

You are being asked to participate in a study of mental health problems. Your participation will supply valuable information to those responsible for the nation's health.

On the following pages you will find a number of statements about health problems. We want to know how much you agree or disagree with each of the statements. To the right of each statement you will find a rating scale. The points on the scale (1, 2, 3, 4, 5, 6, 7) can be interpreted as follows:

1. Completely disagree
2. Mostly disagree
3. Disagree more than agree
4. Neutral
5. Agree more than disagree
6. Mostly agree
7. Completely agree

The use of the scale can be illustrated with the following: "Smoking causes lung cancer." If you completely agreed with this statement, you would place a mark in column 7. If you agreed slightly with the statement, you would place a mark in column 5. If you mostly disagreed with the statement, you would place a mark in column 2. In this manner you can indicate the extent to which you agree or disagree with each of the statements on the following pages.

Like everyone else, you will probably feel that you do not know the answer to some of the statements. When this occurs please make the best guess that you can.

Please make sure that you make a mark for each statement. Leave none of the statements blank and make only one mark for each statement. You should not spend more than a few seconds marking each statement. If it is difficult for you to make up your mind, make the best guess that you can and go on to the next one

---

		Disagree						Agree
1	The mentally ill pay little attention to their personal appearance	1	2	3	4	5	6	7
2	People who keep themselves occupied with pleasant thoughts seldom become mentally ill.	1	2	3	4	5	6	7
3	Few people who enter mental hospitals ever leave.	1	2	3	4	5	6	7

Exhibit 11-2 (Continued)

4	Older people have fewer emotional problems than younger people.	1	2	3	4	5	6	7
5	People cannot maintain good mental health without the support of strong persons in their environment.	1	2	3	4	5	6	7
6	Will power alone will not cure mental disorders.	1	2	3	4	5	6	7
7	Women have no more emotional problems than men do.	1	2	3	4	5	6	7
8	X-rays of the head will not tell whether a person is likely to become insane.	1	2	3	4	5	6	7
9	Emotional problems do little damage to the individual.	1	2	3	4	5	6	7
10	Psychiatrists try to teach mental patients to hold in their strong emotions.	1	2	3	4	5	6	7
11	Mental illness can usually be helped by a vacation or a change of scene.	1	2	3	4	5	6	7
12	Disappointments affect children as much as they do adults.	1	2	3	4	5	6	7
13	The main job of the psychiatrist is to recommend hobbies and other ways for the mental patient to occupy his time.	1	2	3	4	5	6	7
14	The insane laugh more than normal people.	1	2	3	4	5	6	7
15	Psychiatrists try to show the mental patient where his ideas are incorrect.	1	2	3	4	5	6	7
16	Mental disorder is not a hopeless condition.	1	2	3	4	5	6	7
17	Mental health is one of the most important national problems.	1	2	3	4	5	6	7
18	Mental disorder is usually brought on by physical causes.	1	2	3	4	5	6	7
19	It is easier for women to get over emotional problems that it is for men.	1	2	3	4	5	6	7
20	A change of climate seldom helps an emotional disorder.	1	2	3	4	5	6	7

Exhibit 11-2 (Continued)

21	The best way to mental health is by avoiding morbid thoughts.	1	2	3	4	5	6	7
22	There is not much that can be done for a person who develops a mental disorder.	1	2	3	4	5	6	7
23	mental disorder is one of the most damaging illnesses that a person can have.	1	2	3	4	5	6	7
24	Children sometimes have mental breakdowns as severe as those of adults.	1	2	3	4	5	6	7
25	Nervous breakdowns seldom have a physical origin.	1	2	3	4	5	6	7
26	Most of the people in mental hospitals speak in words that can be understood.	1	2	3	4	5	6	7
27	Mental health is largely a matter of trying hard to control emotions.	1	2	3	4	5	6	7
28	If a person concentrates on happy memories, he will not be bothered by unpleasant things in the present.	1	2	3	4	5	6	7
29	The mentally ill have not received enough guidance from the important people in their lives.	1	2	3	4	5	6	7
30	Women are as emotionally healthy as men.	1	2	3	4	5	6	7
31	the seriousness of the mental-health problem in this country has been exaggerated.	1	2	3	4	5	6	7
32	Helping the mentally ill person with his financial and social problems often improves his condition.	1	2	3	4	5	6	7
33	Mental patients usually make a good adjustment to society when they are released.	1	2	3	4	5	6	7
34	The good psychiatrist acts like a father to hid patients.	1	2	3	4	5	6	7
35	Early adulthood is more of a danger period for mental illness than later years.	1	2	3	4	5	6	7
36	Almost any disease that attacks the nervous system is likely to bring on insanity.	1	2	3	4	5	6	7

Exhibit 11-2 (Continued)

37	You can tell a person who is mentally ill from his appearance.	1	2	3	4	5	6	7
38	People who become mentally ill have little will power.	1	2	3	4	5	6	7
39	Women are more likely to develop mental disorders than men.	1	2	3	4	5	6	7
40	Most mental disturbances in adults can be traced to emotional experiences in childhood.	1	2	3	4	5	6	7
41	People who have little sexual desire are more likely to have a "nervous breakdown" than are other people.	1	2	3	4	5	6	7
42	A person can avoid worry by keeping busy.	1	2	3	4	5	6	7
43	A poor diet often leads to feeblemindedness.	1	2	3	4	5	6	7
44	Emotionally upset persons are often found in important positions in business.	1	2	3	4	5	6	7
45	Good emotional habits can be taught to children in school as easily as spelling can.	1	2	3	4	5	6	7
46	The eyes of the insane are glassy.	1	2	3	4	5	6	7
47	When a person is recovering from a mental illness, it is best not to discuss the treatment that he has had.	1	2	3	4	5	6	7
48	People who go from doctor to doctor with many complaints know that there is nothing really wrong with them.	1	2	3	4	5	6	7
49	A person cannot rid himself of unpleasant memories by trying hard to forget them.	1	2	3	4	5	6	7
50	The main job of the psychologist is to explain to the patient the origin of his troubles.	1	2	3	4	5	6	7
51	Most suicides occur because of rejection in love.	1	2	3	4	5	6	7

Exhibit 11-2 (Continued)

52	People who are likely to have a nervous breakdown pay little attention to their personal appearance.	1	2	3	4	5	6	7
53	Most of the time psychiatrists have difficulty in telling whether or not a patient's mental disorder is curable.	1	2	3	4	5	6	7
54	Children usually do not forget about frightening experiences in a short time.	1	2	3	4	5	6	7
55	Books on "peace of mind" prevent many people from developing nervous breakdowns.	1	2	3	4	5	6	7
56	Most clergymen will encourage a person with a mental disorder to see a psychiatrist.	1	2	3	4	5	6	7
57	Physical exhaustion does not lead to a nervous breakdown.	1	2	3	4	5	6	7
58	The adult who needs a great deal of affection is likely to have had little affection in childhood.	1	2	3	4	5	6	7
59	Physical rest will not prevent a mental disorder.	1	2	3	4	5	6	7
60	Most of the people who seek psychiatric help need the treatment.	1	2	3	4	5	6	7

Reprinted from Nunnally, J. C. (1961). Popular conceptions of mental health: Their development and change. New York: Holt, Rhinehart and Winston.

OPINIONS ABOUT MENTAL ILLNESS SCALE (OMI)

Description

The Opinions About Mental Illness (OMI) Scale was developed by Cohen and Struening (1959, 1960) to measure attitudes toward mentally ill people and their personal characteristics, and toward mental illness, its etiology and treatment. The scale consists of 51 items derived from extensive factor analytic studies with over 8,000 respondents. The items are organized into five factorially-derived subscales: Authoritarianism (A, 11 items), Unsophisticated Benevolence (UB, 14 items), Mental Illness (also called Hygiene) Ideology (MII, nine items), Social Restrictiveness (SR, ten items), and Interpersonal Etiology (IE, seven items) (Cohen and Struening, 1962, 1963; Struening and Cohen, 1963).

Response Format

Respondents to the scale choose (i.e., check on the form) one of six alternatives, reflecting their level of agreement with each statement. The six options—"Strongly agree," "Agree," "Not sure but probably agree," "Not sure but probably disagree," "Disagree," and "Strongly disagree"—are then assigned numerical values ranging from 1 to 6, respectively. No neutral responses are permitted.

Administration and Scoring

The OMI was originally planned for group administration. It may, however, also be administered individually. Instructions for group administration include assurance of respondents' anonymity. Scoring of the scale requires separate computations for each of the five subscales. In computing the subscale scores, the subtotals of the respondents' responses to the positive and negative items on that subscale are added or subtracted according to formulae provided by the authors (Struening and Cohen, 1963, p. 294). The scores on the subscales may range from 1 to 56 (for subscale A) 1 to 66 (for subscale UB), 1 to 46 (subscale MII), 1 to 51 (subscale SR), and from 1 to 36 (subscale IE). A high score on a subscale indicates a positive or accepting attitude toward mentally ill people and mental illness. The OMI Scale takes up to 15 minutes for administration.

Reliability

Struening and Cohen (1963) reported the results of a series of internal consistency studies conducted at three separate hospitals. These values ranged from +.77 to +.80 for subscale A, +.70 to +.72 for subscale UB, +.29 to +.39 for subscale MII, +.71 to +.76 for subscale SR, and +.65 to +.66 for subscale IE. No other reliability data were reported by the authors.

Validity

In order to identify the dimensions underlying attitudes toward mental illness, the authors pooled approximately 200 opinion items relating to the cause, nature, treatment, and prognosis of mental illness. These items were later reviewed by experienced hospital researchers, and 55 items were selected for the final instrument. Fifteen additional items from three independent existing scales were later supplemented to bring the total number of items to 70. The 70-item set was then administered anonymously to hospital personnel in two separate large mental hospitals (sample sizes of 541 and 653). Five factors were extracted from the scales intercorrelation matrix for each of the two samples. The rotated factor loadings for the two hospitals were then correlated with the resulting correlation coefficients ranging from + .38 (Factor 3) to + .86 (Factor 1) (Cohen and Struening, 1962). Factor invariance, in a cross-validation study using personnel in three additional large hospitals, was also reported by the authors (Struening and Cohen, 1963). Factorial similarity over time and among hospitals was, therefore, further established. These extensive factor analytic studies serve as evidence of the OMI Scale's validity, and are a model for sound psychometric investigation of a scale's structure.

Further construct validation was rendered by demonstrating the ability of each subscale's factor scores to discriminate among ten occupational groups employed in hospitals (e.g., aides, nurses, physicians, psychiatrists, psychologists). This known-groups construct validation procedure was later extended to the construction of four hospital occupational group profiles (i.e., white-collar workers, blue-collar workers, non-medical professionals, clergymen), differentiated by their five subscale mean scores, through the use of cluster analysis. In addition, analyses of variance conducted on the original occupational groups, for each subscale, resulted in statistically significant differences among the groups' subscale mean scores. Respondents' educational level was also found to be related to the OMI Scale's factor scores. Age and sex, however, demonstrated no relationship, or only a weak relationship, to the factor scores.

One study (Costin and Kerr, 1962) investigated the scale's criterion-related validity. The authors reported a single academic course on abnormal psychology was found to positively alter attitudes (as measured by the OMI Scale) held by students toward mentally ill persons and mental illness.

Comments

The OMI Scale appears to possess satisfactory degrees of internal consistency reliability (with the exception of the MII subscale). However, an investigation of its temporal reliability is clearly needed. Although the factorial validity of the scale seems to have been established by Cohen and Struening's original studies, more recent investigations of intercorrelations among the OMI factors reveal equivocal results (Moore and Castles, 1978). Lawton (1964), who administered the OMI Scale and several other personality measures to a total of 72 psychiatric aides at a large state mental hospital, reported four significant subscale intercorrelations (mean $|r|$ = .43). Allon and Graham (1970) reported three significant subscale intercorrelations (mean $|r|$ = .41) from data from 31 psychiatrists and psychiatric residents, 29 nurses, and 97 nursing aides in a large urban psychiatric facility. Fracchia, Pintyr, Crovello, Sheppard, and Merlis (1972) reported four significant subscale intercorrelations (mean $|r|$ = .30) among data from 77 female psychiatric attendants on the wards of a large urban mental hospital.

In an effort to resolve the question of the factorial validity of the OMI, and recognizing that the original factor analysis of the scale by Cohen and Struening in 1959 used fairly crude statistical techniques, Dielman, Stiefel, and Cattell (1973) factor analyzed two sets of OMI data from 138 students in courses at the University of Illinois obtained two weeks apart. Their factorial congruence procedure confirmed the existence of the original five factors with one or two minor differences in the item loadings on the factors. They found, however, a persistent two-item factor, which they termed "Medical Model Orientation," and a new one-item factor which they chose not to name. Dielman et al. (1973) concluded that the replication of the original five factors across samples and within samples across time supported the original factorial structure of the OMI.

The reasons for these differences may be due to different occupational groups studied, different types of institutions sampled, and temporal changes in attitudes toward mental impairments. Further up-to-date estimates of the scale's criterion-related validity should shed more light on its predictive validity. Since no studies were found which report on how the OMI Scale is affected by social desirability and response styles, its use should be confined to research and experimental purposes.

Finally, most of the investigations of the scale's psychometric properties appear to have taken place in the early 1960's. The recent emphasis on deinstitutionalization of the mentally ill patient and his or her community reintegration should renew the interest of researchers in this seemingly useful scale. Its use is contraindicated, however, unless additional analyses directed toward the scale's content (item) representation, factorial stability, and convergent and predictive validity are undertaken.

Exhibit 11-3

Opinions about Mental Illness Scale

Directions:

The statements that follow are opinions or ideas about mental ill and mental patients. By mental illness, we mean the kinds of illness which bring patients to mental hospitals, and by mental patients we mean mental hospital patients. There are many differences of opinion about this subject. In other words, many people agree with each of the following statements while many people disagree with each of the statements. We would like to know what you think about these statements. Each of them is followed by six choices:

strongly agree ___ agree ___ not sure but probably agree ___ not sure but probably disagree ___ disagree ___ strongly disagree ___

Please check (✓) in the space provided that choice which comes closest to saying how you feel about each statement. you can be sure that many people, including doctors, will agree with your choice. There are no right or wrong answers: we are interested only in your opinion. It is very important that you answer every item. Please do NOT sign your name.

---

1 Nervous breakdowns usually result when people work too hard.

strongly agree ___ agree ___ not sure but probably agree ___ not sure but probably disagree ___ disagree ___ strongly disagree ___

2 Mental illness is an illness like any other.

strongly agree ___ agree ___ not sure but probably agree ___ not sure but probably disagree ___ disagree ___ strongly disagree ___

3 Most patients in mental hospitals are not dangerous.

strongly agree ___ agree ___ not sure but probably agree ___ not sure but probably disagree ___ disagree ___ strongly disagree ___

4 Although patients discharged from mental hospitals may seem all right, they should not be allowed to marry.

strongly agree ___ agree ___ not sure but probably agree ___ not sure but probably disagree ___ disagree ___ strongly disagree ___

Exhibit 11-3 (Continued)

---

5 If parents loved their children more, there would be less mental illness.

strongly agree ___ agree ___ not sure but probably agree ___ not sure but probably disagree ___ disagree ___ strongly disagree ___

6 It is easy to recognize someone who once had a serious mental illness.

strongly agree ___ agree ___ not sure but probably agree ___ not sure but probably disagree ___ disagree ___ strongly disagree ___

7 People who are mentally ill let their emotions control them: normal people think things out.

strongly agree ___ agree ___ not sure but probably agree ___ not sure but probably disagree ___ disagree ___ strongly disagree ___

8 People who were once patients in mental hospitals are no more dangerous than the average citizen.

strongly agree ___ agree ___ not sure but probably agree ___ not sure but probably disagree ___ disagree ___ strongly disagree ___

9 When a person has a problem or a worry, it is best to think about it, but keep busy with more pleasant things.

strongly agree ___ agree ___ not sure but probably agree ___ not sure but probably disagree ___ disagree ___ strongly disagree ___

10 Although they usually aren't aware of it, many people become mentally ill to avoid the difficult problems of everyday life.

strongly agree ___ agree ___ not sure but probably agree ___ not sure but probably disagree ___ disagree ___ strongly disagree ___

11 There is something about mental patients that makes it easy to tell them from normal people.

strongly agree ___ agree ___ not sure but probably agree ___ not sure but probably disagree ___ disagree ___ strongly disagree ___

Exhibit 11-3 (Continued)

---

12 Even though patients in mental hospitals behave in funny ways, it is wrong to laugh about them.

strongly agree ___ agree ___ not sure but probably agree ___ not sure but probably disagree ___ disagree ___ strongly disagree ___

13 Most mental patients are willing to work.

strongly agree ___ agree ___ not sure but probably agree ___ not sure but probably disagree ___ disagree ___ strongly disagree ___

14 The small children of patients in mental hospitals should not be allowed to visit them.

strongly agree ___ agree ___ not sure but probably agree ___ not sure but probably disagree ___ disagree ___ strongly disagree ___

15 People who are successful in their work seldom become mentally ill.

strongly agree ___ agree ___ not sure but probably agree ___ not sure but probably disagree ___ disagree ___ strongly disagree ___

16 People would not become mentally ill if they avoided bad thoughts.

strongly agree ___ agree ___ not sure but probably agree ___ not sure but probably disagree ___ disagree ___ strongly disagree ___

17 Patients in mental hospitals are in many ways like children.

strongly agree ___ agree ___ not sure but probably agree ___ not sure but probably disagree ___ disagree ___ strongly disagree ___

18 More tax money should be spent in the care and treatment of people with severe mental illness.

strongly agree ___ agree ___ not sure but probably agree ___ not sure but probably disagree ___ disagree ___ strongly disagree ___

Exhibit 11-3 (Continued)

---

19 A heart patient has just one thing wrong with him, while a mentally ill person is completely different from other patients.

strongly agree ___ agree ___ not sure but probably agree ___ not sure but probably disagree ___ disagree ___ strongly disagree ___

20 Mental patients come from homes where the parents took little interest in their children.

strongly agree ___ agree ___ not sure but probably agree ___ not sure but probably disagree ___ disagree ___ strongly disagree ___

21 People with mental illness should never be treated in the same hospital with people with physical illness.

strongly agree ___ agree ___ not sure but probably agree ___ not sure but probably disagree ___ disagree ___ strongly disagree ___

22 Anyone who tries to better himself deserves the respect of others.

strongly agree ___ agree ___ not sure but probably agree ___ not sure but probably disagree ___ disagree ___ strongly disagree ___

23 If our hospitals had enough well-trained doctors, nurses, and aides, many of the patients would get well enough to live outside the hospital.

strongly agree ___ agree ___ not sure but probably agree ___ not sure but probably disagree ___ disagree ___ strongly disagree ___

24 A woman would be foolish to marry a man who had a severe mental illness, even though he seems fully recovered.

strongly agree ___ agree ___ not sure but probably agree ___ not sure but probably disagree ___ disagree ___ strongly disagree ___

Exhibit 11-3 (Continued)

---

25 If the children of mentally ill parents were raised by normal parents, they would not become mentally ill.

strongly agree ___	agree ___	not sure but probably agree ___	not sure but probably disagree ___	disagree ___	strongly disagree ___

26 People who have been patients in a mental hospital will never be their old selves again.

strongly agree ___	agree ___	not sure but probably agree ___	not sure but probably disagree ___	disagree ___	strongly disagree ___

27 Many mental patients are capable of skilled labor, even though in some ways they are very disturbed mentally.

strongly agree ___	agree ___	not sure but probably agree ___	not sure but probably disagree ___	disagree ___	strongly disagree ___

28 Our mental hospitals seem more like prisons than like places where mentally ill people can be cared for.

strongly agree ___	agree ___	not sure but probably agree ___	not sure but probably disagree ___	disagree ___	strongly disagree ___

29 Anyone who is in a hospital for a mental illness should not be allowed to vote.

strongly agree ___	agree ___	not sure but probably agree ___	not sure but probably disagree ___	disagree ___	strongly disagree ___

30 The mental illness of many people is caused by the separation or divorce of their parents during childhood.

strongly agree ___	agree ___	not sure but probably agree ___	not sure but probably disagree ___	disagree ___	strongly disagree ___

Exhibit 11-3 (Continued)

---

31 The best way to handle patients in mental hospitals is to keep them behind locked doors.

strongly agree ___ agree ___ not sure but probably agree ___ not sure but probably disagree ___ disagree ___ strongly disagree ___

32 To become a patient in a mental hospital is to become a failure in life.

strongly agree ___ agree ___ not sure but probably agree ___ not sure but probably disagree ___ disagree ___ strongly disagree ___

33 The patients in mental hospital should be allowed more privacy.

strongly agree ___ agree ___ not sure but probably agree ___ not sure but probably disagree ___ disagree ___ strongly disagree ___

34 If a patient in a mental hospital attacks someone, he should be punished so he doesn't do it again.

strongly agree ___ agree ___ not sure but probably agree ___ not sure but probably disagree ___ disagree ___ strongly disagree ___

35 If the children of normal parents were raised by mentally ill parents, they would probably become mentally ill.

strongly agree ___ agree ___ not sure but probably agree ___ not sure but probably disagree ___ disagree ___ strongly disagree ___

36 Every mental hospital should be surrounded with a high fence and guards.

strongly agree ___ agree ___ not sure but probably agree ___ not sure but probably disagree ___ disagree ___ strongly disagree ___

37 The law should allow a woman to divorce her husband as soon as he has been confined in a mental hospital with a severe mental illness.

strongly agree ___ agree ___ not sure but probably agree ___ not sure but probably disagree ___ disagree ___ strongly disagree ___

Exhibit 11-3 (Continued)

---

38 People (both veterans and non-veterans) who are unable to work because of mental illness should receive money for living expenses.

strongly agree ___ agree ___ not sure but probably agree ___ not sure but probably disagree ___ disagree ___ strongly disagree ___

39 Mental illness is usually caused by some disease of the nervous system.

strongly agree ___ agree ___ not sure but probably agree ___ not sure but probably disagree ___ disagree ___ strongly disagree ___

40 Regardless of how you look at it, patients with severe mental illness are no longer really human.

strongly agree ___ agree ___ not sure but probably agree ___ not sure but probably disagree ___ disagree ___ strongly disagree ___

41 Most women who were once patients in a mental hospital could be trusted as baby sitters.

strongly agree ___ agree ___ not sure but probably agree ___ not sure but probably disagree ___ disagree ___ strongly disagree ___

42 Most patients in mental hospitals don't care how they look.

strongly agree ___ agree ___ not sure but probably agree ___ not sure but probably disagree ___ disagree ___ strongly disagree ___

43 College professors are more likely to become mentally ill than are business men.

strongly agree ___ agree ___ not sure but probably agree ___ not sure but probably disagree ___ disagree ___ strongly disagree ___

44 Many people who have never been patients in a mental hospital are more mentally ill than many hospitalized mental patients.

strongly agree ___ agree ___ not sure but probably agree ___ not sure but probably disagree ___ disagree ___ strongly disagree ___

Exhibit 11-3 (Continued)

---

45 Although some mental patients seem all right, it is dangerous to forget for a moment that they are mentally ill.

strongly agree ___ agree ___ not sure but probably agree ___ not sure but probably disagree ___ disagree ___ strongly disagree ___

46 Sometimes mental illness is punishment for bad deeds.

strongly agree ___ agree ___ not sure but probably agree ___ not sure but probably disagree ___ disagree ___ strongly disagree ___

47 Our mental hospitals should be organized in a way that makes the patient feel as much as possible like he is living at home.

strongly agree ___ agree ___ not sure but probably agree ___ not sure but probably disagree ___ disagree ___ strongly disagree ___

48 One of the main causes of mental illness is a lack of moral strength or will power.

strongly agree ___ agree ___ not sure but probably agree ___ not sure but probably disagree ___ disagree ___ strongly disagree ___

49 There is little that can be done for patients in a mental hospital except to see that they are comfortable and well-fed.

strongly agree ___ agree ___ not sure but probably agree not sure but probably disagree ___ disagree ___ strongly disagree ___

50 Many mental patients would remain in the hospital until they were well, even if the doors were unlocked.

strongly agree ___ agree ___ not sure but probably agree ___ not sure but probably disagree ___ disagree ___ strongly disagree ___

Exhibit 11-3 (Continued)

---

51 All patients in mental hospitals should be prevented from having children by a painless operation.

strongly agree ___ agree ___ not sure but probably agree ___ not sure but probably disagree ___ disagree ___ strongly disagree ___

PLEASE CHECK BACK AND MAKE SURE THAT YOU HAVE NOT LEFT OUT ANY STATEMENTS OR PAGES OF STATEMENTS

Reprinted from Cohen, J., & Struening, E. L. (1959). Factors underlying opinions about mental illness in the personnel of a large mental hospital. *American Psychologist*, *14*, 339.

Chapter 12

ATTITUDES TOWARD PEOPLE WHO ARE MENTALLY RETARDED

ATTITUDES TOWARD THE RETARDED SCALE (ATR)

Description

THE ATR WAS constructed by Efron and Efron (1967) to explore the dimensions of attitudes toward people who are mentally retarded. Attitude instruments available to that date were, in their view, unidimensional scales of favorability which provided little useable information on the attitudes of the public and of professionals. The 70 items comprising the ATR were selected from a pool of items including eight items from the California F scale (Adorno et al., 1964) and three from the OMI (Cohen and Struening, 1959). The authors state that nine of the 70 items, which were selected from a 1962 publication (unnamed) of the President's Panel on Mental Retardation, measure knowledge of the field of mental retardation. No item revision or item reduction procedures were reported, and presumably none were undertaken.

Factor analysis of data obtained from a sample of 235 individuals, the majority of whom were students enrolled in courses at Newark State College, yielded six factors which the authors titled: Segregation via Institutionalization (14 items), Cultural Deprivation (seven items), Noncondematory Etiology (eight items), Personal Exclusion (12 items), Authoritarianism (11 items), and Hopelessness (six items). These factors accounted for 22 percent, 14 percent, 14 percent, 20 percent, 18 percent, and 12 percent of the shared item variance, respectively.

Response Format

The items are arranged on a scale with six-point response continua ranging from 1, to signify "Strongly disagree," to 6, to signify "Strongly agree." A definition of the referent "Educable mental retardate" was provided at the top of the questionnaire for the respondent.

Administration and Scoring

The questionnaires were administered in group settings in the original study. The subjects' responses were scored on the six factors using the weighting formula:

$$w = a \,/\, [(1 - a^2)^* s]$$

where $w =$ the item weight, $a =$ the item's factor loading, and $s =$ the item's standard deviation.

Reliability

Subscale internal consistency reliability coefficients ranged from +.57 to +.79. No reliability data for the total scale or for the knowledge subscale were reported. The mean intercorrelation between pairs of factors was +.23 (range −.26 to +.43).

Validity

Analyses of differences in the factor scores by occupational group were used to assess criterion-related validity. Scores were "relatively independent" of age, sex, marital status, and educational level of the respondents. Experienced teachers of mentally retarded children and students training to enter the profession were more favorable on four of the factors than were regular education teachers and people employed in "other professions." No other validity analyses were reported by the authors.

One study was located which analyzed the subscale scores and variables representing sex and experience of 41 ward attendants at a state residential facility for the mentally retarded (Overbeck, 1971). None of the factor scores were significantly correlated with a variable representing the level of retardation of the people with whom the attendants worked. One of the six factors was significantly related to the sex of the attendants. The mean of the pairwise factor correlations was +.19 (range −.24 to +.54). An analysis of data using the ATR with ward attendants at another large institution for the mentally retarded produced seven factors with only limited similarity in item loadings to those suggested by Efron and Efron (Easley, 1976).

Comments

Although the ATR is one of the earliest scales to measure attitudes toward people who are mentally retarded, and has been referred to in more than a dozen published research reports since 1967, it has not been used in any significant research since its publication. The factorial structure is not at all clear considering the highly significant intercorrelations between several pairs of factors. Factor homogeneity and specificity analyses are needed, as well as studies of the predictive and criterion-related validity of the scale. Unless these additional detailed psychometric and validity studies are undertaken, the ATR must be considered an incomplete attempt to construct a summated rating scale of attitudes toward mentally retarded people.

ATTITUDES TOWARD MENTALLY RETARDED PEOPLE SCALE (AMRP)

Description

Bartlett, Quay, and Wrightsman (1960) developed the AMRP to assess the effectiveness of a program designed to change the attitudes of attendants employed in a large residential facility for the mentally retarded. An initial pool of 175 items was created and presented to a total of 99 attendants on a questionnaire. Factor analyses of data obtained from a sample led the authors to select 24 items with loadings of + .30 or greater on a general factor of attitude. A second sample of 97 attendants, from a different institution for the mentally retarded, was used for a subsequent study of the scale's reliability and validity.

Response Format

Respondents are asked to express their belief in the truth of each statement by circling the letter T, to signify "True," the letter F, to signify "False," or a question mark (?), to signify "Undecided."

Administration and Scoring

A total of 14 items were worded so that a T response expressed an unfavorable attitude. Four of the items concerned expressions of the respondents' views of their job. Ten of the items were oppositely-worded pairs. All favorable responses were scored as 2, all undecided responses as 1, and all unfavorable responses as 0. A sum of the item scores (range 0 to 48) is an index of the respondent's attitude, with a high score representing a favorable attitude.

Reliability

A Spearman-Brown corrected reliability estimate of + .80 was reported for the data from 68 of the 97 attendants in the second sample who completed the questionnaire both before and after an educational lecture. (The five pairs of oppositely-worded items make this coefficient spurious.) A test-retest reliability estimate of + .71 was reported based on the scores of respondents two weeks apart.

Validity

The authors' attempt to validate the scale in a subsequent study (Quay, Bartlett, Wrightsman, and Catron, 1961), by measuring attitude change after an intervention, was not successful. No additional validity analyses have been located. In fact, no studies have been found, other than the two by the authors, in which the scale has been used.

Comments

This scale must be considered as another reasonable, although incomplete, attempt to construct a summated rating scale to measure attitudes toward people who are mentally retarded. Its use cannot be recommended unless adequate reliability and validity data on samples other than institutional ward attendants are reported.

Exhibit 12-1

Attitudes Toward Mentally Retarded People Scale

Directions

Read each of the following sentences and decide whether the sentence is true or false. If you think the sentence is true, make a circle around the T. If you think it is false, make a circle around the F. If you cannot decide whether it is true or false, make a circle around the ?. There is no right or wrong answer to any of the sentences. Just give your personal opinion about each sentence.

1	I don't get paid enough for this job.	T	?	F
2	I don't trust retarded people.	T	?	F
3	I don't want to work with the mentally retarded all my life.	T	?	F
4	I want to work with the mentally retarded all my life.	T	?	F
5	I would like this job even if I didn't get paid.	T	?	F
6	Mentally retarded people are dangerous.	T	?	F
7	Mentally retarded people are mean.	T	?	F
8	Mentally retarded people are not crazy.	T	?	F
9	Mentally retarded people are not dangerous.	T	?	F
10	Mentally retarded people are not mean.	T	?	F
11	Mentally retarded people are not stubborn.	T	?	F
12	Mentally retarded people are not very easy to take care of.	T	?	F
13	Mentally retarded people should not be allowed to vote.	T	?	F
14	Mentally retarded people try to outsmart you.	T	?	F
15	Mentally retarded people will listen to reason.	T	?	F
16	Mentally retarded people won't listen to reason.	T	?	F
17	Most retarded people wouldn't steal.	T	?	F
18	Most mentally retarded people would steal if they had a chance.	T	?	F

Exhibit 12-1 (Continued)

19	Retarded people can be trusted.	T	?	F
20	Retarded people like to be dirty.	T	?	F
21	The church should not provide religious training for the retarded.	T	?	F
22	The mentally retarded are born stubborn.	T	?	F
23	The retarded can't learn right from wrong.	T	?	F
24	The retarded have something to live for.	T	?	F

Reprinted from Bartlett, C. J., Quay, L. C., & Wrightsman, L. S., Jr. (1960). A comparison of two methods of attitude measurement: Likert-type and forced choice. Educational and Psychological Measurement, 20, 699-704.

MULTIDIMENSIONAL ATTITUDE SCALE ON MENTAL RETARDATION (MASMR)

Description

The MASMR, originally published under the name Mental Retardation Attitude Inventory (MRAI) by Harth (1971), was created to measure attitudes toward people who are mentally retarded using the construct of attitudes toward minority groups. In particular, items were selected from the Woodmansee and Cook (1967) multidimensional scale to measure attitudes toward Negroes. A total of ten items were selected from each of five of the ten subtests of the Woodmansee and Cook scale. These subtests were: Integration-Segregation, referring to the respondent's view of the integration of mentally retarded children in regular classrooms; Overfavorableness, concerning characteristics which make mentally retarded children superior to non-retarded children; Social Distance, expressing a willingness to recognize, live near, or be associated with mentally retarded people; Private Rights, expressing the view that school personnel, landlords, and others have a private right to exclude people who are mentally retarded from schools, communities, and the workplace; and Subtle Derogatory Beliefs, expressing degrading views of people who are mentally retarded.

Harth rewrote each of the Woodmansee and Cook items by replacing the word Negro with the word retarded (or its grammatic equivalent). In certain cases, other parts of the original items were revised to reflect situations which were applicable to people who are mentally retarded. In a second step, a list of the revised items was presented to a panel of six special education experts who were asked to comment on the quality of the items and their appropriateness for the subtest on which they appeared. Changes in several items were made following this step, but the exact number and rationale for the changes are not described. The final version of the scale contains 50 items.

Response Format

The 50 items of the MASMR are presented in a booklet labelled an Opinion Inventory. Respondents are asked to express their agreement with each of the statements by selecting one of four alternatives: "Strongly agree," "Agree," "Disagree," and "Strongly disagree." Neutral responses are not permitted.

Administration and Scoring

The MASMR was administered by the author in a group setting to 86 undergraduates in an introductory special education course at the University of Missouri-Columbia. Directions to the respondents are printed on the cover of the MASMR booklet. The directions state that the booklet presents opinions about children who are mentally retarded, that the respondent should mark one of the four categories of responses for all 50 items, and that they should "WORK FAST!" A spearate answer sheet is provided which also asks the respondent for demographic information (e.g., age, sex, major, etc.).

To score the MASMR, the four response alternatives are converted to points ranging from 1 to 4, with 4 representing the most favorable attitude. Half the number of items for each subscale are worded positively, so that an agree response represents a favorable attitude, and half are worded negatively, so that a disagree response represents a favorable attitude. The numerical values for the former items range from 1 (for "Strongly disagree") to 4 (for "Strongly agree"), while the values range from 1 to 4 for these same responses for the letter set of items. Total score on the MASMR ranges from 50 to 200, while scores on each of the five subscales range from 10 to 40, with a higher score representing a more favorable attitude in all cases.

Reliability

Coefficient alpha reliability estimates for the subscales ranged from + .55 to + .89 (mean $r = +.71$). Substantial correlations of the majority of items with the subscale on which the item was scored were interpreted as evidence for the homogeneity of the subscales. Correlations of the subscales with the total scale ranged from + .44 to + .76 (mean $r = +.63$). Pairwise subscale intercorrelations ranged from − .15 to + .43. These data would appear to support a conclusion that the scale is reliable, and that the subscales are reasonably homogeneous and specific.

Validity

The respondents were divided into special and general education majors, and MASMR scores were compared to determine if the scale discriminates between these groups. The special education majors were more favorable on two of the subscales and the total scale, suggesting partial criterion-related validity of the scale. A study by Kennon and Sandoval (1978) using the MASMR revealed that those teachers who had more experience with mildly mentally retarded children in their classrooms expressed more favorable attitudes than those teachers who had limited experience teaching mildly mentally retarded children.

Harth (1981) modified and renamed the scale by using as the referent either trainable (moderately) mentally retarded or educable (mildly) mentally retarded, and gave the two scales to 102 students in an introductory special education class. Mildly mentally retarded children were evaluated more favorably on the total scale and on three of the subscales than were moderately mentally retarded children.

Feldman, Jay, Kinnison, and Harth (1984) modified the scale for use in a study of attitudes toward minority learning handicapped children. Analyses of the factorial structure of this revised version generally confirmed the original structure, with several significant differences as would be expected.

Comments

The scale development and reliability data reported by the author are reasonable. While the face validity of the scale may have been high at the time it was written, this is no longer the case. Because of the passage of federal legislation requiring the integration of mentally retarded children into public schools, and the integration of mentally retarded adults into the workplace and community, a number of the 50 items are, in 1987, clearly invalid (e.g., #9, 14, 19, 29, 34, 39, 44, 49). Following revision of the scale (e.g., elimination or substitution of these items), factorial and convergent validity analyses will be needed before it can be concluded that the five subscales remain conceptually and psychometrically valid as measures of significant domains of attitudes toward people who are mentally retarded. This effort to create a multidimensional scale based on the notion that attitudes toward people who are mentally retarded share a similar structure with attitudes toward other minority groups is sound. Until the data necessary to refine this potentially useful scale are collected, we cannot recommend its use for research attempting to measure attitudes toward people who are mentally retarded.

Exhibit 12-2

Multidimensional Attitude Scale on Mental Retardation

Directions

Here are some questions we are asking different people. Please give your own opinion. DO NOT PUT YOUR NAME ON THIS BOOKLET. This booklet contains numbered statements. Read each statement carefully.

--If you strongly agree with it put a check in the column marked "Strongly Agree."
--If you only mildly agree with it put a check in the column marked "agree."
--If you mildly disagree with it put a check in the column marked "disagree."
--If you strongly disagree with it put a check in the column marked "Strongly Disagree."

Respond to each statement. Put only one check for each statement.

WORK FAST!

	Strongly Agree	Agree	Disagree	Strongly Disagree
1. The mentally retarded child should be integrated into regular class.	---	---	---	---
2. There is nothing to the idea that the retarded child's problems in many situations have built in him a stronger character than the non-retarded child.	---	---	---	---
3. I would allow my child to accept an invitation to a birthday party given by a retarded child.	---	---	---	---
4. A Sunday school teacher ought to have the right to decide for himself whether he is going to let a retarded child enter his class.	---	---	---	---
5. Retarded children sometimes imagine they have been discriminated against even when they have been treated fairly.	---	---	---	---
6. School officials should not try placing retarded and non-retarded children in the same class because problems would arise.	---	---	---	---

Exhibit 12-2 (Continued)

	Strongly Agree	Agree	Disagree	Strongly Disagree
7. I think that retarded children have a kind of quiet courage which few non-retarded children have.	---	---	---	---
8. I would not take a retarded child to eat with me in a restaurant where I was well known.	---	---	---	---
9. There should be a strictly enforced law requiring school personnel to admit children regardless of whether or not they are retarded.	---	---	---	---
10. Some retarded children are so touchy that it is difficult to get along with them.	---	---	---	---
11. We should not put retarded and non-retarded children in the same class until retarded children can behave as well as non-retarded children.	---	---	---	---
12. Suffering and trouble have made retarded children better able to understand the stresses and strains of modern life than most non-retarded children.	---	---	---	---
13. I would rather not have retarded children swim in the same pool as I do.	---	---	---	---
14. A person should not have the right to run a school in this counrty if he will not admit retarded children.	---	---	---	---
15. Although some equality between retarded and non-retarded children may be the democratic way, a good many retarded children are not yet ready to practice the self-control that goes with it.	---	---	---	---
16. Integrating retarded children and non-retarded children in the same classes will result in greater understanding between retarded and non-retarded children.	---	---	---	---

Exhibit 12-2 (Continued)

	Strongly Agree	Agree	Disagree	Strongly Disagree
17. There is no basis in fact for the idea that retarded children withstand misfortune more courageously than do most non-retarded children.	---	---	---	---
18. I am willing for my child to have retarded children as close personal friends.	---	---	---	---
19. Playground officials have the right to refuse services to anyone they please, even if it means refusing retarded children.	---	---	---	---
20. Many retarded children waste time playing in class instead of trying to do better.	---	---	---	---
21. Placing retarded and non-retarded children in the same class will be beneficial to both the retarded and non-retarded.	---	---	---	---
22. There is no reason to believe that because retarded childrn have suffered in the past it has made them more noble people than are non-retarded children.	---	---	---	---
23. I would be willing to go to a competent retarded barber.				
24. In areas where they have been given an opportubity to advance, retarded childrn have shown that they are good sports and gentlemen.	--	---	---	---
25. Even if there were completer equality of social opportunity, it would take a long time for retarded children to show themselves equal to non-retarded children in social situations.	---	---	---	---
26. Integrating the retarded and non-retarded into the same classes should not be attempted because of the turmoil it would cause.	---	---	---	---

Exhibit 12-2 (Continued)

	Strongly Agree	Agree	Disagree	Strongly Disagree
27. I think that retarded children have a sense of dignity that you see in few non-retarded children.	---	---	---	---
28. I would rather not have retarded people as dinner guests with most of my non-retarded friends.	--	---	---	---
29. If I were a school principal I would resent it if I were told that I had to serve retarded children.	---	---	---	---
30. Even though retarded children are in public school, it is doubtful whether they will gain much from it.	---	---	---	---
31. Assigning retarded and non-retarded children into the same class is more trouble than it is worth.	---	---	---	---
32. There is nothing to the idea that retarded children have more sympathy for other handicapped children than most non-retarded children do.	---	---	---	---
33. I have no objection to attending the movies or a play in conjunction with retarded children.	---	---	---	---
34. Real estate agents should be required to show homes to families with retarded children regardless of the desires of the home owners.	---	---	---	---
35. Even though some retarded children have some cause for complaint, they would get what they want if they were more patient.	---	---	---	---
36. I feel in sympathy with responsible people who are trying to integrate retarded and non-retarded children into the same classes.	---	---	---	---

Exhibit 12-2 (Continued)

	Strongly Agree	Agree	Disagree	Strongly Disagree
37. In this day of rush and hurry, the retarded child has met the problems of society in a much calmer manner than the non-retarded child.	---	---	---	---
38. If my child were invited to be a guest of a group of retarded and non-retarded children on a weekend pleasure trip, I would probably not let her go.	---	---	---	---
39. If I were a landlord, I would want to pick my own tenents even if this meant only renting to families with non-retarded children.	---	---	---	---
40. The problem of prejudice towards retarded children has been greatly overexaggerated by parents of retarded children and by special educators.	---	---	---	---
41. Since grouping on the basis of ability has been declared illegal in Washington, DC, we should integrate the retarded and the non-retarded in the same classes.	---	---	---	---
42. There is no basis in fact for the idea that the retarded child's misfortunes have made him more understanding than the average non-retarded child.	---	---	---	---
43. I would rather not have retarded children live in the same apartment building I live in.	---	---	---	---
44. Laws forcing schools to admit retarded children often violate the rights of the individual who does not want to have to associate with retarded children.	---	---	---	---
45. Although social mixing of retarded and non-retarded childrn may be right, it is impractical until retardates learn to accept more "don'ts" in the relations between boys and girls.	---	---	---	---

Exhibit 12-2 (Continued)

	Strongly Agree	Agree	Disagree	Strongly Disagree
46. It is a good idea to have separate classes for retarded and non-retarded children.	---	---	---	---
47. The retarded child's own experiences with unfair treatment has given him a sensitivity and understanding that will make him an excellent worker with non-retarded people.	---	---	---	---
48. I would be willing to introduce retarded children visiting my home to friends and neighbors in my home town.	---	---	---	---
49. Regardless of his own views, a nursery school principal should be required to admit retarded children.	---	---	---	---
50. If I were retarded, I would not want to go places where I was really not wanted.	---	---	---	---

Reprinted with permission of the author; from Harth, R. (1974). Attitudes toward minority groups as a construct in assessing attitudes toward the mentally retarded. Education and Training of the Mentally Retarded, 6, 142-147.

MENTAL RETARDATION QUESTIONNAIRE (MRQ)

Description

The MRQ of Gan, Tymchuck, and Nishihara (1977) is unique because it was devised to measure the attitudes and level of knowledge of mildly mentally retarded adults toward mental retardation and the issue of community integration. The majority of previous theoretical reports suggested that adults who are mentally retarded are unable to display the insight and sensitivity necessary to respond meaningfully to an attitude questionnaire. Consequently, previous empirical research has investigated the attitudes of the parents, siblings, relatives, or caretakers of mentally retarded adults. The authors proposed to test the validity of these assertions.

A total of 40 items were selected, equally divided into eight information subscales: Knowledge of Mental Retardation, General Attitude Toward Mental Retardation, and scales measuring General Ability, Job Skills, Integration, Rights, Special Needs, and Personality of the Mentally Retarded. The items were written so that half of the items were positively worded and half were negatively worded. These items were then randomly presented on the subscales. The criteria for item preparation and inclusion are not presented.

Response Format

Each item is presented with a five-option response format, ranging from 1 to signify "I agree," to "I think I agree," "Not sure," "I think I disagree," to 5 to signify "I disagree."

Administration and Scoring

A sample of 50 mildly mentally retarded adults who were attending a meeting of the California Adult Council participated in the development of the MRQ. The Council was established to provide a forum for mentally retarded adults to discuss issues of importance to them. The purpose of the research was explained to the group as was the response format. Each item was read out loud and the respondents were asked to circle their response. Counselors were available in the room to assist with questions and to enhance "comprehension of the statement." The data from 33 subjects who completed all the items were analyzed by percentage of respondents selecting each option for each item.

Reliability

A pilot study with 31 nonretarded adults yielded an alpha reliability coefficient of + .97 for the scale. This seems to be a curious procedure for a scale purporting to have eight subscales. No reliability data for the subscales are reported, nor are reliability coefficients available for data obtained from mentally retarded respondents.

Validity

No validity data are presented, and no research using the scale, other than the authors' original study, has been located.

Comments

The MRQ is unique because of the intended audience and use of the scale. While the scale purports to measure attitudes and knowledge with eight subscales, no data supporting this claim are available. The MRQ may be useful for the investigation of the attitudes and knowledge of mentally retarded people about mental retardation and society's responses to mentally retarded people. Additional studies are needed to establish the scale's reliability and validity before its use can be recommended in any other than expeirmental settings.

Exhibit 12-3

Mental Retardation Questionnaire

Key

1	2	3	4	5
I agree	I think I agree	Not sure	I think I disagree	I disagree

---

1	The mentally retarded are not generally late for work.	1	2	3	4	5
2	Special marriage and family counseling should be available for the mentally retarded.	1	2	3	4	5
3	The worth of a human being should not be measured by how smart he or she is.	1	2	3	4	5
4	Most people do not like to talk about the mentally retarded.	1	2	3	4	5
5	If a person is retarded, his or her children will be retarded.	1	2	3	4	5
6	There are different kinds of mental retardation.	1	2	3	4	5
7	There is no reason to fear mentally retarded people.	1	2	3	4	5
8	The mentally retarded should be allowed to vote.	1	2	3	4	5
9	The mentally retarded are always happy and carefree.	1	2	3	4	5
10	Mentally retarded people do not need other people to help them with everything they do.	1	2	3	4	5
11	The mentally retarded should marry if they want to.	1	2	3	4	5
12	Most mentally retarded people can hold some kind of job that they can be paid for.	1	2	3	4	5
13	Mentally retarded people should be able to play along with people who are not retarded.	1	2	3	4	5
14	The mentally retarded cannot get around town on public buses.	1	2	3	4	5
15	On the job, mentally retarded workers and other workers get along well.	1	2	3	4	5

Exhibit 12-3 (Continued)

16	Being crazy is not the same as being mentally retarded.	1	2	3	4	5
17	The mentally retarded can handle their own money.	1	2	3	4	5
18	You cannot tell if a person is retarded by his or her looks.	1	2	3	4	5
19	Mentally retarded people know that they are retarded.	1	2	3	4	5
20	The mentally retarded do not always need someone around to help them make up their minds.	1	2	3	4	5
21	The mentally retarded should have lawyers who are concerned with they special kinds of problems.	1	2	3	4	5
22	The mentally retarded should not be in special classes in school.	1	2	3	4	5
23	Once someone is mentally retarded, they will always be that way.	1	2	3	4	5
24	The mentally retarded need to be able to talk to someone about their feelings and their problems.	1	2	3	4	5
25	The mentally retarded should be allowed to drive.	1	2	3	4	5
26	Mentally retarded people can control their feelings.	1	2	3	4	5
27	The mentally retarded should have children if they want to.	1	2	3	4	5
28	On the job, the mentally retarded person cannot follow simple directions from the boss like other people can.	1	2	3	4	5
29	Mentally retarded people cannot live alone and take care of themselves.	1	2	3	4	5
30	I would not mind if a mentally retarded person moved into my neighborhood.	1	2	3	4	5
31	Mentally retarded people do not have a difficult time saying what they mean.	1	2	3	4	5
32	Most mentally retarded people should not be hospitalized.	1	2	3	4	5

Exhibit 12-3 (Continued)

33	Mentally retarded people can play sports as well as other people who are considered normal.	1	2	3	4	5
34	The mentally retarded should not be allowed to have credit or take out loans.	1	2	3	4	5
35	It is fine for other children to play with mentally retarded children.	1	2	3	4	5
36	Normal people feel sorry for the mentally retarded.	1	2	3	4	5
37	Most mentally retarded people do things slower than people who are not retarded.	1	2	3	4	5
38	The mentally retarded do not know right from wrong.	1	2	3	4	5
39	I would like to have someone who is mentally retarded as a friend.	1	2	3	4	5
40	Other people do not make fun of the mentally retarded.	1	2	3	4	5

Reprinted with permission of the authors; from Gan, J., Tymchuk, A. J., & Nishihara, A. (1977). Mildly retarded adults: Their attitudes toward retardation. Mental Retardation, 15, 5-9.

Chapter 13

SOCIETAL RESPONSIBILITIES TOWARD PEOPLE WITH DISABILITIES

ATTITUDES TOWARD DISABLEMENT SCALE (ATDS)

Description

THE ATDS WAS developed by Antonak (1985c) to investigate the extent to which service providers endorse the premise that components of society disable people who are impaired. This premise was derived from the theoretical work of Finkelstein (1980) who argued that people with impairments should not be considered passive, dependent, and helpless, nor should disability be viewed as a tragic misfortune of the person who is impaired. Rather, disability should be defined, in Finkelstein's view, as a "special form of discrimination, or social oppression" (pp. 1-2) that is created by the "material and social components of society" (p. 38).

The scale consists of five statements of the research hypothesis with the attitude referent changed from chronic health impairment, to emotional impairment, to mental impairment, to physical impairment, to sensory impairment. Each statement is presented at the top of a page followed by a listing of 13 components of society. The 13 stimuli listed (architecture, communication systems, economic conditions, educational practices, employment requirements, health care, public attitudes, recreation facilities, technology, transportation, vocational opportunities, welfare policies, and zoning ordinances) were selected from an original list of 31 stimuli because they were consistently selected by three judges as representing the major material, social, and environmental components of society. The 13 components were randomized independently for each category of impairment and five different booklets were created with the category of impairment presented in orders corresponding to a Latin square design. These steps were undertaken to permit measurement of the influence of any carryover effects on the respondent's attitudes to later appearing impairments, and to disrupt any possible acquiescence response style within impairments.

Each respondent's booklet includes a page of definitions of each impairment, in alphabetical order, to insure that the respondents referred to a common attitude referent (Gottlieb and Siperstein, 1976). These definitions were brief statements (less than 50 words) taken from professional handbooks or from widely used textbooks, together with exemplars in some cases (e.g., chronic health impairments "include asthma, leukemia, hemophilia, diabetes, rheumatic fever, and heart disease").

Response Format

The respondent is asked to express the degree of his or her agreement or disagreement with the statement as applied to each component on a six-point scale from NO!, to signify "Not at all," through NO., NO?, YES?, YES., or YES!, to signify "Very much."

Administration and Scoring

The five different booklets were distributed in approximately equal numbers to samples of 150 individuals who were enrolled in a variety of courses in human services at the University of New Hampshire. The instructions emphasize that the scale is not a test, but rather an opinion questionnaire, that there are no right or wrong answers, and that responses are evaluated anonymously. The last page of the booklet asked the respondents to provide information about their sex, age, educational level, and professional training and experience. A weighted sum of the 13 responses provides what is considered to be a measure of the respondent's endorsement of the disablement premise for people with each type of impairment. The scores range from 13 to 78 for each of the five impairment subscales (i.e., 1 to 6 for each of 13 items), and from 65 to 390 for the total scale (i.e., 13 to 78 for each of five impairments), with high scores indicating strong endorsement of the disablement premise.

Reliability

No evidence was found that the respondents' endorsement scores were influenced by the order of presentation of the categories of impairments within the booklets. Item analyses of the respondents' data for the total scale yielded a corrected Spearman-Brown split-half reliability coefficient of + .97, and a coefficient alpha homogeneity index of + .84. The various item statistics (e.g., item mean, standard deviation, difficulty, and discrimination indices) were satisfactory in all cases. The mean value for the item-to-total-scale correlations corrected for redundancy was + .50 (range + .26 to + .67). The reliability indices for each subscale were uniformly high (Spearman-Brown corrected split-half values of + .91, + .80, + .81, + .84, and + .88), as were the coefficient alpha homogeneity indices (+ .83, + .78, + .78, + .74, and + .78). Together with the interscale correlations (mean $r = +.58$, range from + .47 to + .87) and the subscale-to-total-scale correlations (mean $r = +.81$, range from $+.76$ to $+.84$), these homogeneity coefficients demonstrate that the five impairment subscales are both reliable and specific.

Validity

Investigation of the relationships of the demographic variables to the total scale score and to each of the five impairment subscale scores with multiple regression analyses showed that the special service providers (e.g., special educators, rehabilitation counselors, occupational therapists) expressed stronger endorsement of the disablement premise for each impairment category, and for all impairments combined, than did the regular service providers (e.g., elementary and secondary teachers, administrators). There were no significant relationships between any of the other demographic variables and scores on either the total scale or any of the five impairment subscales. Factor analyses of the subjects' responses to the 13 items on each subscale revealed different structures for each of the five impairment subscales. Order analysis of the endorsement data for the five impairments revealed a hierarchical relationships in the respondents' views concerning the different types of social situations and barriers faced by, and the interventions required by, people who are impaired in different ways.

Comments

The ATD Scale shows that scales can be written which do not focus on the people who are impaired but rather on the environmental situations faced by them. Clearly, the categories of impairments and the components of society used on the ATD Scale could be varied by other investigators who may be interested in exploring other premises. The scales and methods of analyses used by Antonak (1985c) are a modest contribution to the research methodology available to researchers who are investigating the attitudes of service professionals toward people who are impaired and their participation in society.

Exhibit 13-1

Attitudes Toward Disablement Scale

General Directions

This booklet contains statements which express opinions or ideas about situations and conditions faced by people who are impaired in some way. There are differences of opinion about each statement; many people agree while many people disagree. We would like to know your opinion about them.

In the space provided on each sheet, put an "X" through the response which best corresponds to how you feel about the statement. There are no right or wrong responses.

On the next page you will find brief definitions of five different impairments of an individual which result in functional loss, Read each one carefully before proceeding.

A CHRONIC HEALTH IMPAIRMENT weakens an individual's physical condition, reduces vitality, or renders him or her relatively inactive. Such impairments include asthma, leukemia, hemophilia, diabetes, rheumatic fever, and heart disease.

AN EMOTIONAL IMPAIRMENT is a functional loss of an individual due to behavior which significantly interfers with either the individual's own growth and development, or the lives of others. Such impairments may be labeled depression, withdrawal, autism, impulsive-aggression, schizophrenia, delinquency, and social maladjustment.

A MENTAL IMPAIRMENT of an individual includes both significantly subaverage general intellectual functioning as well as impairment in adaptive behavior, and is manifest during the developmental period. Such impairments are classified as mild, moderate, severe, and profound.

A PHYSICAL IMPAIRMENT of an individual interferes with the normal function of the bones, joints, or muscles, and includes arthritis, poliomyelitis, muscular dystrophy, amputation, and spinal cord injury.

A SENSORY IMPAIRMENT is a functional loss of hearing or sight due to defects in one or more of the parts of the ear, eye, or associated nerve pathways.

Exhibit 13-1 (Continued)

To what extend do the following material, social, or environmental components of society effectively disable people with chronic health impairments?

	NOT AT ALL					VERY MUCH
Educational policies	NO!	NO.	NO?	YES?	YES.	YES!
Public attitudes	NO!	NO.	NO?	YES?	YES.	YES!
Welfare policies	NO!	NO.	NO?	YES?	YES.	YES!
Communication systems	NO!	NO.	NO?	YES?	YES.	YES!
Zoning ordinances	NO!	NO.	NO?	YES?	YES.	YES!
Vocational opportunities	NO!	NO.	NO?	YES?	YES.	YES!
Architecture	NO!	NO.	NO?	YES?	YES.	YES!
Economic conditions	NO!	NO.	NO?	YES?	YES.	YES!
Recreation facilities	NO!	NO.	NO?	YES?	YES.	YES!
Health care	NO!	NO.	NO?	YES?	YES.	YES!
Transportation	NO!	NO.	NO?	YES?	YES.	YES!
Technology	NO!	NO.	NO?	YES?	YES.	YES!
Employment requirements	NO!	NO.	NO?	YES?	YES.	YES!

Exhibit 13-1 (Continued)

To what extend do the following material, social, or environmental components of society effectively disable people with emotional impairments?

	NOT AT ALL					VERY MUCH
Vocational opportunities	NO!	NO.	NO?	YES?	YES.	YES!
Public attitudes	NO!	NO.	NO?	YES?	YES.	YES!
Employment requirements	NO!	NO.	NO?	YES?	YES.	YES!
Economic conditions	NO!	NO.	NO?	YES?	YES.	YES!
Technology	NO!	NO.	NO?	YES?	YES.	YES!
Health care	NO!	NO.	NO?	YES?	YES.	YES!
Communication systems	NO!	NO.	NO?	YES?	YES.	YES!
Recreation facilities	NO!	NO.	NO?	YES?	YES.	YES!
Transportation	NO!	NO.	NO?	YES?	YES.	YES!
Zoning ordinances	NO!	NO.	NO?	YES?	YES.	YES!
Architecture	NO!	NO.	NO?	YES?	YES.	YES!
Welfare policies	NO!	NO.	NO?	YES?	YES.	YES!
Educational policies	NO!	NO.	NO?	YES?	YES.	YES!

Exhibit 13-1 (Continued)

To what extend do the following material, social, or environmental components of society effectively disable people with mental impairments?

	NOT AT ALL					VERY MUCH
Transportation	NO!	NO.	NO?	YES?	YES.	YES!
Employment requirements	NO!	NO.	NO?	YES?	YES.	YES!
Communication systems	NO!	NO.	NO?	YES?	YES.	YES!
Welfare policies	NO!	NO.	NO?	YES?	YES.	YES!
Educational policies	NO!	NO.	NO?	YES?	YES.	YES!
Technology	NO!	NO.	NO?	YES?	YES.	YES!
Public attitudes	NO!	NO.	NO?	YES?	YES.	YES!
Architecture	NO!	NO.	NO?	YES?	YES.	YES!
Health care	NO!	NO.	NO?	YES?	YES.	YES!
Zoning ordinances	NO!	NO.	NO?	YES?	YES.	YES!
Recreation facilities	NO!	NO.	NO?	YES?	YES.	YES!
Vocational opportunities	NO!	NO.	NO?	YES?	YES.	YES!
Economic conditions	NO!	NO.	NO?	YES?	YES.	YES!

Exhibit 13-1 (Continued)

To what extend do the following material, social, or environmental components of society effectively disable people with physical impairments?

	NOT AT ALL					VERY MUCH
Communication systems	NO!	NO.	NO?	YES?	YES.	YES!
Zoning ordinances	NO!	NO.	NO?	YES?	YES.	YES!
Transportation	NO!	NO.	NO?	YES?	YES.	YES!
Vocational opportunities	NO!	NO.	NO?	YES?	YES.	YES!
Health care	NO!	NO.	NO?	YES?	YES.	YES!
Technology	NO!	NO.	NO?	YES?	YES.	YES!
Architecture	NO!	NO.	NO?	YES?	YES.	YES!
Economic conditions	NO!	NO.	NO?	YES?	YES.	YES!
Employment requirements	NO!	NO.	NO?	YES?	YES.	YES!
Recreation facilities	NO!	NO.	NO?	YES?	YES.	YES!
Educational policies	NO!	NO.	NO?	YES?	YES.	YES!
Welfare policies	NO!	NO.	NO?	YES?	YES.	YES!
Public attitudes	NO!	NO.	NO?	YES?	YES.	YES!

Exhibit 13-1 (Continued)

To what extend do the following material, social, or environmental components of society effectively disable people with sensory impairments?

	NOT AT ALL					VERY MUCH
Health care	NO!	NO.	NO?	YES?	YES.	YES!
Communication systems	NO!	NO.	NO?	YES?	YES.	YES!
Architecture	NO!	NO.	NO?	YES?	YES.	YES!
Zoning ordinances	NO!	NO.	NO?	YES?	YES.	YES!
Vocational opportunities	NO!	NO.	NO?	YES?	YES.	YES!
Technology	NO!	NO.	NO?	YES?	YES.	YES!
Recreation facilities	NO!	NO.	NO?	YES?	YES.	YES!
Transportation	NO!	NO.	NO?	YES?	YES.	YES!
Economic conditions	NO!	NO.	NO?	YES?	YES.	YES!
Public attitudes	NO!	NO.	NO?	YES?	YES.	YES!
Educational policies	NO!	NO.	NO?	YES?	YES.	YES!
Employment requirements	NO!	NO.	NO?	YES?	YES.	YES!
Welfare policies	NO!	NO.	NO?	YES?	YES.	YES!

Reprinted with permission of the author; from Antonak, R. F. (1985). Societal factors in disablement. Rehabilitation Counseling Bulletin, 28, 188-201.

ATTITUDES TOWARD MAINSTREAMING SCALE (ATMS)

Description

The ATMS (Berryman and Neal, 1980) was developed to measure attitudes toward the practice of mainstreaming (integrating) handicapped children into public school classrooms. A pool of items concerning opinions about, rather than knowledge of, mainstreaming was written and revised to yield 22 items. No information is provided on the analyses used to accomplish the item selection. Of these 22 items, six dealt with the feasibility of teaching nondisabled and disabled students in the same classroom, and the remaining 16 dealt with the feasibility of regular classes as the least restrictive educational environment for six different groups of disabled students: that is, students with mental retardation, sensory impairments, physical impairments, speech handicaps, health impairments, and behavior disorders. Learning disability was not included because of the difficulty in composing an acceptable and unambiguous definition. The 22 items were prepared on a scale which included brief descriptions of each type of disability and a brief definition of the educational practice of mainstreaming. An original sample of 159 students in introductory education classes were asked to respond to the questionnaire.

A factor analysis of the original data (Berryman and Neal, 1980) led to the retention of 18 items comprising three subscales: Learning Capability, dealing with the pragmatic aspects of mainstreaming (eight items); General Mainstreaming, which expresses the view that mainstreaming is a desirable goal for all disabled students (seven items); and Traditional Limiting Disability, concerning the inadvisability of mainstreaming students with severe sensory, physical, or behavioral disabilities (three items).

Response Format

The items are presented on a questionnaire with six-point agree-disagree continuum. The anchors and the points on this continuum are not reported in the authors' publications. All of the items appear to have been stated so that an agree response represents a favorable attitude.

Administration and Scoring

The ATMS was designed to be administered to subjects in group situations, although the printed directions provided would presumably permit data to be collected from mailed questionnaires. No scoring directions are reported, although it is presumed from the statistics reported that the responses to the items are summed to obtain subscale and scale totals.

Reliability

Alpha reliability coefficients for the total scale were reported by Berryman and

Neal (1980) to be + .88 for both samples. Alpha reliability coefficients for the subscales ranged from + .76 to + .84, subscale intercorrelations ranged from + .42 to + .55, and subscale-to-total scale correlations ranged from + .77 to + .88. A subsequent analysis of ATMS data was conducted (Berryman, Neal, and Robinson, 1980) from another sample of 161 students in a course on exceptionality required of all teachers and administrators in Georgia. A total of 17 fields within education were represented by the respondents. A Spearman-Brown corrected reliability coefficient of + .92 was reported.

Validity

Factor analysis results of Berryman et al. (1980) led to the retention of four factors, rather than three as in the Berryman and Neal (1980) study. The first factor, named as before, was reported to have nine items, and the second factor, also named as before, was reported to have seven items. The third factor appeared to concern the mainstreaming of students with severe disabilities, and the fourth factor appeared to concern mainstreaming of children with inappropriate social behavior.

A cross-cultural validation (Green and Harvey, 1983) on a sample of New Zealand teachers and teachers-in-training confirmed the existence of the first two factors. The third factor discovered in this study was similar to the third factor in the Berryman and Neal (1980) report, while a fourth factor was similar to the fourth factor in the Berryman et al. (1980) study. Correlations of the four factor scores with the total scale scores, as well as investigations of internal consistency and subscale intercorrelations led Green and Harvey (1983) to conclude that the four factor solution was the most defensible.

Comments

These results show that the ATMS is a reasonably reliable scale, but that its factorial structure is somewhat unclear. It may be that any factors beyond the first two are merely artifacts of measurement. We support the recommendation of Green and Harvey (1983) who suggested that Berryman and her colleagues undertake to write three or four additional items for the last two factors and to conduct additional validity analyses of this expanded scale. Additional studies of the modified (either expanded or reduced) scale's criterion-related and predictive validity will be required before this scale can be used in situations other than experimental research.

Exhibit 13-2

Attitudes Toward Mainstreaming Scale

---

1 In general, mainstreaming is a desirable educational practice.

2 Students should have the right to be in regular classrooms.

3 It is feasible to teach gifted, normal, and mentally retarded students in the same class.

4 Educable mentally retarded students should be in regular classrooms.

5 Visually handicapped students who can read standard printed material should be in regular classrooms.

6 Blind students who cannot read standard printed material should be in regular classrooms.

7 Hearing impaired students, who are not deaf, should be in regular classrooms.

8 Deaf students should be in regular classrooms.

9 Physically handicapped students confined to wheelchairs should be in regular classrooms.

10 Physically handicapped students not confined to wheelchairs should be in regular classrooms.

11 Students with cerebral palsy who cannot control movement of one or more limbs should be in regular classrooms.

12 Students who stutter should be in regular classrooms.

13 Students with speech difficult to understand be in regular classrooms.

14 Students with epilepsy should be in regular classrooms.

15 Students with diabetes should be in regular classrooms.

Exhibit 13-2 (Continued)

---

16 Students with behavior disorders who cannot readily control their own behavior should be in regular classrooms.

17 Students who present persistent discipline problems should be in regular classrooms.

18 Mainstreaming will be sufficiently successful to be retained as a required educational practice.

Reprinted with permission of the authors; from Berryman, J. D., Neal, W. R., Jr., & Robinson, J. E. (1980). The validation of a scale to measure attitudes toward the classroom integtration of disabled students. Journal of Educational Research, 73, 199-203.

EDUCATIONAL ATTITUDE SURVEY (EAS)

Description

The EAS was created by Reynolds and Greco (1980) to provide educators and researchers with a measure for evaluating teachers' attitudes toward mainstreaming. This work was motivated in part by the authors' view that previous instruments to measure these attitudes were lacking in sophistication and psychometric adequacy. The scale's item content was derived from a review of the literature on mainstreaming and previous attitude instruments. An initial set of 20 items was written and presented in a pilot study to a sample of 70 teachers from upstate New York. Half of these teachers were from schools which mainstreamed handicapped students. A total of 16 items were retained following psychometric analyses of the pilot study data.

In particular, items which were deleted failed to reach a cutoff value of + .30 for item-to-total scale correlation. The revised form of the EAS was written and given to a second sample of 112 teachers from the same population as in the pilot study. The responses of the 70 pilot study teachers were added to this sample (a procedure which is not recommended). The Crowne-Marlowe SDS (Crowne and Marlowe, 1960) was also given to the respondents. A factor analysis of these data suggested that the scale consisted of two subscales: Administrative Aspects of Mainstreaming (seven items), and Educational Aspects of Mainstreaming (nine items).

Response Format

Items are presented on the EAS with five response options, ranging from 1, to signify "Strongly agree," to 5, to signify "Strongly disagree." The anchors for the values of 2, 3, and 4 are "Agree," "Neither agree nor disagree," and "Disagree," respectively.

Administration and Scoring

Respondents are asked to circle the number following each item which corresponds to the level of their agreement with the item. The directions in the introductory paragraphs specifically state that the EAS contains statements "concerning attitudes toward mainstreaming and self-contained special education classrooms." No specific information is provided by the authors concerning administration of the scale, although in the original report the questionnaire was administered to the respondents as a group.

Four of the 16 items are worded so that an agree response is the favorable response. The respondent's selection is subtracted from six to yield his or her item response. The other 12 items are worded so that a disagree response is the favorable response. The respondent's score on the EAS is the sum of his or her item responses to the 12 negatively-worded items, plus the converted responses to the four positively-worded items. A high score (range from 16 to 80) signifies a more favorable attitude toward the concept of mainstreaming.

Reliability

The alpha homogeneity indices for the total scale and the two subscales were reported to be +.90, +.83, and +.86, respectively. Similarly, the test-retest reliability indices after two to three weeks were +.85, +.70, and +.80. (It is unclear from the authors report who was retested or how this was accomplished.) The correlations of the items with the scale ranged from +.38 to +.72, while similar item-to-subscale correlations ranged from +.49 to +.67 for subscale 1, and from +.45 to +.70 for subscale 2. The correlation of subscale 1 to subscale 2 was +.63.

Validity

The analysis of the SDS data showed that responding to the scale and subscales was not influenced by social desirability. No other validity data are presented by the authors.

Comments

Additional investigations are needed before the validity of the scale and the specificity and homogeneity of the subscales can be accepted. The overwhelming number of negatively worded items on the scale may limit the scale's validity. The EAS does appear, however, to be a reliable and useful measurement instrument for the investigation of attitudes toward mainstreaming.

Exhibit 13-3

Educational Attitude Survey

In recent years, Federal and State legislation has mandated that several changes be instituted in the education of handicapped students. One of these changes has been that, to the extent possible, handicapped students must be mainstreamed, i.e., integrated into regular classroom placements. This is a change from the more traditional approach to education of the handicapped, which centered around the use of "self-contained" special education classrooms which consisted only of handicapped students.

Listed below are a number of statements concerning attitudes toward mainstreaming and self-contained special education classrooms. Read each item and decide how it relates to you. Use the following scale to rate each statement:

strongly agree	agree	neither agree nor disagree	disagree	strongly disagree
1	2	3	4	5

For each item, circle the number which corresponds to the level of agreement.

---

1) Those who favor the integration of handicapped students into regular classroom placements are not really concerned with the quality of education.	1	2	3	4	5
2) If advocates of mainstreaming took the time to see what happens to handicapped students who are integrated into regular class placements, they would come to recommend self-contained special education classes for these students.	1	2	3	4	5
3) Administrators who favor mainstreaming are more concerned with financial decisions than with the educational adequacy of the school or district.	1	2	3	4	5
4) When handicapped students are integrated into regular classrooms, it is usually done against the advice of the regular classroom teacher.	1	2	3	4	5
5) The resource room in a mainstreaming program will simply become another form of a self-contained classroom for handicapped students.	1	2	3	4	5
6) Having handicapped students in regular classrooms lowers the quality of instruction to all students.	1	2	3	4	5
7) Being in a regular class helps a handicapped child develop a positive self-image.	1	2	3	4	5
8) Mainstreaming is being imposed rather than explained.	1	2	3	4	5

Exhibit 13-3 (Continued)

---

9) Children with special needs could best be served through instruction in a special education classroom.	1	2	3	4	5
10) The move toward mainstreaming is more of a legal and political matter than an educational one.	1	2	3	4	5
11) Self-contained classes for the education of handicapped students enable teachers to provide more adequate instruction for those students than would be possible if those students were integrated into regular classrooms.	1	2	3	4	5
12) The handicapped child in a special education classroom which is self-contained is likely to be socially isolated.	1	2	3	4	5
13) Being in a self-contained class restricts the participation of handicapped students in extra-currucular activities.	1	2	3	4	5
14) Having handicapped students in regular classrooms is not fair to either the handicapped or non-handicapped students.	1	2	3	4	5
15) Education of handicapped students through self-contained classes prevents these students from being accepted by non-handicapped students.	1	2	3	4	5
16) While theoretically mainstreaming may seem to be a good idea, in reality mainstreamed students have great difficulty adjusting to the regular classroom.	1	2	3	4	5

Reprinted with permission of the authors: from Reynolds, W. M., & Greco, V. T. (1980). The reliability and factorial validity of a scale for measuring teachers' attitudes toward mainstreaming. Educational and Psychological Measurement, 40, 463-468.

MAINSTREAMING OPINIONNAIRE (MO)

Description

The Mainstreaming Opinionnaire was developed by Schmelkin (1981) to study the attitudes of special education teachers, regular teachers, and non-teachers (e.g., administrators, counselors) toward mainstreaming handicapped students. Schmelkin argued that investigations of the attitudes toward mainstreaming had, until that time, focused only on unitary acceptance-rejection issues, failing to consider the complexity of these attitudes. Consequently, the development of a multidimensional scale of attitudes was undertaken.

A review of the literature on mainstreaming led to the creation of a large item pool concerned with the social, academic, emotional, and behavioral characteristics of handicapped children, as well as items concerned with the effects of mainstreaming on the non-handicapped children, teachers, and the teaching process. Following review and refinement, 67 items were presented on a pilot questionnaire to a group of 222 graduate students in the School of Education, Health, Nursing, and Arts Professions at New York University. Factor analyses of the data led to the decision to retain two factors. Items loading at least + .40 on one factor and no more than + .40 on any other factor were considered for inclusion on the final scale. Additional criteria included item dispersion characteristics, lack of redundancy with other items, and logical consistency of the items on each factor. A total of 30 items were retained with 15 items scored on each of the two subscales.

The first subscale, Academic Costs of Mainstreaming (ACM), concerned the detrimental effects of mainstreaming on the academic progress of both handicapped and non-handicapped students. The second subscale, Socio-Emotional Costs of Segregation (SECS), concerned the negative effects on social and emotional development of segregating handicapped children in special classrooms. Scores on the two subscales were found to correlate – .44, indicating that they are measuring two different aspects of the complex issue of mainstreaming.

The final version of the scale was subsequently administered to three new samples of 40 individuals representing special education teachers, regular education teachers, and nonteachers. Differences in the subscale scores among the groups were explored to uncover the relationships of these components of attitudes toward mainstreaming to the respondents' experiential characteristics. In a later study, Schmelkin and Lieberman (1984) administered the MO to a sample of 142 students in the School of Education at Hofstra University. These individuals also responded to the ATDP Scale and a 13-item scale of knowledge of various aspects of mainstreaming. In addition to the investigation of the attitudes toward mainstreaming among subgroups of this sample, the research was also designed to investigate the relationship between the knowledge and attitude domains.

Garvar and Schmelkin (1986) have recently reported on their investigation of the attitudes of school administrators toward mainstreaming using a scale based, in part, on the two subscales of the Mainstreaming Opinionnaire. Analyses of the psychometric properties of this scale are presently in progress, and may yield either a revision of the MO, or a new summated rating scale to compliment the MO.

Response Format

Each of the 30 items on the MO is responded to on a six-point scale, ranging from −3, to signify "Disagree very strongly," to +3, to signify "Agree very strongly." Respondents are asked to write the number corresponding to their agreement with each item in the test booklet on a short line preceding each statement. No neutral response option is permitted. Missing or ambiguous responses are given the value of 0 for scoring.

Administration and Scoring

The MO can be administered in both individual and group settings. The instructions state that the opinionnaire is an opportunity for the respondent to express his or her beliefs and opinions about the issue of mainstreaming. This is indirectly defined as "whether handicapped children should be educated in special classes or placed in regular classes." The term handicapped is explicitly limited to those children classified as learning disabled, mentally retarded, or emotionally disturbed, "or the like." These groups are not defined, and no reference is made to severity of handicap or age in the instructions. Assurance is given that the responses are evaluated anonymously. The respondent is urged to work rapidly and not to omit a response to any item. It is estimated that the MO would take about ten minutes to administer.

To score the MO, the value of four is added to each response. This transforms all values to a positive whole number from 1 to 7 (e.g., −3 = 1, −2 = 2, −1 = 3, missing = 4, +1 = 5, +2 = 6, and +3 = 7). The respondent's score on the ACM subscale is calculated by adding the responses to the items #1, 3, 4, 8, 9, 10, 12, 16, 18, 19, 20, 26, 27, 28, and 30. The total is divided by 15 to yield a mean value ranging from 1 to 7, with a low value representing a positive attitude toward this aspect of mainstreaming. The respondent's score on the SECS subscale is calculated by adding the responses to the remaining 15 items (#2, 5, 6, 7, 11, 13, 14, 15, 17, 21, 22, 23, 24, 25, and 29). As with the first subscale, a mean value is calculated by dividing the total by 15, with the result ranging from 1 to 7. A positive attitude toward this aspect of mainstreaming, however, is reflected by a high score. No grand total scale score is calculated, in keeping with the author's view that the MO is a multidimensional measure of attitudes and not a measure of global acceptance or rejection of mainstreaming as an educational practice.

Reliability

Schmelkin (1981) reported coefficient alpha reliability estimates of +.90 for the ACM subscale and + .88 for the SECS subscale. Alpha values of + .89 and + .81 are reported by Schmelkin and Lieberman (1984) for the two subscales, respectively. No analyses of stability estimates are reported to date, nor is there any report of the investigation of the specificity of the subscales.

Validity

Evidence of the validity of the MO is obtained in the information on its development, and in two sources of data: the results of the factor analytic investigations, and the data on differences in the MO subscale scores for samples of different known characteristics. The specification of the multidimensional nature of the practice of mainstreaming, the preparation of the item pool using these specifications, and the procedures followed for the selection of items for the final subscales supports the content validity of the MO. The high alpha reliabilities for the subscales, the moderate negative correlation between these two subscales, and the data on the factor loadings of the 30 items, support the factorial validity of the MO.

Schmelkin's (1981) analyses of data from special education teachers, regular education teachers, and nonteachers led her to conclude that the MO measures meaningful differences among the three groups. Special education teachers expressed more favorable attitudes toward mainstreaming on both of the two subscale, as predicted by the author. The analyses of data concerning both knowledge and attitudes toward mainstreaming (Schmelkin and Lieberman, 1984) supported a conclusion, as predicted, that increased knowledge is associated with a more positive attitude toward mainstreaming. Taken together, these results lend reasonable support to a conclusion that the MO is a valid measure of the construct of mainstreaming.

Comments

The procedures which Schmelkin followed to develop and validate the Mainstreaming Opinionnaire are a good illustration of the procedures recommended in the three chapters in Part II of this book. The construct to be measured was carefully specified, the item pool was developed to match these specifications, the item selection criteria were based on detailed item and factor analyses, and the reliability and validity analyses reported to date are well-conceived and psychometrically sound. Additional investigations of the criterion-related validity of the MO should be undertaken, perhaps using one of the other measures of attitudes toward mainstreaming reported on in this chapter. The investigation of the attitudes expressed by the Hofstra University sample (Schmelkin and Lieberman, 1984) would seem to provide a basis for a predictive validity analysis based on the students' career choices and experiences after graduation.

The author has yet to document that the respondents' scores on the MO subscales are free from the biasing influences of response styles. With regard to the acquiescence response style, it is noted that all of the items on a subscale have the same valence. That is, all of the ACM items will be responded to negatively, and all of the SECS items will be responded to positively, by an individual with a positive attitude toward mainstreaming. While this is in keeping with the definitions of the subscale constructs, it may also influence the respondent to select only a positive (or negative) alternative if he or she discerns the binary factor structure of the scale.

Finally, the MO items include four different attitude referents: the handicapped, handicapped child (or children), handicapped student, and special class pupil. The first can be easily modified to the second. The difference between the second and the third reflects the difference between children who are handicapped with reference to societal standards (e.g., a limitation of mobility which does not impair learning or educational achievement) and those who are handicapped with reference to educational standards. The definition of the term handicapped in the instructions may eliminate this potential confounding influence. The last referent appears in only one item (#3) and should be changed to handicapped student.

Exhibit 13-4

Mainstreaming Opinionnaire

An issue that is currently being debated among educators and laymen is whether or not handicapped children should be educated in special classes or placed in regular classes. This scale is an attempt to let you express your beliefs and opinions on this issue. A number of conflicting and opposing points of view are included. You will find yourself agreeing strongly with some of the statements, disagreeing just as strongly with others, and agreeing or disagreeing less strongly with still others. Whether you agree or disagree with any statement, you can be sure that many other people feel pretty much the way you do. Please try to respond to all 30 statements as honestly and frankly as you can. No one will know how you respond because we are not asking you to identify yourself.

There is no universal agreement about the meaning of the term handicapped. In the present context, the term handicapped children is limited to those who are learning disabled, mentally retarded, emotionally disturbed, and the like. Please use this frame of reference when responding to the items of this scale.

Instructions: Respond to each of the items as follows:

Agree very strongly:	+3	Disagree very strongly:	-3
Agree strongly:	+2	Disagree strongly:	-2
Agree:	+1	Disagree:	-1

For example, if you agree very strongly with a statement, write a +3 on the short line preceeding the statement, but if you should happen to disagree with it, write -1 in front of it. Respond to each of the statements as best you can. Please do not omit any. Go rapidly but carefully. Do not spend too much time on any one statement; try to respond and then go on. Do not sign your name.

___ 1. The presence of a handicapped child in the regular classroom reduces teaching efficiency and learning.

___ 2. Regular classes help prepare the handicapped to live in an integrated world.

___ 3. Special class pupils fail to make appropriate academic progress when they are integrated into the regular classroom.

___ 4. The shorter attention span of handicapped students makes them unable to benefit from placement in a regular classroom.

___ 5. The special self-contained classroom cannot serve the social needs of handicapped children.

___ 6. Special class placement leads to a feeling of being neglected and rejected on the part of handicapped students.

___ 7. Potential problems of the handicapped student associated with being placed in a regular class, such as heightened awareness of disability, are outweighed by the stigma associated with special class placement.

Exhibit 13-4 (Continued)

___ 8. The handicapped child cannot deal with the challenges of a regular class as well as the normal child.

___ 9. The handicapped are not bothered much by their differences unless they are confronted with normal children.

___ 10. The inclusion of handicapped children in regular classes leads to disruption of regular routines.

___ 11. Contact with the handicpped in regular classes helps the non-handicapped to realize that their own problems are not unique.

___ 12. Placing handicapped children in a regular classroom accentuates the differences between them and their non-handicapped peers.

___ 13. Special classes for the handicapped are not conducive to the fostering of the motive to achieve.

___ 14. Chilren placed in self-contained special education classes are more likely to be perceived as different as opposed to when they are placed in regular classes.

___ 15. Special class placement leads to an estrangement between the handicapped and their normal peers.

___ 16. The handicapped child in the regular classroom consumes too much of the teacher's time and attention.

___ 17. Special class placement results in a loss of self-esteem in the part of handicapped students.

___ 18. When placed in a regular class, handicapped children exhibit inappropriate behavior.

___ 19. Integrating handicapped children in regular education contributes to negative behavior patterns on the part of the non-handicapped children.

___ 20. The presence of a handicapped child in a regular classroom inhibits the progress of his or her non-handicapped peers.

___ 21. Segregration of the handicapped in education provided them with a distorted view of reality, thus aggravating the handicap.

___ 22. Segregrating the handicapped in special classes contributes to a self-fulfilling prophecy that operates when children are labeled.

___ 23. The social status of handicapped children as perceived by their non-handicapped peers will be enhanced through their interaction in regular classrooms.

Exhibit 13-4 (Continued)

___ 24. In the special class, emphasis is placed more on disability than on ability.

___ 25. Integrating handicapped children with normal children provides the handicapped with appropriate role models.

___ 26. The range of abilities confronting a regular teacher when handicapped students are present in the class reduces the effectiveness of the teacher.

___ 27. Handicapped children cannot profit greatly from ordinary schooling.

___ 28. Segregrating the handicapped frees normal pupils from restrictions imposed upon them when they are made to interact with the handicapped.

___ 29. Handicapped children placed in special classes hold more negative attitudes toward school when compared with those placed in regular classes.

___ 30. Due to their lack of self-control, it is inadvisable to integrate handicapped children into regular classes.

Reprinted with permission of the author; from Schmelkin, L. P. (1981). Teachers' and non-teachers' attitudes toward mainstreaming. <u>Exceptional Children</u>, <u>48</u>, 42-47.

OPINIONS RELATIVE TO MAINSTREAMING (ORM)

Description

Larrivee and Cook (1979) developed the ORM Scale as part of a large sample investigation of teachers' attitudes toward mainstreaming handicapped children into regular classrooms. The item selection procedure involved the preparation of items within eight hypothesized dimensions of attitudes toward mainstreaming (Larrivee, 1981): views of education in general; philosophy of mainstreaming; effects of regular classroom placement of handicapped students on their social, emotional, and cognitive development; similar effects on the typical child; the handicapped student's classroom behavior; the handicapped student's cognitive functioning; the views of the parents of handicapped students about mainstreaming; and the regular classroom teacher's perceived ability to teach handicapped children. An original pool of 41 items was narrowed to 30 following item and scale analyses of pilot study data. The criterion for inclusion was an item-total scale correlation value exceeding + .30. The items were presented on a revised questionnaire to a sample of 941 regular classroom teachers in grades K through 12 in New England using a multistage random sampling process. Two-thirds of the respondents taught in elementary schools; 54 percent taught in suburban schools, 28 percent in rural schools, and 18 percent in urban schools. Multiple regression analyses were performed to investigate the relationships of respondent experiential and demographic variables.

Response Format

The respondents are asked to express the extent of their agreement with each statement on a five-point continuum ranging from 1, to signify "Strongly agree," to 5, to signify "Strongly disagree."

Administration and Scoring

The respondent is directed to circle the appropriate response on the questionnaire. The directions state that there are no right or wrong answers, and that a response for all 30 items should be marked. A total of 12 of the items are worded so that an agree response indicates a favorable attitude. The remaining are worded so that a disagree response indicates a favorable attitude. The sum of the positive item responses is subtracted from 72, and that result is added to the sum of the responses to the negative items. The total scores range from 30 to 150, with a high score indicating a more favorable attitude toward mainstreaming.

Reliability

A Spearman-Brown corrected reliability coefficient of + .92 was reported. Green, Rock, and Weisenstein (1983), who gave the ORM to 168 undergraduate and graduate teacher education students at the University of Washington, reported an internal consistency correlation coefficient of + .89. They suggest that five items did not contribute to the reliability of the scale, but do not explain how this was determined.

Validity

Larrivee and Cook (1979) found that teachers' perceptions of their success in mainstreaming handicapped children accounted for the majority of variance in their attitude scores. In addition, regular classroom teachers' attitude toward mainstreaming became less positive as grade level increased, as the authors hypothesized. Larrivee (1981) studied the ORM scores of three groups of teachers: (a) those who received a year-long weekly intensive inservice training program on mainstreaming techniques, (b) those who participated in a year-long monthly inservice training program, and (c) those of a large random sample of regular classroom teachers who did not participate in training. The research data showed that the mean ORM Scale scores for the first group were significantly more positive than the mean ORM Scale scores of either of the other two groups. The mean scores of these last two groups did not differ significantly from each other.

A subsequent study (Larrivee, 1982) reported factor analysis results. Five factors were retained accounting for 52 percent of the total variance in the item responses. These factors were named: General Philosophy of Mainstreaming (32% of the variance with eight items), Classroom Behavior of Special Needs Children (6.6% of the variance with six items), Perceived Ability to Teach Special Needs Children (6.2% of the variance with four items), Classroom Management of Special Needs Children (4.5% of the variance with four items), and Academic and Social Growth of Special Needs Children (3.5% of the variance with four items). Data concerning the homogeneity and specificity of these subscales were not provided. A principal components analysis of ORM data by Green et al. (1983) yielded one general factor and seven specific factors.

Comments

The ORM scale was carefully developed from a theoretical base and its psychometric characteristics are sound. Additional investigations of the factorial structure are warranted in light of the conflicting results in the two studies located. Additional investigations of the scale's criterion and predictive validity would increase the strength of our recommendation for this useful scale.

Exhibit 13-5

Opinions Relative to Mainstreaming

Recent legislation requires that children with special needs be integrated into the regular classroom to the extent that such integration is possible. Educators have long realized that one of the most important influences on a child's educational progress is the classroom teacher. The purpose of this questionnaire is to obtain information that will aid school systems in maximizing the classroom teacher's effectiveness with special needs children placed in his or her classroom.

Please circle the number under the column that best describes your agreement or disagreement with the following statements. There are no correct answers: the best answers are those that honestly reflect your feelings.

KEY

SA = Strongly Agree U = Undecided D = Disagree

A = Agree SD = Strongly Disagree

SA	A	U	D	SD	
1	2	3	4	5	1. Many of the things teachers do with regular students in a classroom are appropriate for special-needs students.
1	2	3	4	5	2. The needs of handicapped students can best be served through special separate classes.
1	2	3	4	5	3. A special-needs child's classroom behavior generally requires more patience from the teacher than does the behavior of a normal child.
1	2	3	4	5	4. The challenge of being in a regular classroom will promote the academic growth of the special-needs child.
1	2	3	4	5	5. The extra attention special-needs students require will be to the detriment of the other students.
1	2	3	4	5	6. Mainstreaming offers mixed-group interaction which will foster understanding and acceptance of differences.
1	2	3	4	5	7. It is difficult to maintain order in a regular classroom that contains a special-needs child.
1	2	3	4	5	8. Regular teachers possess a great deal of the expertise necessary to work with special-needs students.

Exhibit 13-5 (Continued)

1	2	3	4	5	9. The behavior of special-needs students will set a bad example for the other students.
1	2	3	4	5	10. Isolation in a special class has a negative effect on the social and emotional development of a special-needs student.
1	2	3	4	5	11. The special-needs child will probably develop academic skills more rapidly in a special classroom than in a regular classroom.
1	2	3	4	5	12. Most special-needs children do not make an adequate attempt to complete their assignments.
1	2	3	4	5	13. Integration of special-needs children will require significant changes in regular classroom procedures.
1	2	3	4	5	14. Most special needs children are well-behaved in the classroom.
1	2	3	4	5	15. The contact regular-class students have with mainstreamed students will be harmful.
1	2	3	4	5	16. Regular classroom teachers have sufficient training to teach children with special needs.
1	2	3	4	5	17. Special-needs students will monopolize the teacher's time.
1	2	3	4	5	18. Mainstreaming the special-needs child will promote his or her social independence.
1	2	3	4	5	19. It is unlikely that a special-needs child will exhibit behavior problems in a regular classroom setting.
1	2	3	4	5	20. Diagnostic-prescriptive teaching is better done by resource-room or special teachers that by regular-classroom teachers.
1	2	3	4	5	21. The integration of special-needs students can be beneficial for regular students.
1	2	3	4	5	22. Special-needs children need to be told exactly what to do and how to do it.
1	2	3	4	5	23. Mainstreaming is likely to have a negative effect on the emotional development of the special-needs child.
1	2	3	4	5	24. Increased freedom in the classroom creates too much confusion.

Exhibit 13-5 (Continued)

---

1 2 3 4 5 25. The special-needs child will be socially isolated by regular-classroom students.

1 2 3 4 5 26. Parents of a special-needs child present no greater problem for a classroom teacher than those of a normal child.

1 2 3 4 5 27. Integration of a special-needs child will necessitate extensive retraining of regular teachers.

1 2 3 4 5 28. Special-needs students should be given every opportunity to function if the regular-classroom setting, where possible.

1 2 3 4 5 29. Special-needs children are likely to create confusion in the regular classroom.

1 2 3 4 5 30. The presence of special-needs students will promote acceptance of differences on the part of regular students.

Reprinted with permission of the authors; from Larrivee, B., & Cook, L. B. (1979). Mainstreaming: A study of the variables affecting teacher attitudes. Journal of Special Education, 13, 315-324.

Part IV

CONCLUDING COMMENTS

THIS LAST part consists of a final chapter in which we will begin by presenting a summary of the previous 13 chapters of the book. This will be followed by a presentation of 15 recommendations which we consider to be essential for the design of innovative research investigations and the development of sound attitude measurement instruments. We conclude the chapter and the book with an appeal for assistance in continuing the work we have begun.

Chapter 14

SUMMARY AND RECOMMENDATIONS

SUMMARY

RECENT LEGISLATIVE efforts have guaranteed the provision of a variety of educational, social, and vocational services to people who are physically, mentally, and psychosocially disabled. While these efforts have increased the integration of disabled children and adults into our schools, communities, and workplaces, barriers to complete acceptance remain. It is generally agreed that complete integration and acceptance of disabled people by non-disabled people will only come about following long-term changes in attitudes. Understanding the nature and structure of these attitudes must precede the development and implementation of intervention strategies designed to improve attitudes and to ultimately remove barriers to serving people who are disabled.

Our goal in writing this book was to contribute to the understanding of the nature and structure of attitudes toward disabled people. This book has presented a taxonomy of methods for the measurement of attitudes, a set of psychometric guidelines for attitude scales, and a compilation of previously published scales which possess minimal technical adequacy for the measurement of attitudes toward disability and disabled people. It is hoped that this information will constitute one significant part of the "framework for thinking about, investigating, and intervening in attitudes" (p.11) which Jones and Guskin (1984) have called for.

We began by introducing various definitions of the concept of attitude and suggested that these definitions can be organized along two dimensions. The first dimension concerns the concreteness or specificity of the definition, and the second dimension concerns the extensiveness of the components included in the definition. With regard to the second dimension, typical definitions refer to at least one of the following: cognitive, affective, behavioral, or conative components. Next, the functions served by, and the importance of scientifically investigating, attitudes were discussed, followed by an explication of the importance of studying attitudes toward people who are disabled. Finally, a history of the measurement of attitudes toward people who are disabled was presented, emphasizing the development of scales measuring attitudes toward a variety of disabling conditions which have been developed during the past quarter of a century.

Following the introductory discussion in Chapter 1, attitude measurement methods were presented in Chapter 2. This included an overview of basic concepts of measurement, definitions of indirect and direct methods of measurement, and a discussion of the concept of scaling. A total of ten direct methods of attitude measurement, all of which inform the subject that he or she is participating in an attitude measurement experiment, were dealt with in Chapter 3. Of these methods, the summated rating scale (pioneered by Rensis Likert) has been the method of choice by most researchers investigating attitudes toward disabled people.

In Chapter 4, Professor Schmelkin discussed the limitations of traditional direct methods for measuring attitudes, focusing on the constraints of their unidimensional assumptions and of the researcher's a priori conceptions of the important dimensions. As an alternative, nonmetric multidimensional scaling was presented, augmented by two examples illustrating the methodology and results. Considerations relevant to MDS studies were summarized and suggestions for the use of MDS in disability attitude research were offered.

The discussion of indirect methods of attitude measurement in Chapter 5 concentrated on four general methods typically found in the literature. Projective techniques provide the respondent with a set of ambiguous stimuli to which he or she is expected to react by projecting, and thereby revealing, his or her true attitudes toward a particular referent. Disguised procedures dupe the respondent into believing that he or she is participating in an experiment other than what it really is, or they may provide the respondent with no or ambiguous information of the true purpose of the investigation. Behavioral observations are simply attempts to measure the respondent's specific actions toward the referent group in natural or simulated settings. Finally, physiological methods allow for the measurement of presumably uncontrollable bodily reactions (e.g., skin conductance or pupil dilation) toward the referent group. Indirect methods have the advantage, compared to direct methods, of providing better control over the respondent's sensitization to the experimental task, the respondent's awareness that he or she is being assessed or observed, and unintentional confounding of the attitude to be measured with the subject's response style or personality characteristics.

To assist the researcher to select an existing attitude scale, or to construct a new scale, the chapters in the second part of the book sought to provide comprehensive guidelines for the psychometric adequacy of attitude scales. To achieve this aim, the concepts of reliability (Chapter 6), validity (Chapter 7), and item and scale analyses (Chapter 8) were introduced and discussed. Reliability concerns both the degree of consistency of scale scores over time, and the precision with which a scale samples the attitude domain of interest. Factors known to affect a scale's reliability estimate are the scale's length, the level of difficulty and power of discrimination of the scale items, the objectivity of the scale, and the conditions under which the scale is administered.

Validity refers to the capability of the scale to achieve its intended measurement aims. In other words, how successful the scale is in measuring what it sets out to measure. Three classes of validity were presented and discussed: content validity, or the degree to which the items represent the attitude domain; criterion-related validity, or the degree of correspondence between the scale and some independent measure of the criterion; and construct validity, or the degree to which the scale presumably measures the particular attitude or set of attitudes it intends to measure. Factors known to affect a scale's validity estimate include the reliabilities of both the scale and the criterion, the heterogeneity of the group studied, the similarity of the demographic and personality composition of the respondents to the scale's normative group, and contamination due to the respondent's prior knowledge of the criterion measure.

Because rating scales are the most widely used method to measure attitudes toward people who are disabled, Chapter 8 was devoted to a detailed examination of the psychometric characteristics of these scales. This examination followed a sequence which the researcher proposing to construct a new scale should follow: item preparation, collecting pilot study data to refine the scale's format and to select suitable items, analyzing the characteristics of the selected items (e.g., difficulty, discrimination), analyzing the structure of the scale (e.g., scale score distribution characteristics, scale dimensionality), and determining the extent to which the respondent's score is influenced by non-relevant personality traits and response determinants (i.e., acquiescence, social desirability, and extreme position response styles). Chapter 8 concluded with a discussion of the needs for and means to present normative data which permit interpretation of a respondent's scale score.

The third part of the book (Chapters 9 through 13) presented and discussed 22 scales for the measurement of attitudes toward people with disabilities, organized into five categories. These categories included general attitudes toward disabled people (six scales), attitudes toward physically disabled people (four scales), attitudes toward psychiatrically disabled people (three scales), attitudes toward people who are mentally retarded (four scales), and scales measuring societal responsibilities to disabled people (five scales). Each of the scales was described (i.e., origins, rationale, development, content), and the scale's item response format, administration, and scoring were discussed. Results of studies of each scale's reliability and validity were reviewed, and a general critique was provided to assist the reader who is considering the scale for research purposes.

RECOMMENDATIONS

This book demonstrates that the concept of attitudes toward people who are disabled is complex, and that the measurement of these attitudes is not a simple task. Far too often researchers investigating attitudes have been responsible for perpetuating the myth that this area of research is simple and, therefore, simplistic. It is easy to create a useless instrument and to collect useless data. Nor is there any doubt that the report of such useless research can be published if the researcher looks hard enough for a publication source that looks the other way on issues of psychometric adequacy of the measurement instrument. Researchers and faculty members in university settings must also share the criticism for the psychometric inadequacy of instruments created by their students pursuing graduate degrees.

The investigation of the formation, structure, correlates, and modification of attitudes toward disabled people requires innovative experimental methods and psychometrically sound instruments which are reliable, valid, and multidimensional. Without such instruments, it will not be possible to obtain conclusive answers to important research questions concerning the relationship between these attitudes and the acceptance and integration of disabled people into society. In this last section we will present a series of recommendation which we consider to be essential for the design of innovative research investigations, the critical review of existing measurement scales, and the development of sound attitude measurement instruments.

Refine Rather Than Create Scales

The creation of the so-called "Likert-format scale" to measure attitudes toward disabled people should cease. Summated rating scales (which were pioneered by Rensis Likert) are a sound and useful type of probabilistic rating scale. The rules for the creation of a summated rating scale are very clear and have been available since 1932. Why researchers persist in violating most of these rules, and then presenting and using what they term a "Likert-format scale" is beyond comprehension. Little evidence is provided for the assumptions underlying the construction of summated rating scales (e.g., equality of units necessary for interval scaling, monotonically increasing item functions, item homogeneity or a single common factor). The only resemblance these objects have to a summated rating scale in most cases is that the subject is asked to respond to each item by selecting one of several alternatives arranged on a pseudo-continuum of favorability or agreement.

The rating scales reviewed in Chapters 9 through 13, as well as those scales which use other direct methods to measure attitudes (e.g., adjective checklists, semantic differential scales) should be carefully examined and used in research on attitudes toward people who are disabled. In this way these scales can be periodically refined and improved (or withdrawn) by their authors. Others should pay particular attention to the efforts of Yuker and his colleagues to monitor the use of their venerable ATDP Scale and to publish periodic summaries of the characteristics of the scale, as well as summaries of the results of research in which the scale was used to operationalize the concept of attitude (e.g., Yuker and Block, 1986; Yuker, et al., 1970).

Use Indirect Attitude Measures

The use of valid and reliable indirect attitude measures is encouraged for future research investigating attitudes toward people with disabilities. Due to their relative immunity from the influences of respondent sensitization and confounding variables (e.g., response styles), and the natural embeddedness of observational methods in the broader social research context, these methods hold the promise of providing answers to significant research questions concerning the structure of attitudes. For example, the investigation of the relationship of attitudes to behavior can best be studied using one of the indirect methods described in Chapter 5. Researchers interested in questions in the domain of attitudes toward disabled people would do well to review the previous research in other social psychology domains, and design investigations incorporating these novel and powerful methods.

Use Multidimensional Scaling Methods

While MDS applications within the disability and rehabilitation literature are relatively recent, the general MDS literature has grown in the past 20 years, both in methodological advances and in the range of topics to which it has been applied. The traditional unidimensional measurement methods impose several limitations on the research results and subsequent interpretations. These include the inability of the methods to consider the commonalities or differences that may exist in the perception of various disabilities, and the imposition of the researcher's a priori conceptions of the relevant dimensions and constructs of the attitude domain. MDS overcomes these limitations and permits the exploration of the internal psychological structure of a respondent group's perceptions of disabilities and of people who are disabled. The technique can help the researcher to determine whether the structure is multidimensional, and to discover the salient dimensions. Due to the relatively unconstraining assumptions and methods of response elicitation required, MDS methods are particularly useful for investigating questions in the complex areas of attitudes, perceptions, behaviors, and interactions among individuals with and without disabilities.

Report Psychometric Properties of Scales

Researchers must be cognizant of and must report the psychometric properties of the attitude scales which they use in their investigations; that is, the reliability and validity of the scale, and the characteristics of the items and scale. All too frequently, researchers assume that the attitudes they are investigating have been reliably and validly measured just because they have used one of the standard methods. In reality, these attitude measures may not have been constructed according to sound procedures, and evidence of their psychometric adequacy is at best incomplete and often questionable. [See also the discussions by Shaw and Wright (1967).]

Use the Correct Reliability Estimate

The most frequently used reliability estimate is the internal consistency estimate. Yet in many cases, the wrong one is calculated and reported (four different estimates of internal consistency alone are described in Chapter 6). In many cases, this is because a particular statistical software package calculates many values and leaves it up to the researcher to determine which one is appropriate for the type of attitude data being studied. If the researcher is unaware of the differences among these various estimates, and the statistical assumptions which are required to be met before the estimates can be calculated, he or she may report the one which is the most common rather than the most appropriate one (e.g., one of the Kuder-Richardson formulas). Although seldom done (the authors of the ATDP Scale provide a notable exception), the researcher should report not only an internal consistency estimate but also a temporal stability estimate and an equivalence estimate between two or more forms. Finally, reliability estimates should be calculated for every sample of data, and not just reported from the original article or monograph in which the scale was published.

Report Data-Based Validity Estimates

The most commonly used validation method is content validation. Most developers of attitude scales select their items based on more or less extensive reviews of the literature, and may submit a prototype version of their scale to experts (e.g., their faculty advisor) for review and criticism. Of the three classes of validity discussed in Chapter 7, content validity is the weakest, primarily because it relies not on data but rather on subjective judgment and opinion, which is limited by the psychometric competence of the developer and expert. Rarely are the data-based validation procedures used by scale developers. Of the data-based criterion-related validity estimates, the concurrent validation methods are most frequently used, while the more powerful predictive validation methods are less frequently undertaken.

Construct validity of attitude scales is seldom established, although many times we discover extensive factor analytic studies of data obtained from an attitude measure. Often these same studies fail to investigate and report the reliability of the scale. The point we made previously about computer software applies here as well. Factor and cluster analyses of data are glamorous analytic procedures which are all too frequently undertaken by novices who have little background in statistics and, consequently, little understanding of the requisite assumptions and limitations of the methods. There is an over-reliance on factor analysis for the construct validation of attitude scales, and a notable lack of effort to relate the measured attitudes (e.g., scores on an attitude scale) to behavioral acts presumed to be influenced by those attitudes.

Investigate Attitude-Behavior Relationships

The need to investigate the relationship between the subject's verbalized expressions of his or her attitudes toward disabled people and the subject's overt behavior has been emphasized by previous authors (Rabkin, 1971, 1974; Siller, 1984) and is shared by us. Because some of the components of attitudes are more directly related to the subject's propensity to engage in certain behaviors than are other components, it is incumbent upon the researcher to select a measuring scale that appropriately taps those components of interest and relevance when planning an investigation of the correspondence between subjects' attitudes and their behaviors.

Investigate Attitude Correlates

It is recommended that researchers focus on the reciprocal relationships among empirically-derived attitude components drawn from several scales and predetermined sets of demographic (e.g., age, gender, educational level, professional background), personality (e.g., anxiety, hostility, ambiguity tolerance), and situational variables. Canonical and discriminant function analyses of data relating to these relationships would shed light on how attitudes vary with the psychological, educational, and vocational characteristics of respondents. Moreover, these data can be used as empirical evidence for the construct validity of the attitude studied. Researchers planning to design strategies to alter the structure of attitudes toward disabled people would ultimately benefit from these efforts.

Select a Multidimensional Scale

Although most of the attitude scales reviewed in this book were constructed as unidimensional instruments (e.g., the ATDP, CMI, AB, and AMRP scales), recent research strongly supports the multidimensionality of attitudes toward disabled people. As a result, a growing number of measures can presently be located that are constructed as multidimensional scales (e.g., the DFS, OMI, and MASMR). Researchers should carefully consider the multidimensional structure of these newer attitude scales when planning their research designs. The analyses of data derived from these measures will require that the appropriate multivariate statistical analysis procedures be used to derive the most useful information from these data.

Search for Fundamental Domains of Attitudes

It is recommended that researchers undertake investigations designed to explicate and validate the existence of fundamental domains of attitudes toward people who are disabled. This should be possible through the factor, cluster, and order analyses of the responses of large and diverse samples of subjects to collections of items from well-developed scales. Examples of research designs related to this activity are the studies reported by Antonak (1979a, 1980b, 1985c) and by Livneh (1982a, 1983, 1985a, 1985b, 1985c). If such a fundamental structure of attitudes can be established and validated, and if it can be shown that this structure accounts for differences in attitudes related to the demographic and experiential characteristics of respondents, then it may be possible to direct attitude intervention and modification strategies to these fundamental domains, and yield more permanent results.

Investigate the Context of Attitudes

An often neglected part of the design of studies of attitudes toward disabled people is an investigation of the situational or environmental context within which attitudes and their behavioral correlates occur. It is also clear that some of the components of attitudes are a function of relatively enduring personality traits, such as authoritarianism, dogmatism, and ethnocentrism (Rabkin, 1974). Other attitudes are related to less ingrained personality characteristics, such as those contingent upon specific situational interactions (e.g., role ambiguity, state anxiety, stress). It is recommended that the study of the interaction between specific social-situational variables and the various attitude components should be undertaken in future investigations. [See also the discussions in Altman (1981), Siller (1984), and Sloat and Frankel (1972).] This will allow a more accurate prediction of attitudes and behaviors. Since both attitudes and behaviors are multiply-determined and are subject to the influences of content-based (i.e., social situation) events, strategies for altering components of negative attitudes toward specific disability groups in particular situations could be ultimately undertaken.

Beware of Biasing Factors

The influence of outside factors on responses to attitude scale items, especially the biasing influence of socially desirable responding, has often been unnoticed by researchers using direct attitude measurement methods. The fortuitous confounding of subject personality characteristics and response style with substantive attitude scale content has led to problems interpreting the results of studies using these methods. Researchers involved with the measurement of attitudes are cautioned to be aware of these potential effects and either to control for them or, barring that possibility, to measure and report their influence so that others may judge for themselves which conclusions are warranted.

Not Everyone Is a College Freshman Taking Introductory Psychology

Researchers and practitioners are interested in measuring the attitudes of diverse groups of people toward people who are disabled. To do so requires a measure that has been developed and tested using data from samples which resemble the population to be sampled. Most attitude scales, however, have been developed by university faculty and have been used almost exclusively with samples of respondents who are college students. Most often these students are taking an introductory course in psychology or education, or are majoring in some discipline concerned with the provision of services to disabled people. These narrowly-defined, non-random, and unrepresentative samples of respondents are biased toward younger and more highly educated individuals, and toward those professionally-trained in providing human services. The usefulness of scales developed with these samples is seriously compromised for studies of other populations.

Few scales, for example, have included disabled people in their samples measured during the scale development process (the ATDP is again a notable exception). The authors of attitude scales purporting to measure attitudes toward people who are disabled are encouraged to undertake validation studies with diverse respondent samples and not just those who are readily available in their university setting. Researchers in other settings can participate in this effort by undertaking and reporting the results of these validation studies, and transmitting their data to the scale's author for inclusion in future normative tables and technical reports. In this way, the research community can build a small set of highly useful measures rather than continue to develop and publish measures for single-shot studies which are useless for others.

Specify the Attitude Referent

Respondents to an attitude scale can be expected to react differently when faced with attitude referents phrased in terms of disabling conditions (e.g., blindness, mental illness) than when provided with references to individuals who have a specific disability (e.g., blind person, psychiatrically disabled person). The ambiguous and overlapping use of the terms "disability," "the disabled," and "disabled person" on an attitude scale leads to concern about the scale's validity. It is recommended that researchers should be clear about whether they are focusing on attitudes toward people with a specific disability or on attitudes toward the disability per se.

The results of the study by Gottlieb and Siperstein (1976) suggested a similar recommendation. Researchers should take care to specify exactly the characteristics or definition of the attitude referent. Being asked to express the extent of one's agreement with the statement:

> Mentally retarded children should be afforded a free and appropriate education with their peers in regular classrooms.

will be answered quite differently if the referent (mentally retarded children) is defined to be mildly mentally retarded or profoundly mentally retarded. Similarly, the subject's response may vary if the age of the referent is specified to be three years or 11 years or 20 years. While there is justification for not specifying the characteristics or definition of the attitude referent in some studies, in most cases such specificity is necessary.

Update Old Scales

Many of the scales measuring attitudes toward disabled people were developed and validated in the late 1950s and early 1960s. The past two decades have seen tremendous changes in society's views of and moral judgments toward people who are disabled, coupled with significant changes in legislation and public policy concerning the provision of comprehensive educational, psychosocial, and vocational services. There is a significant need to revise, update, and revalidate many of the older scales. In most cases the original authors of these scales would welcome this work and contribute to its completion.

CONCLUDING COMMENTS

The attitude scales reviewed in this book should not, under any circumstances, be used for clinical, diagnostic, assessment, selection, or placement purposes. At best, these scales should be regarded as adequate for research and experimental purposes. Moreover, researchers must carefully and judiciously select, use, and interpret the results of analyses of data from existing scales measuring attitudes toward disabled people. As Shaw and Wright (1967) appropriately cautioned us, "An inadequate measuring instrument has nullified many research efforts" (p. 568).

The decision to include and review an attitude scale in this book was ours alone. Our judgments were based on the extent to which a scale met the objective criteria for the psychometric adequacy of attitude scales which were presented and discussed in the chapters in Part II of this book (i.e., reliability, validity, and item and scale characteristics). In those cases when a scale was clearly deficient in some areas, yet reasonably adequate in most areas, we decided to include it and to clearly point out in our reviews the areas of deficiency. We provided a manuscript copy of our reviews to the primary authors we were able to locate for their comments and suggestions. In those cases when we were granted permission, we reproduced a copy of the scale. Appendix A provides the names and addresses for the primary authors of each of the 22 scales presented in Part III to enable researchers to participate in the review and revision processes we have recommended.

We have attempted to present a balance of scales in as many areas as possible related to the measurement of attitudes toward disabled people. We encourage researchers and authors who know of, or who have authored, other scales in these or other domains to write to us and share their information. It is our intention to continually update the work we started in this book.

REFERENCES

Abroms, K.I., and Kodera, T.L. (1979). Acceptance hierarchy of handicaps: Validation of Kirk's statement "Special education often begins where medicine stops." *Journal of Learning Disabilities, 12,* 15-20.

Adorno, T.W., Frenkel-Brunswik, E., Levinson, D.J., and Sanford, R.N. (1964). *The authoritarian personality.* New York: John Wiley and Sons.

Airasian, P.W., and Bart, W.M. (1973). Ordering theory: A new and useful measurement model. *Educational Technology, 13,* 56-60.

Ajzen, I., and Fishbein, M. (1977). Attitude-behavior relations: A theoretical analysis and review of empirical research. *Psychological Bulletin, 84,* 888-918.

Ajzen, I., and Fishbein, M. (1980). *Understanding attitudes and predicting social behavior.* Englewood Cliffs, NJ: Prentice-Hall.

Allen, M.J., and Yen, W.M. (1979). *Introduction to measurement theory.* Monterey, CA: Brooks/Cole.

Allon, R., and Graham, J.R. (1970). Intercorrelations of factor scores from the Opinions About Mental Illness Scale. *Psychological Reports, 26,* 805-806.

Allport, G.W. (1935). Attitudes. In C. Murchison (Ed.), *Handbook of social psychology* (pp. 798-884). Worcester, MA: Clark University Press.

Allport, G.W. (1954). *The nature of prejudice.* Reading, MA: Addison-Wesley.

Altman, B.M. (1981). Studies of attitudes toward the handicapped: The need for a new direction. *Social Problems, 28,* 321-337.

American Psychological Association. (1974). *Standards for educational and psychological tests.* Washington, DC: Author.

Anastasi, A. (1982). *Psychological testing* (5th ed.). New York: Macmillan.

Antonak, R.F. (1979a). An ordering-theoretic analysis of attitudes toward disabled persons. *Rehabilitation Psychology, 26,* 136-144.

Antonak, R.F. (1979b). ITEM3: A general purpose FORTRAN 10 test scoring and item analysis program. *Behavior Research Methods and Instrumentation, 11,* 81-82.

Antonak, R.F. (1980a). A FORTRAN program to analyze summated rating scales. *The American Statistician, 34,* 59.

Antonak, R.F. (1980b). A hierarchy of attitudes toward exceptionality. *Journal of Special Education, 14,* 231-241.

Antonak, R.F. (1980c). Psychometric analysis of the Attitude Toward Disabled Persons Scale, Form-O. *Rehabilitation Counseling Bulletin, 23,* 169-176.

Antonak, R.F. (1981a). *Development and psychometric analysis of the Scale of Attitudes Toward Disabled Persons* (Technical Report No. 1). Durham, NH: University of New Hampshire, Education Department.

Antonak, R.F. (1981b). Prediction of attitudes toward disabled persons: A multivariate analysis. *Journal of General Psychology, 104,* 119-123.

Antonak, R.F. (1982). Development and psychometric analysis of the Scale of Attitudes Toward Disabled Persons. *The Journal of Applied Rehabilitation Counseling, 13*(2), 22-29.

Antonak, R.F. (1985a). Construct validation of the Scale of Attitudes Toward Disabled Persons. *Journal of Applied Rehabilitation Counseling, 16*(1), 7-10, 48.

Antonak, R.F. (1985b). *Construct validation and psychometric analysis of the Scale of Attitudes Toward Disabled Persons* (Technical Report No. 2). Durham, NH: University of New Hampshire, Education Department.

Antonak, R.F. (1985c). Societal factors in disablement. *Rehabilitation Counseling Bulletin, 28,* 188-201.

Antonak, R.F., Bart, W.M., and Lele, K. (1979). ORDER2: A program to perform ordering-theoretic data analysis. *Behavior Research Methods and Instrumentation, 11,* 457-458.

Antonak, R.F., and Rankin, P.R. (1981). *Measurement and analysis of knowledge and attitudes about epilepsy* (Technical Report No. 1). Durham, NH: University of New Hampshire, Education Department.

Antonak, R.F., and Rankin, P.R. (1982). Measurement and analysis of knowledge and attitudes about epilepsy and persons with epilepsy. *Social Science and Medicine, 16,* 1591-1593.

Attneave, F. (1950). Dimensions of similarity. *American Journal of Psychology, 63,* 516-556.

Baird, J.C., and Noma, E. (1978). *Fundamentals of scaling and psychophysics.* New York: Wiley.

Baker, F.B. (1985). *The basics of item response theory.* Portsmouth, NH: Heinemann.

Baker, L.D., and Reitz, H.J. (1978). Altruism toward the blind: Effects of sex of helper and dependency of victim. *The Journal of Social Psychology, 104,* 19-28.

Barker, D.G. (1964). Concepts of disabilities. *Personnel and Guidance Journal, 43,* 371-374.

Barker, R.G. (1948). The social psychology of physical disability. *Journal of Social Issues, 4*(4), 28-38.

Barngrover, E. (1971). A study of educator's preferences in special education programs. *Exceptional Children, 37,* 754-755.

Barsch, R.H. (1964). The handicapped ranking scale among parents of handicapped children. *American Journal of Public Health, 54,* 1560-1567.

Bart, W.M. (1972a). A hierarchy of attitudes toward animals. *Journal of Environmental Education, 3*(4), 4-6.

Bart, W.M. (1972b). A hierarchy of attitudes toward the environment. *Journal of Environmental Education, 4*(1), 10-14.

Bart, W.M., and Krus, D. (1973). An ordering theoretic method to determine hierarchies among items. *Educational and Psychological Measurement, 33,* 291-300.

Bartlett, C.J., Quay, L.C., and Wrightsman, L.S., Jr. (1960). A comparison of two methods of attitude measurement: Likert-type and forced choice. *Educational and Psychological Measurement, 20,* 699-704.

Begab, M.J. (1970). Impact of education on social work students' knowledge and attitudes about mental retardation. *American Journal of Mental Deficiency, 74,* 801-808.

Berryman, J.D., and Neal, W.R., Jr. (1980). The cross validation of the Attitudes Toward Mainstreaming Scale. *Educational and Psychological Measurement, 40,* 469-474.

Berryman, J.D., Neal, W.R., Jr., and Robinson, J.E. (1980). The validation of a scale to measure attitudes toward the classroom integration of disabled students. *Journal of Educational Research, 73,* 199-203.

Betz, N.E., and Weiss, D.J. (1976). Validity. In B. Bolton (Ed.), *Handbook of measurement and evaluation in rehabilitation* (pp. 39-60). Baltimore, MD: University Park Press.

Billings, H.K. (1963). An exploratory study of the attitudes of non-crippled children in three selected elementary schools. *Journal of Experimental Education, 31,* 381-387.

Block, J. (1961). *The Q-sort method in personality assessment and psychiatric research.* Springfield, IL: Charles C Thomas.

Block, J.R. (1974). *Recent research with the Attitude Toward Disabled Persons Scale: Some research abstracts.* Rehabilitation Series No. 7. Albertson, NY: Human Resources Center.

Bogdan, R.C., and Biklen, S.K. (1982). *Qualitative research for education: An introduction to theory and methods.* Boston: Allyn and Bacon.

Bogardus, E.S. (1925a). Social distance and its origins. *Journal of Applied Sociology, 9,* 216-226.

Bogardus, E.S. (1925b). Measuring social distances. *Journal of Applied Sociology, 9,* 299-308.

Bogardus, E.S. (1931). *Fundamentals of social psychology.* New York: Century.

Bogardus, E.S. (1933). A social distance scale. *Sociology and Social Research, 17,* 265-271.

Bolton, B. (1974). *Introduction to rehabilitation research.* Springfield, IL: Charles C Thomas.

Bolton, B. (1976). (Ed.). *Handbook of measurement and evaluation in rehabilitation.* Baltimore, MD: University Park Press.

Bolton, B. (1979). *Rehabilitation counseling research.* Baltimore, MD: University Park Press.

Bolton, B., Lawlis, G.F., and Brown, R.H. (1976). Scores and norms. In B. Bolton (1976). (Ed.), *Handbook of measurement and evaluation in rehabilitation* (pp. 3-14). Baltimore, MD: University Park Press.

Borg, I., and Lingoes, J.C. (1980). A model and algorithm for multidimensional scaling with external constraints on the distances. *Psychometrika, 45,* 25-38.

Brindberg, D., and Kidder, L. (1982). *Forms of validity in research.* San Francisco: Jossey-Bass.

Bruininks, R.H., Rynders, J.E., and Gross, J.C. (1974). Social acceptance of mildly retarded pupils in resource rooms and regular classes. *American Journal of Mental Deficiency, 78,* 377-383.

Buss, A.H., and Durkee, A. (1957). An inventory for assessing different kinds of hostility. *Journal of Consulting Psychology, 21,* 343-348.

Bryan, T.H. (1978). Social relationships and verbal interactions of learning disabled children. *Journal of Learning Disabilities, 11,* 107-115.

Bryan, T.H., Wheeler, R., Felcan, J., and Henek, T. (1976). "Come on, Dummy": An observational study of children's communications. *Journal of Learning Disabilities, 9,* 661-669.

Buck, J.N. (1948). The H-T-P technique, a qualitative and quantitative scoring manual. Monograph supplement. *Journal of Clinical Psychology, 4,* 1-120.

Campbell, D.T. (1950). The indirect assessment of social attitudes. *Psychological Bulletin, 47,* 15-38.

Campbell, D.T., and Fiske, D.W. (1959). Convergent and discriminant validation by the multitrait-multimethod matrix. *Psychological Bulletin, 56,* 81-105.

Campbell, D.T., and Stanley, J.C. (1966). *Experimental and quasi-experimental designs for research.* Chicago: Rand McNally.

Cannon, B.J., and Szuhay, J.A. (1986). Faking can elevate scores on the Attitudes Toward Disabled Persons Scale. *Rehabilitation Counseling Bulletin, 30,* 120-123.

Carmines, E.G., and Zeller, R.A. (1979). *Reliability and validity assessment.* Beverly Hills, CA: Sage.

Carroll, J.D., and Chang, J.J. (1970). Analysis of individual differences in multidimensional scaling via an n-way generalization of "Eckart-Young" decomposition. *Psychometrika, 35,* 283-319.

Carroll, J.D., and Wish, M. (1974). Multidimensional perceptual models and measurement methods. In E.C. Carterette and M.P. Friedman (Eds.). *Handbook of perception* (Vol. 2, pp. 391-447). New York: Academic Press.

Carver, C.S., Glass, D.C., and Katz, I. (1978). Favorable evaluations of Blacks and the handicapped: Positive prejudice, unconscious denial, or social desirability. *Journal of Applied Social Psychology, 8,* 97-106.

Centra, J.A. (1971). Validation by the multigroup-multiscale matrix: An adaptation of Campbell and Fiske's convergent and discriminant validation procedure. *Educational and Psychological Measurement, 31,* 675-683.

Chan, F., Hua, M-S., Ju, J.J., and Lam, C.S. (1984). Factorial structure of the Chinese Scale of Attitudes Toward Disabled Persons: A cross-cultural validation. *International Journal of Rehabilitation Research, 7,* 317-319.

Chigier, E., and Chigier, M. (1968). Attitudes to disability of children in the multi-cultural society of Israel. *Journal of Health and Social Behavior, 9,* 310-317.

Cialdini, R.B., Petty, R.E., and Cacioppo, J.T. (1981). Attitude and attitude change. *Annual Review of Psychology, 32,* 357-404.

Clark, A.N., and Binks, N.M. (1966). Relation of age and education to attitudes toward mental illness. *Psychological Reports, 19,* 649-650.

Cleland, C., Manaster, G., King, M., and Iscoe, I. (1975). The mentally ill and mentally retarded via adjectival descriptions. *Mental Retardation, 13,* 28-30.

Cline, R. (1981). Principals' attitudes and knowledge about handicapped children. *Exceptional Children, 48,* 172-174.

Cloerkes, G. (1981). Are prejudices against disabled persons determined by personality characteristics? *International Journal of Rehabilitation Research, 4,* 35-46.

Cohen, J.S. (1963). Employer attitudes toward hiring mentally retarded individuals. *American Journal of Mental Deficiency, 67,* 705-713.

Cohen, J.S., and Struening, E.L. (1959). Factors underlying opinions about mental illness in the personnel of a large mental hospital. *American Psychologist, 14,* 339.

Cohen, J.S., and Struening, E.L. (1960). Attitudes toward the mental ill of psychiatric hospital personnel as a function of occupation, education, age, and sex. *American Psychologist, 15,* 417.

Cohen, J.S., and Struening, E.L. (1962). Opinions about mental illness in the personnel of two large mental hospitals. *Journal of Abnormal and Social Psychology, 64,* 349-360.

Cohen, J.S., and Struening, E.L. (1963). Opinions about mental illness: Mental hospital occupational profiles and profile clusters. *Psychological Reports, 12,* 111-124.

Comer, R.J., and Piliavin, J.A. (1972). The effects of physical deviance upon face to face interaction: The other side. *Journal of Personality and Social Psychology, 23,* 33-39.

Comer, R.J., and Piliavin, J.A. (1975). As others see us: Attitudes of physically handicapped and normals toward own and other groups. *Rehabilitation Literature, 36,* 206-221.

Conant, S., and Budoff, M. (1982). The development of sighted people's understanding of blindness. *Journal of Visual Impairment and Blindness, 76,* 86-90.

Cook, S.W., and Selltiz, C. (1964). A multi-indicator approach to attitude measurement. *Psychological Bulletin, 62,* 36-55.

Coombs, C.H. (1964). *A theory of data.* New York: John Wiley and Sons.

Cooper, J., and Croyle, R.T. (1984). Attitudes and attitude change. *Annual Review of Psychology, 35,* 395-426.

Costin, F., and Kerr, W.D. (1962). The effects of abnormal psychology source on student's attitudes toward mental illness. *Journal of Educational Psychology, 53,* 214-218.

Couch, A., and Kenniston, K. (1960). Yeasayers and naysayers: Agreeing response set as a personality variable. *Journal of Abnormal and Social Psychology, 60,* 151-174.

Cowen, E.L., Bobrove, P.H., Rockway, A.M., and Stevenson, J. (1967). Development and evaluation of an attitude to deafness scale. *Journal of Personality and Social Psychology, 6,* 183-191.

Cowen, E.L., Underberg, R.P., and Verrillo, R.T. (1958). The development and testing of an attitude to blindness scale. *The Journal of Social Psychology, 48,* 297-304.

Coxon, A.P.M. (1982). *The user's guide to multidimensional scaling.* Exeter, NH: Heinemann Educational Books.

Cronbach, L.J. (1951). Coefficient alpha and the internal structure of tests. *Psychometrika, 16,* 297-334.

Cronbach, L.J. (1984). *Essentials of psychological testing* (4th ed.). New York, Harper and Row.

Crowne, D.P., and Marlowe, D. (1960). A new scale of social desirability independent of psychopathology. *Journal of Consulting Psychology, 24,* 349-354.

D'Agostino, R.B., and Cureton, E.E. (1976). The 27 percent rule revisited. *Educational and Psychological Measurement, 35,* 47-50.

Davison, M.L. (1983). *Multidimensional scaling.* New York: Wiley.

Davison, M.L., and Jones, L.E. (1976). A similarity-attraction model for predicting sociometric choice from perceived group structure. *Journal of Personality and Social Psychology, 33,* 601-612.

Dawes, R.M. (1984). Approaches to attitude measurement. In R.L. Jones (Ed.). *Attitude and attitude change in special education: Theory and practice* (pp. 70-92). Reston, VA: Council for Exceptional Children.

Dawes, R.M., and Smith, T.L. (1985). Attitude and opinion measurement. In G. Lindzey and E. Aronson (Eds.), *The handbook of social psychology* (3rd ed.) (pp. 509-566). New York: Random House.

Deri, S.K. (1949). *Introduction to the Szondi Test: Theory and practice.* New York: Grune and Stratton.

Dielman, T.E., Steifel, G., and Cattell, R.B. (1973). A check on the factor structure of the Opinions of [sic] Mental Illness Scale. *Journal of Clinical Psychology, 29,* 92-95.

Dunlop, K.H., Stoneman, Z., and Cantrell, M.L. (1980). Social interaction of exceptional and other children in a mainstreamed preschool classroom. *Exceptional Children, 47,* 132-141.

Easley, V.A. (1976). Attitudes of professional and para-professional staff of a state hospital for the retarded toward the mentally retarded (Doctoral dissertation, Catholic University of America, 1976). *Dissertation Abstracts International, 37,* 1819A-1820A.

Edwards, A.L. (1957a). *Techniques of attitude scale construction.* New York: Appleton-Century-Crofts.

Edwards, A.L. (1957b). *The social desirability variable in personality assessment and research.* New York: Dryden Press.

Edwards, A.L., and Kilpatrick, F.P. (1948). A technique for the construction of attitude scales. *Journal of Applied Psychology, 32,* 374-384.

Efron, R.E., and Efron, H.Y. (1967). Measurement of attitudes toward the retarded and an application with educators. *American Journal of Mental Deficiency, 72,* 100-106.

Ehrlich, H.J., and Rinehart, J.W. (1965). A brief report on the methodology of stereotype research. *Social Forces, 43,* 564-575.

Elsberry, N.L. (1975). Comparison of two scales measuring attitudes toward persons with physical disabilities. *Psychological Reports, 36,* 473-474.

English, H.B., and English, A.C. (1958). *A comprehensive dictionary of psychological and psychoanalytic terms: A guide to usage.* New York: McKay.

English, R.W. (1971). Correlates of stigma toward physically disabled persons. *Rehabilitation Research and Practice Review, 2,* 1-17.

Eysenck, H.J. (1954). *The psychology of politics.* London: Routledge and Kegan Paul.

Farina, A., Holland, C.H., and Ring, K. (1966). Role of stigma and set in interpersonal interaction. *Journal of Abnormal Psychology, 71,* 421-428.

Farina, A., and Ring, K. (1965). The influence of perceived mental illness on interpersonal relations. *Journal of Abnormal Psychology, 70,* 47-51.

Farina, A., Sherman, M., and Allen, J.G. (1968). Role of physical abnormalities in interpersonal perception and behavior. *Journal of Abnormal Psychology, 73,* 590-593.

Feinberg, L.B. (1967). Social desirability and attitudes toward the disabled. *Personal and Guidance Journal, 46,* 375-381.

Feldman, D., Jay, R., Kinnison, L., and Harth, R. (1984). Attitudes toward minority learning handicapped students as a function of differential labelling. *Education and Training of the Mentally Retarded, 19,* 141-149.

Ferguson, L.T. (1970). Components of attitudes toward the deaf. *Proceedings of the Annual Convention of the American Psychological Association, 5,* 693-694.

Finkelstein, V. (1980). Attitudes and disabled people: Issues for discussion. In V. Finkelstein (Ed.), *Attitudes and disabled people,* (pp. 1-42). New York: World Rehabilitation Fund.

Fishbein, M. (Ed.). (1967). *Readings in attitude theory and measurement.* New York: John Wiley and Sons.

Fishbein, M., and Ajzen, I. (1972). Attitudes and opinions. *Annual Review of Psychology, 23,* 487-544.

Fishbein, M., and Ajzen, I. (1975). *Belief, attitude, intention, and behavior: An introduction to theory and research.* Reading, MA: Addison-Wesley.

Fitting, E.A. (1954). *Evaluation and adjustment to blindness.* (Research Series No. 2) New York; American Foundation for the Blind.

Fitts, W.H. (1965). *Manual: Tennessee Self-Concept Scale.* Nashville, TN: Counselor Recordings and Tests.

Force, D.G., Jr. (1956). Social status of physically handicapped children. *Exceptional Children, 23,* 104-107, 132-133.

Ford, A.B., Liske, R.E., and Ort, R.S. (1962). Reactions of physicians and medical students to chronic illness. *Journal of Chronic Diseases, 15,* 785-794.

Fracchia, J., Pintyr, J., Crovello, J., Sheppard, C., and Merlis, S. (1972). Comparison of intercorrelations of scale scores from the Opinions about Mental Illness scale. *Psychological Reports, 30,* 149-150.

Fulkerson, S.C. (1958). *An acquiescence key to the MMPI.* United States Air Force School of Aviation Medicine, Report No. 58-71, pp. 1-11.

Funk, S.G., Horowitz, A.D., Lipshitz, R., and Young, F.W. (1976). The perceived structure of American ethnic groups; the use of multidimensional scaling in stereotype research. *Sociometry, 39,* 116-130.

Gan, J., Tymchuk, A.J., and Nishihara, A. (1977). Mildly retarded adults: Their attitudes toward retardation. *Mental Retardation, 15,* 5-9.

Gargiulo, R.M., and Yonker, R.J. (1983). Assessing teachers' attitudes toward the handicapped: A methodological investigation. *Psychology in the Schools, 20,* 229-233.

Garver, A., and Schmelkin, L.P. (1986, October). *Administrators' and teachers' attitudes toward mainstreaming.* Paper presented at the annual meeting of the Northeastern Educational Research Association, Kerhonksen, New York.

Gibbons, F.X., Stephan, W.G., Stephenson, B., and Petty, C.R. (1980). Reactions to stigmatized others: Response amplification vs. sympathy. *Journal of Experimental Social Psychology, 16,* 591-605.

Gilbert, D.C., and Levinson, D.J. (1956). Ideology, personality, and institutional policy in the mental hospital. *Journal of Abnormal and Social Psychology, 53,* 263-271.

Goldberg, L.R., and Werts, C.E. (1966). The reliability of clinicians' judgments: A multitrait-multimethod approach. *Journal of Consulting Psychology, 30,* 199-206.

Goldstein, M.J. (1960). The social desirability variable in attitude research. *Journal of Social Psychology, 52,* 103-108.

Goldstein, K., and Blackman, S. (1975). Generalizations regarding deviant groups. *Psychological Reports, 37,* 279-283.

Golin, A.K. (1970). Stimulus variables in the measurement of attitudes toward disability. *Rehabilitation Counseling Bulletin, 14,* 20-26.

Golledge, R.C., and Raynor, J.N. (Eds.) (1982). *Proximity and preference: Problems in the multidimensional analysis of large data sets.* Minneapolis: University of Minnesota Press.

Gottlieb, J. (1975). Public, peer, and professional attitudes toward mentally retarded persons. In M.J. Begab and S.A. Richardson, (Eds.). *The mentally retarded in society: A social science perspective.* Baltimore, MD: University Park Press.

Gottlieb, J., and Budoff, M. (1973). Social acceptability of retarded children in nongraded schools differing in architecture. *American Journal of Mental Deficiency, 78,* 215-219.

Gottlieb, J., Corman, L., and Curci, R. (1984). Attitudes toward mentally retarded children. In R.L. Jones (Ed.), *Attitude and attitude change in special education: Theory and practice* (pp. 143-156). Reston, VA: Council for Exceptional Children.

Gottlieb, J., and Siperstein, G.N. (1976). Attitudes toward mentally retarded persons: Effects of attitude referent specificity. *American Journal of Mental Deficiency, 80,* 376-381.

Gough, H.G. (1960). The Adjective Check List as a personality assessment research scale. *Psychological Reports, 6,* 107-122.

Graham, S., and Deaton, W. (1983). A factor analysis of the Rucker-Gable Educational Programming Scale. *Educational and Psychological Measurement, 43,* 927-933.

Graham, S., and Henry, N. (1981). Reliability of the Rucker-Gable Educational Programming Scale. *Diagnostique, 7,* 130-132.

Graham, S., and Henry, N. (1982). An examination of the construct validity of the Rucker-Gable Educational Programming Scale. *Teacher Education and Special Education, 5,* 30-35.

Grand, S.A., Bernier, J.E., and Strohmer, D.C. (1982). Attitudes toward disabled persons as a function of social context and specific disability. *Rehabilitation Psychology, 27,* 165-173.

Granofsky, J. (1956). Modification of attitudes toward the visibly disabled: An experimental study of the effectiveness of social contact in producing a modification of the attitudes of non-disabled females toward visibly disabled males. *Dissertation Abstracts International, 16,* No. 1, 1182. (University Microfilms No., 56-1863).

Green, K., and Harvey, D. (1983). Cross-cultural validation of the Attitudes Toward Mainstreaming Scale. *Educational and Psychological Measurement, 43,* 1255-1261.

Green, K., Rock, D.L., and Weisenstein, G.R. (1983). Validity and reliability of a scale assessing attitudes toward mainstreaming. *Exceptional Children, 50,* 182-183.

Guilford, J.P. (1954). *Psychometric methods* (2nd ed.). New York: McGraw-Hill.

Guilford, J.P., and Fruchter, B. (1978). *Fundamental statistics in psychology and education* (6th ed.). New York: McGraw-Hill.

Guion, R.M. (1977). Content validity—The source of my discontent. *Applied Psychological Measurement, 1,* 1-10.

Guttman, L. (1944). A basis for scaling qualitative data. *American Sociological Review, 9,* 139-150.

Guttman, L. (1947). The Cornell technique for scale and intensity analysis. *Educational and Psychological Measurement, 7,* 247-280.

Guttman, L. (1950). The basis for scalogram analysis. In S.A. Stouffer, L. Guttman, E.A. Suchman, P.F. Lazarsfeld, S.A. Star, and J.A. Clausen (Eds.), *Measurement and prediction* (pp. 60-90). New York: Wiley.

Hafer, M., Wright, W.R., and Godley, S.H. (1983). Dimensionality of the Attitudes Toward Disabled Persons Scale. *Educational and Psychological Measurement, 43,* 459-463.

Harasymiw, S.J., Horne, M.D., and Lewis, S.C. (1976). A longitudinal study of disability group acceptance. *Rehabilitation Literature, 37,* 98-102.

Harth, R. (1974). Attitudes toward minority groups as a construct in assessing attitudes toward the mentally retarded. *Education and Training of the Mentally Retarded, 6,* 142-147.

Harth, R. (1981). Personally relevant and personally irrelevant attitude differences toward educable and trainable retarded children. *Educational and Training of the Mentally Retarded, 16,* 213-216.

Hartke, A.R. (1979). The development of conceptually independent subscales in the measurement of attitudes. *Educational and Psychological Measurement, 39,* 585-592.

Henry, N., and Graham, S. (1980). Validity of the Rucker-Gable Educational Programming Scale. *Diagnostique, 6,* 24-28.

Henry, N., and Graham, S. (1983). The Rucker-Gable Educational Programming Scale: Stability over time. *Psychology in the Schools, 20,* 494-497.

Hess, E.H. (1965). Attitude and pupil size. *Scientific American, 212,* 46-54.

Hess, E.H., and Polt, J.M. (1960). Pupil size as related to interest value of visual stimuli. *Science, 132,* 349-350.

Hess, E.H., Seltzer, A.L., and Shlien, J.M. (1965). Pupil response of hetero- and homosexual males to pictures of men and women. *Journal of Abnormal Psychology, 70,* 165-168.

Hicks, J.M. (1967). Comparative validation of attitude measures by the multitrait-multimethods matrix. *Educational and Psychological Measurement, 27,* 985-995.

Hilgard, E.R., and Atkinson, R.C. (1967). *Introduction to psychology* (4th ed.). New York: Harcourt and Brace.

Hollinger, C.S., and Jones, R.L. (1970). Community attitudes toward slow learners and mental retardates. What's in a name. *Mental Retardation, 8,* 19-23.

Holtzman, W.H. (1968). Holtzman Inkblot Technique. In A.I. Rabin (Ed.), *Projective techniques in personality assessment* (pp. 136-170). New York: Springer.

Hood, R.W., Jr. (1973). Dogmatism and opinions about mental illness. *Psychological Reports, 32,* 1283-1290.

Horenstein, D. (1978). Social pressure as a factor influencing sex differences in attitudes toward disability. *Rehabiliation Psychology, 25,* 209-213.

Horne, M.D. (1978). Cultural effect on attitudes toward labels. *Psychological Reports, 43,* 1051-1058.

Horne, M.D. (1980). *How attitudes are measured: A review of investigations of professional, peer, and parent attitudes toward the handicapped.* (Report No. TM-78). Princeton, NJ: ERIC Clearinghouse on Tests, Measurements, and Evaluation. (ERIC Document Reproduction Service No. ED 198 154).

Horne, M.D. (1985). *Attitudes toward handicapped students: Professional, peer, and parent reactions.* Hillsdale, NJ: Lawrence Erlbaum.

Horney, K. (1945). *Our inner conflicts.* New York: W.W. Norton.

Horowitz, L.S., Rees, N.S., and Horowitz, M.W. (1962). *Attitudes toward deafness.* A Paper presented at the Convention of the American Speech and Hearing Association, New York.

Horowitz, L.S., Rees, N.S., and Horowitz, M.W. (1965). Attitudes toward deafness as a function of increasing maturity. *Journal of Social Psychology, 66,* 331-336.

Horst, P. (1966). *Psychological measurement and prediction.* Belmont, CA: Wadsworth.

Hoyt, C.J. (1941). Test reliability estimated by analysis of variance. *Psychometrika, 6,* 153-160.

Insko, C.A., and Schopler, J. (1967). Triadic consistency: A statement of affective—cognitive—conative consistency. *Psychological Review, 74,* 361-376.

Jaccard, J., Weber, J., and Lundmark, J. (1975). A multitrait-multimethod analysis of four attitude assessment procedures. *Journal of Experimental Social Psychology, 11,* 149-154.

Jackson, D.N. (1969). The multidimensional nature of human social perception. *Canadian Journal of Behavioral Sciences, 1,* 227-262.

Jaffee, J. (1972). The effects of work conferences on attitudes toward the mentally retarded. *Rehabilitation Counseling Bulletin, 15,* 220-227.

Janicki, M.P. (1970). Attitudes of health professionals toward twelve disabilities. *Perceptual and Motor Skills, 30,* 77-78.

Jones, E.E., and Sigall, H. (1971). The bogus pipeline: A new paradigm for measuring affect and attitude. *Psychological Bulletin, 76,* 349-364.

Jones, R.L. (Ed.). (1984). *Attitudes and attitude change in special education: Theory and practice.* Reston, VA: Council for Exceptional Children.

Jones, R.L., Gottfried, N.W., and Owens, A. (1966). The social distance of the exceptional: A study at the high school level. *Exceptional Children, 32,* 551-556.

Jones, R.L., and Guskin, S.L. (1984). Attitudes and attitude change in special education. In R.L. Jones (Ed.). *Attitudes and attitude change in special education: Theory and practice* (pp. 1-20). Reston, VA: Council for Exceptional Children.

Jones, R.L., and Sisk, D.A. (1967). Early perceptions of orthopedic disability. *Exceptional Children, 34,* 42-43.

Jordan, J.E. (1971). Attitude-behavior research on physical-mental-social disability and racial-ethnic differences. *Psychological Aspects of Disability, 18,* 5-26.

Jung, C.G. (1910). The association method. *American Journal of Psychology, 21,* 219-269.

Katz, D. (1960). The functional approach to the study of attitudes. *Public Opinion Quarterly, 24,* 163-205.

Katz, I., Glass, D.C., Lucido, D.J., and Farber, J. (1977). Ambivalence, guilt, and the denigration of a physically handicapped victim. *Journal of Personality, 45,* 419-429.

Katz, P.A., Katz, I., and Cohen, S. (1976). White children's attitudes toward Blacks and the physically handicapped: A developmental study. *Journal of Educational Psychology, 68,* 20-24.

Kelley, T.L. (1939). The selection of upper and lower groups for the validation of test items. *Journal of Educational Psychology, 30,* 17-24.

Kenon, A.F., and Sandoval, J. (1978). Teacher attitudes toward the educable mentally retarded. *Education and Training of the Mentally Retarded, 13,* 139-145.

Kent, G.H., and Rosanoff, A.J. (1910). A study of association in insanity. *American Journal of Insanity, 67,* 37-96, 317-390.

Kidder, L.H., and Campbell, D.T. (1970). The indirect testing of social attitudes. In G.F. Summers (Ed.), *Attitude measurement* (pp. 333-385). Chicago: Rand-McNally.

Kleck, R. (1968). Physical stigma and nonverbal cues emitted in face-to-face interaction. *Human Relations, 21,* 19-28.

Kleck, R. (1969). Physical stigma and task oriented interactions. *Human Relations, 22,* 53-60.

Kleck, R., Buck, P.L., Goller, W.L., London, R.S., Pfeiffer, J.R., and Vukcevic, D.P. (1968). Effect of stigmatizing conditions on the use of personal space. *Psychological Reports, 23,* 111-118.

Kleck, R., Ono, H., and Hastorf, A.H. (1966). The effects of physical deviance upon face-to-face interaction. *Human Relations, 19,* 425-436.

Kleck, R., Richardson, S.A., and Ronald, L. (1974). Physical appearance cues and interpersonal attraction in children. *Child Development, 45,* 305-310.

Kohler, E.T., and Graves, W.H. (1973). Factor analysis of the Disability Factor Scales with the Little Jiffy, Mark III. *Rehabilitation Psychology, 20,* 102-107.

Krech, D., Crutchfield, R.S., and Ballachey, E.L. (1962). *Individual in society.* New York: McGraw-Hill.

Krus, D.J. (1975). *Order analysis of binary data matrices.* Los Angeles: Theta Press.

Krus, D.J. (1977). Order analysis: An inferential model of dimensional analysis and scaling. *Educational and Psychological Measurement, 37,* 587-602.

Krus, D.J., and Bart, W.M. (1974). an ordering-theoretic method of multidimensional scaling of items. *Educational and Psychological Measurement, 34,* 525-535.

Krus, D.J., Bart, W.M., and Airasian, P.W. (1975). *Ordering theory and methods.* Los Angeles: Theta Press.

Kruskal, J.B. (1964a). Multidimensional scaling by optimizing goodness of fit to a nonmetric hypothesis. *Psychometrika, 29,* 1-27.

Kruskal, J.B. (1964b). Nonmetric multidimensional scaling: A numerical method. *Psychometrika, 29,* 115-129.

Kruskal, J.B., and Wish, M. (1978). *Multidimensional scaling.* Beverly Hills, CA: Sage.

Kuder, G.F., and Richardson, M.W. (1937). The theory of estimation of test reliability. *Psychometrika, 2,* 151-160.

Langer, E.J., Fiske, S., Taylor, S.E., and Chanowitz, B. (1976). Stigma, staring, and discomfort: A novel-stimulus hypothesis. *Journal of Experimental and Social Psychology, 12,* 451-463.

Larrivee, B. (1981). Effect of inservice training intensity on teachers' attitudes toward mainstreaming. *Exceptional Children, 48,* 34-39.

Larrivee, B. (1982). Factors underlying regular classroom teachers' attitudes to mainstreaming. *Psychology in the Schools, 19,* 374-379.

Larrivee, B., and Cook, L. (1979). Mainstreaming: A study of the variables affecting teacher attitude. *Journal of Special Education, 13,* 315-324.

Lawler, E.E. (1976). The multitrait-multirater approach to measuring managerial job performance. *Journal of Applied Psychology, 51,* 369-381.

Lawton, M.P. (1964). Correlates of the Opinions about Mental Illness Scale. *Journal of Consulting Psychology, 28,* 94.

Lazar, A.L., Gensley, J.T., and Orpet, R.E. (1971). Changing attitudes of young mentally retarded children toward handicapped persons. *Exceptional Children, 37,* 600-602.

Lazar, A.L., Stodden, R.L., and Sullivan, N.V. (1976). A comparison of attitudes held by male and female future school administrators toward instructional goals, personal adjustment, and the handicapped. *Rehabilitation Literature, 37,* 198-201.

Lazarsfeld, P.F., and Henry, N.W. (1968). *Latent structure analysis.* Boston: Houghton-Mifflin.

Lehmann, E.L. (1975). *Nonparametrics: Statistical methods based on ranks.* Oakland, CA: Holden-Day.

Lemon, N. (1973). *Attitudes and their measurement.* New York: John Wiley and Sons.

Leyser, Y., and Abrams, P.D. (1982). Teacher attitudes toward normal and exceptional groups. *Journal of Psychology, 110,* 227-238.

Likert, R. (1932). A technique for the measurement of attitudes. *Archives of Psychology,* No. 140.

Lindzey, G. (1959). On the classification of projective techniques. *Psychological Bulletin, 56,* 158-168.

Lingoes, J.C. (1963). Multiple scalogram analysis: A set theoretic model for analyzing dichotomous items. *Educational and Psychological Measurement, 23,* 501-524.

Linkowski, D.C., Jaques, M.E., and Gaier, E.L. (1969). Reactions to disabilities: A thematic analysis. *Journal of Social Psychology, 77,* 201-214.

Livneh, H. (1982a). Factor analysis of the Attitudes Toward Disabled Persons Scale—Form A. *Rehabilitation Psychology, 27,* 235-243.

Livneh, H. (1982b). On the origins of negative attitudes toward people with disabilities. *Rehabilitation Literature, 43,* 338-347.

Livneh, H. (1983). Application of smallest space analysis to the study of attitudes toward disabled persons. *Journal of Professional Psychology, 14,* 406-413.

Livneh, H. (1985a). The attitudinal structure of the Disability Factor Scale-General: A cluster analytic study. *International Journal of Rehabilitation Research, 8,* 189-193.

Livneh, H. (1985b). The Disability Factor Scale-General: Second-order factor structure. *Journal of General Psychology, 112,* 279-283.

Livneh, H. (1985c). Factor structure of attitudes toward individuals with disabilities: A replication. *Rehabilitation Counseling Bulletin, 29,* 53-58.

Loevinger, J., Wessler, R., and Redmore, C. (1970). *Measuring ego development. Vol. 1: Construction and use of a sentence completion test.* San Francisco: Josey-Bass.

Lord, F.M. (1980). *Application of item response theory to practical testing problems.* Hillsdale, NJ: Lawrence Erlbaum.

Lowenfeld, M. (1939). The world pictures of children. *British Journal of Medical Psychology, 18,* 65-101.

Lukoff, I.F., and Whiteman, M. (1959). *Components and correlates of attitudes toward blindness* (OVR Project No. 346-C). Washington, DC: Department of Health, Education, and Welfare.

Lukoff, I.F., and Whiteman, M. (1961). Attitudes toward blindness: Some preliminary findings. *New Outlook for the Blind, 55,* 39-44.

Luscher, M. (1969). *The Luscher Color Test.* New York: Random House.

Lustig, P. (1965). *The Color Vector Test.* Madison, WI: University of Wisconsin.

Lyth, M. (1973). Employers' attitudes to the employment of the disabled. *Occupational Psychology, 47* (1-2), 67-70.

MacCallum, R.C. (1979). Recovery of structure in incomplete data by ALSCAL. *Psychometrika, 44,* 69-74.

Machover, K. (1949). *Personality projection in the drawing of the human figure: A method of personality investigation.* Springfield, IL: Charles C Thomas.

MacMillan, D.L., and Morrison, G.M. (1984). Sociometric research in special education. In R.L. Jones (Ed.), *Attitudes and attitude change in special education: Theory and practice* (pp. 70-92). Reston, VA: Council for Exceptional Children.

Maher, B.A., Watt, N., and Campbell, D.T. (1960). Comparative validity of two projective and two structured attitude tests in a prison population. *Journal of Applied Psychology, 44,* 284-288.

Makas, E. (1981). *Attitudes and disability: An annotated bibliography.* 1975-1981. Washington, DC: George Washington University Rehabilitation Research Institute on Attitudinal, Legal and Leisure Barriers.

Marascuilo, L.A., and McSweeney, M. (1977). *Nonparametric and distribution-free methods for the social sciences.* Belmont, CA: Wadsworth.

Marinelli, R.P. (1974). State anxiety in interactions with visibly disabled persons. *Rehabilitation Counseling Bulletin, 18,* 72-77.

Marinelli, R.P., and Kelz, J.W. (1973). Anxiety and attitudes toward visibly disabled persons. *Rehabilitation Counseling Bulletin, 16,* 198-205.

Marlowe, D., and Crowne, D.P. (1961). Social desirability and response to perceived situational demands. *Journal of Consulting Psychology, 25,* 109-115.

McCauley, R.W., Bruininks, R.H., and Kennedy, P. (1976). Behavioral interactions of hearing impaired children in regular classrooms. *Journal of Special Education, 10,* 277-284.

McCauley, R.W., Morris, P.S., and Cooper, J.K. (1978). The placement of handicapped children by Canadian public school personnel. *Education and Training of the Mentally Retarded, 13,* 367-379.

McGuire, W.J. (1960). A syllogistic analysis of cognitive relationships. In C.I. Hovland and M.J. Rosenberg (Eds.), *Attitude organization and change* (pp. 65-111). New Haven, CT: Yale University Press.

McGuire, W.J. (1969). The nature of attitudes and attitude change. In G. Lindzey and E. Aronson (Eds.), *The handbook of social psychology* (Vol. 3, pp. 136-314). Reading, MA: Addison-Wesley.

Mehrens, W.A., and Lehmann, I.J. (1978). *Measurement and evaluation in education and psychology* (2nd ed.). New York: Holt, Rinehart, and Winston.

Mercer, J.R. (1966). Patterns of family crisis related to reacceptance of the retardate. *American Journal of Mental Deficiency, 71,* 19-32.

Messick, S.A. (1980). Test validity and the ethics of assessment. *American Psychologist, 35,* 1012-1027.

Moed, G., Wright, B., Feshbach, S., and Sandry, M. (1963). A picture story test for use in physical disability. *Perceptual and Motor Skills, 17,* 483-497.

Moore, G., and Castles, M.R. (1978). Intercorrelations among factors in the Opinions about Mental Illness Scale in scores of nonpsychiatric nurses: Comparisons with other studies. *Psychological Reports, 43,* 876-878.

Moses, H.A., Rubin, S.E., and Turner, J. (n.d.). *Relationship of attitudes toward the disabled with demographic information and personality measures. Discussion papers.* Little Rock, AK: Arkansas Rehabilitation Research and Training Center.

Mueller, D.J. (1970). Physiological techniques of attitude measurement. In G.F. Summers (Ed.), *Attitude measurement* (pp. 534-552). Chicago, IL: Rand-McNally.

Murray, H.A. (1938). *Explorations in personality.* New York: Oxford University Press.

Mussen, P.H., and Barker, R.G. (1943). Attitudes toward cripples. *Journal of Abnormal and Social Psychology, 39,* 351-355.

Napior, D. (1972). Nonmetric multidimensional techniques of summated ratings. In R.N. Shepard, A.K. Romney, and S.B. Nerlove (Eds.), *Multidimensional scaling: Theory and applications in the behavioral sciences* (Vol. 1, pp. 157-178). New York: Seminar Press.

Newcomb, T.M., Turner, R.H., and Converse, P.E. (1965). *Social psychology: The study of human interactions.* New York: Holt.

Noonan, J.R., Barry, J.R., and Davis, H.C. (1970). Personality determinants in attitudes toward visible disability. *Journal of Personality, 39,* 1-15.

Nunnally, J.C. (1961). *Popular conceptions of mental health: Their development and change.* New York: Holt, Rinehart, and Winston.

Nunnally, J.C. (1970). *Introduction to psychological measurement.* New York: McGraw-Hill.

Nunnally, J.C. (1978). *Psychometric theory* (2nd ed.). New York: McGraw-Hill.

Nunnally, J.C., Knott, P.D., Duchnowski, A., and Parker, R. (1967). Pupillary responses as a general measure of activation. *Perception and Psychophysics, 2,* 149-155.

Oppenheimer, A.N. (1966). *Questionnaire design and attitude measurement.* New York: Basic Books.

Orlansky, M.D. (1979). Active learning and student attitudes toward exceptional children. *Exceptional Children, 46,* 49-52.

Osgood, C.E., Suci, G.J., and Tannenbaum, P.H. (1957). *The measurement of meaning.* Urbana, IL: University of Illinois Press.

Oskamp, S. (1977). *Attitudes and opinions.* Englewood Cliffs, NJ: Prentice-Hall.

Ostrom, T.M. (1969). The relationship between the affective, behavioral, and cognitive components of attitude. *Journal of Experimental Social Psychology, 5,* 12-30.

Overbeck, D. (1971). Attitude sampling of institutional charge attendant personnel: Cues for intervention. *Mental Retardation, 9,* 8-10.

Pancer, S.M., Adams, D.A., Mollard, D., Solsberg, D., and Tammen, L. (1979). Perceived distinctiveness of the handicapped. *Journal of Social Psychology, 108,* 275-276.

Panda, K.C., and Bartel, N.R., (1972). Teacher perception of exceptional children. *The Journal of Special Education, 6,* 261-266.

Parish, T.S., and Taylor, J.C. (1978). The Personal Attribute Inventory for Children: A report on its validity and reliability as a self-concept scale. *Educational and Psychological Measurement, 38,* 565-569.

Parish, T.S., Bryant, W.T., and Shirazi, A. (1976). The personal attribute inventory. *Perceptual and Motor Skills, 42,* 715-720.

Pfeiffer, S.I., and Naglieri, J.A. (1984). Special education placement decisions as a function of professional role and handicapping conditions. *Psychology in the Schools, 21,* 61-65.

Philips, G.B. (1975). An exploration of employer attitudes concerning employment opportunities for deaf people. *Journal of Rehabilitation of the Deaf, 9*(2), 1-9.

Plummer, J.M. (1976). Projective techniques. In B. Bolton (Ed.), *Handbook of measurement and evaluation in rehabilitation.* Baltimore: University Park Press.

Pomazal, R.J., and Clore, G.L. (1973). Helping on the highway: The effects of dependency and sex. *Journal of Applied Social Psychology, 3,* 150-164.

Porier, G.W., and Lott, A.J. (1967). Galvanic skin responses and prejudice. *Journal of Personality and Social Psychology, 5,* 253-259.

Quay, L.C., Bartlett, C.J., Wrightsman, L.S., Jr., and Catron, D. (1961). Attitude change in attendant employees. *Journal of Social Psychology, 55,* 27-31.

Rabinowitz, G. (1986). Nonmetric multidimensional scaling and individual difference scaling. In W.D. Berry and M.S. Lewis-Beck (Eds.), *New tools for social scientists: Advances and applications in research methods* (pp. 77-107). Beverly Hills, CA: Sage.

Rabkin, J.G. (1971). Opinions about mental illness: A review of the literature. *Psychological Bulletin, 77,* 153-171.

Rabkin, J.G. (1974). Public opinions toward mental illness: A review of the literature. *Schizophrenia Bulletin, 10,* 9-33.

Ramsay, J.O. (1977). Maximum likelihood estimation in multidimensional scaling. *Psychometrika, 42,* 241-266.

Ramsey, G.V., and Seipp, M. (1948). Public opinions and information concerning mental health. *Journal of Clinical Psychology, 4,* 397-406.

Rapaport, J. Gill, M.M., and Schafer, R. (1946). *Diagnostic psychological testing.* Chicago: Year Book Publishers.

Rapier, J., Adelson, R., Carey, R., and Croke, K. (1972). Changes in children's attitudes toward the physically handicapped. *Exceptional Children, 39,* 219-223.

Reynolds, W.M., and Greco, V.T. (1980). The reliability and factorial validity of a scale for measuring teachers' attitudes towards mainstreaming. *Educational and Psychological Measurement, 40,* 463-468.

Richardson, S.A., Goodman, N., Hastorf, A.H., and Dornbusch, S. (1961). Cultural uniformity in reaction to physical disabilities. *American Sociological Review, 26,* 241-247.

Rickard, T.E., Triandis, H.C., and Patterson, C.H. (1963). Indices of employer prejudice toward disabled applicants. *Journal of Applied Psychology, 47,* 52-55.

Roeher, G.A. (1959). *A study of certain public attitudes toward the orthopedically disabled.* Unpublished doctoral dissertation, New York University, New York.

Roessler, R., and Bolton, B. (1978). *Psychosocial adjustment to disability.* Baltimore, MD: University Park Press.

Romney, A.K., Shephard, R.N., and Nerlove, S.B. (Eds.). (1972). *Multidimensional scaling: Theory and applications in the behavioral sciences* (Vol. 2). New York: Seminar Press.

Rorer, L.G. (1965). The great response style myth. *Psychological Bulletin, 63,* 129-156.

Rorschach, H. (1942). *Psychodiagnostics: A diagnostic test based on perception.* Berne, Switzerland: Verlag Hans Huber. (U.S. distributor, Grune and Stratton).

Rosenberg, M.J. (1956). Cognitive structure and attitudinal affects. *Journal of Abnormal and Social Psychology, 53,* 367-372.

Rosenberg, M.J., and Hovland, C.I. (Eds.). (1960). *Attitude organization and change.* New Haven, CT: Yale University Press.

Rosenzweig, S. (1950). *Revised scoring manual for the Rosenzweig Picture-Frustration Study, Form for Adults.* St. Louis: Author.

Ross, R.T. (1934). Optimum orders for the presentation of pairs in the method of pairwise comparisons. *The Journal of Educational Psychology, 25,* 375-382.

Rotter, J.B., and Rafferty, J. (1950). *Manual for the Rotter Incomplete Sentences Blank, College form.* New York: Psychological Corporation.

Rotter, J.B., Seeman, M.R., and Liverant, S. (1962). Internal versus external control of reinforcement: A major variable in personality theory. In N.F. Washburne (Ed.). *Decisions, values, and groups.* Vol. 2 (pp. 473-516). London: Pergamon Press.

Rucker, C., and Gable, R. (1974). *The Rucker-Gable Educational Programming Scale.* Storrs, CT: Rucker-Gable Associates.

Rusalem, H. (1950). The environmental supports of public attitudes toward the blind. *New Outlook for the Blind, 44,* 277-288.

Rusalem, H. (1965). A study of college students' beliefs about deaf-blindness. *New Outlook for the Blind, 59,* 90-93.

Sadlick, M., and Penta, F.B. (1975). Changing nurses' attitudes toward quadraplegics through the use of television. *Rehabilitation Literature, 36,* 274-278.

Samerotte, G.C., and Harris, M.B. (1976). Some factors influencing helping: The effects of handicap, responsibility, and requesting help. *Journal of Social Psychology, 98,* 39-45.

Sax, G. (1980). *Principles of educational and psychological measurement and evaluation* (2nd ed.). Belmont, CA: Wadsworth.

Schaie, K.W. (1963). The Color Pyramid Test: A nonverbal technique for personality assessment. *Psychological Bulletin, 60,* 530-547.

Schiffman, S.S., Reynolds, M.L., and Young, F.W. (1981). *Introduction to multidimensional scaling: Theory, methods, and applications.* New York: Academic Press.

Schmelkin, L.P. (in press). Multidimensional perspectives in the perception of disabilities. In H.E. Yuker (Ed.), *Attitudes toward persons with disabilities.* New York: Springer.

Schmelkin, L.P. (1981). Teachers' and nonteachers' attitudes toward mainstreaming. *Exceptional Children, 48,* 42-47.

Schmelkin, L.P. (1982). Perceptions of disabilities: A multidimensional scaling approach. *The Journal of Special Education, 16,* 161-177.

Schmelkin, L.P. (1985). A multidimensional scaling of disability labels. *Rehabilitation Psychology, 30,* 221-233.

Schmelkin, L.P., and Lieberman, L.L. (1984). Education students' awareness of mainstreaming concerns: Implications for improving training programs. *Education, 104,* 258-263.

Schroedel, J.G. (1979). *Attitudes toward persons with disabilities: A compendium of related literature.* Albertson, NY: Human Resources Center.

Schuessler, K., Hittle, D., and Cardascia, J. (1978). Measuring responding desirability with attitude-opinion items. *Social Psychology, 41,* 224-235.

Scott, O., and Rohrbach, J. (1977). A comparison of five criteria for identifying fakable items on an attitude inventory. *Journal of Experimental Education, 45,* 51-55.

Secord, P.F., and Jourard, S.M. (1953). The appraisal of body cathexis: Body cathexis and the self. *Journal of Consulting Psychology, 17,* 343-347.

Shaver, P.R., and Scheibe, K.E. (1967). Transformation of social identity: A study of chronic mental patients and college volunteers in a summer camp setting. *Journal of Psychology, 66,* 19-37.

Shaw, M.E., and Wright, J.M. (1967). *Scales for the measurement of attitudes.* New York: McGraw-Hill.

Shaw, S.F., and Gillung, T.B. (1975). Efficacy of a college course for regular class teachers of the mildly handicapped. *Mental Retardation, 13,* 3-6.

Shepard, R.N. (1962a). The analysis of proximities: Multidimensional scaling with an unknown distance function. I. *Psychometrika, 27,* 125-140.

Shepard, R.N. (1962b). The analysis of proximities: Multidimensional scaling with an unknown distance function. II. *Psychometrika, 27,* 219-246.

Shepard, R.N. (1972). A taxonomy of some principal types of data and of multidimensional methods for their analysis. In R.N. Shepard, A.K. Romney, and S.B. Nerlove (Eds.), *Multidimensional scaling: Theory and applications in the behavioral sciences* (Vol. 1, pp. 21-47). New York: Seminar Press.

Shepard, R.N., Romney, A.K., and Nerlove, S.B. (Eds.). (1972). *Multidimensional scaling: Theory and applications in the behavioral sciences* (Vol. 1). New York: Seminar Press.

Shontz, F.C. (1971). Physical disability and personality. In W.S. Neff (Ed.), *Rehabilitation psychology* (pp. 33-73). Washington, DC: American Psychological Association.

Siller, J. (1963). Reactions to physical disability. *Rehabilitation Counseling Bulletin, 7,* 12-16.

Siller, J. (1969). *The general form of the Disability Factors Scales Series (DFS-G).* Unpublished manuscript: New York University School of Education, New York.

Siller J. (1970). *Generality of attitudes toward the physically disabled.* Proceedings of the 78th Annual Convention of the American Psychological Association, 5, 697-698.

Siller, J. (1984). Attitudes toward the physically disabled. In R.L. Jones (Ed.), *Attitudes and attitude change in special education: Theory and practice* (pp. 184-205). Reston, VA: Council for Exceptional Children.

Siller, J., and Braden, B. (1976). *A factor analytically derived scale to measure attitudes toward cancer.* Unpublished manuscript, New York University School of Education, New York.

Siller, J., and Chipman, A. (1964). Factorial structure and correlates of the Attitudes Toward Disabled Persons Scale. *Educational and Psychological Measurement, 24,* 831-839.

Siller, J., Chipman, A., Ferguson, L.T., and Vann, D.H. (1967). *Attitudes of the non-disabled toward the physically disabled.* Studies in reactions to disability: XI. New York University School of Education, New York.

Siller, J., Ferguson, L.T., Vann, D.H., and Holland B. (1967). *Structure of attitudes toward the physically disabled: The Disability Factor Scales—Amputation, Blindness, Cosmetic Conditions.* Studies in reactions to disability: XII. New York University School of Education, New York.

Siperstein, G.N., and Bak, J.J. (1985). Effects of social behavior on children's attitudes toward their mildly and moderately mentally retarded peers. *American Journal of Mental Deficiency, 90,* 319-327.

Siperstein, G.N., Bak, J.J., and Gottlieb, J. (1977). Effects of group discussions on children's attitudes toward handicapped peers. *Journal of Educational Research, 70,* 131-134.

Skrtic, T.M., Clark, F.L., and White, W.J. (1982). Modification of attitudes of regular education preservice teachers toward visually impaired students. *Journal of Visual Impairment and Blindness, 76,* 49-52.

Sloat, W.L., and Frankel, A. (1972). The contributions of subjects, disabilities, situations, sex of target person, and items to the variation of attitudes toward persons with a disability. *Rehabilitation Psychology, 19,* 3-17.

Snyder, M.L., Kleck, R.E., Strenta, A., and Mentzer, S.J. (1979). Avoidance of the handicapped: An attributional ambiguity analysis. *Journal of Personality and Social Psychology, 37,* 2297-2306.

Sontag, M., and Pedhazur, E. (1972). Dimensions of educational attitudes: Factorial congruence of two scales. *Journal of Educational Measurement, 9,* 189-198.

Spence, I. (1982). Incomplete experimental designs for multidimensional scaling. In R.G. Colledge and J.N. Rayner (Eds.), *Proximity and preference: Problems in the multidimensional analysis of large data sets* (pp. 29-46). Minneapolis: University of Minnesota Press.

SPSS, Inc. (1986). *SPSSx user's guide* (2nd ed.). New York: McGraw-Hill.

Steingisser, E.R. (1954). *The influence of set upon attitudes toward the blind as related to self-concept.* Unpublished Master's thesis, University of New Hampshire, Durham.

Stephenson, W. (1953). *The study of behavior: Q-technique and its methodology.* Chicago: University of Chicago Press.

Strohmer, D.C., Grand, S.A., and Purcell, M.J. (1984). Attitudes toward persons with a disability: An examination of demographic factors, social contact, and specific disability. *Rehabilitation Psychology, 29,* 131-145.

Strong, E.K. (1931). *Changes of interest with age.* Palo Alto, CA: Stanford University Press.

Struening, E.L., and Cohen, J. (1963). Factorial invariance and other psychometric characteristics of five Opinions about Mental Illness factors. *Educational and Psychological Measurement, 23,* 289-298.

Stude, E.W. (1973). Evaluation of short-term training for rehabilitation counselors: Effectiveness of an institute on epilepsy. *Rehabilitation Counseling Bulletin, 16,* 146-154.

Summers, G.F. (Ed.). (1970). *Attitude measurement.* Chicago: Rand-McNally.

Taylor, J.B. (1961). What do attitudes measure? The problem of social desirability. *Journal of Abnormal and Social Psychology, 62,* 386-390.

Thede, D.L., and Antonak, R.F. (1981). An ordering-theoretic analysis of women's attitudes. *Journal of Social Psychology, 114,* 251-258.

Thomas, D. (1980). *The social psychology of childhood disability.* New York: Schoken Books.

Thomas, W.I., and Znaniecki, F. (1918). *The Polish peasant in Europe and America.* Boston: Bader.

Thorndike, R.M. (1976). Reliability. In B. Bolton (Ed.)., *Handbook of measurement and evaluation in rehabilitation* (pp. 15-37). Baltimore, MD: University Park Press.

Thurston, J.R. (1959). A procedure for evaluating parental attitudes toward the handicapped. *American Journal of Mental Deficiency, 64,* 148-155.

Thurstone, L.L. (1927). Psychophysical analysis. *American Journal of Psychology., 38,* 368-389.

Thurstone, L.L. (1928). Attitudes can be measured. *American Journal of Sociology, 33,* 529-554.

Thurstone, L.L. (1929). Theory of attitude measurement. *Psychological Bulletin, 36,* 222-241.

Thurstone, L.L. (1931). The measurement of attitudes. *Journal of Abnormal and Social Psychology, 26,* 249-269.

Thurstone, L.L. (1946). Comment. *American Journal of Sociology, 52,* 39-50.

Thurstone, L.L., and Chave, E.J. (1929). *The measurement of attitude.* Chicago, IL: University of Chicago Press.

Titley, R.W., and Viney, W. (1969). Expression of aggression toward the physically handicapped. *Perceptual and Motor Skills, 29,* 51-56.

Towfighy-Hoshyar, N., and Zingle, H.W. (1984). Regular class students' attitudes toward integrated multiply handicapped peers. *American Journal of Mental Deficiency, 88,* 630-637.

Triandis, H.C. (1971). *Attitude and attitude change.* New York: John Wiley and Sons.

Triandis, H.C., Adamopoulos, J., and Brinberg, D. (1984). Perspectives and issues in the study of attitudes. In R.L. Jones (Ed.), *Attitudes and attitude change in special education: Theory and practice* (pp. 21-40). Reston, VA: Council for Exceptional Children.

Triandis, H.C., and Triandis, L.M. (1965). Race, social class, religion, and nationality as determinants of social distance. *Journal of Abnormal and Social Psychology, 61,* 110-118.

Tringo, J.L. (1968). *The hierarchy of preference: A comparison of attitudes and prejudices toward specific disability groups.* Unpublished doctoral dissertation, University of Connecticut, Storrs.

Tringo, J.L. (1970). The hierarchy of preference toward disability groups. *Journal of Special Education, 4,* 295-306.

VanderKolk, C.J. (1976a). Physiological and self-reported reactions to the disabled and deviant. *Rehabilitation Psychology, 23,* 77-83.

VanderKolk, C.J. (1976b). Physiological measures as a means of assessing reactions to the disabled. *New Outlook for the Blind, 70,* 101-103.

Vann, D.H. (1970). Components of attitudes toward the obese including presumed responsibility for the condition. *Proceedings of the Annual Convention of the American Psychological Association, 5,* 695-696.

Vargo, J.W., and Semple, J.E. (1984). Honest versus fake scores on the Attitudes Toward Disabled Persons Scale—Form A. *Rehabilitation Counseling Bulletin, 27,* 182-185.

Vickers, R.R., and Hervig, L.K. (1981). Comparison of three psychological defense mechanism questionnaires. *Journal of Personality Assessment, 45,* 630-638.

Vidulich, R.N., and Krevanick, F.W. (1966). Racial attitudes and emotional response to visual representations of the Negro. *Journal of Social Psychology, 68,* 85-93.

Voeltz, L.M. (1980). Children's attitudes toward handicapped peers. *American Journal of Mental Deficiency, 84,* 455-464.

Voeltz, L.M. (1982). Effect of structured interactions with severely handicapped peers on children's attitudes. *American Journal of Mental Deficiency, 86,* 380-390.

Wang, C.K. (1932). Suggested criteria for writing attitude statements. *Journal of Social Psychology, 3,* 367-373.

Watson, J.B. (1925). *Behaviorism.* New York: W.W. Norton.

Webb, E.J., Campbell, D.T., Schwartz, R.D., and Sechrest, L. (1966). *Unobtrusive measures: Nonreactive research in the social sciences.* Chicago, IL: Rand McNally.

Wesolowski, M.D., and Diechmann, J. (1980). Physiological activity and attitudes toward disabled persons. *Rehabilitation Counseling Bulletin, 23,* 218-226.

Whiteman, M., and Lukoff, I.F. (1962). Public attitudes toward blindness. *New Outlook for the Blind, 56,* 153-158.

Whiteman, M., and Lukoff, I.F. (1964a). Attitudes toward blindness in two college groups. *Journal of Social Psychology, 63,* 179-191.

Whiteman, M., and Lukoff, I.F. (1964b). A factorial study of sighted people's attitudes toward blindness. *Journal of Social Psychology, 64,* 339-353.

Whiteman, M., and Lukoff, I.F. (1965). Attitudes toward blindness and other physical handicaps. *Journal of Social Psychology, 66,* 135-145.

Wicas, E.A., and Carluccio, L.W. (1971). Attitudes of counselors toward three handicapped client groups. *Rehabilitation Counseling Bulletin, 15,* 25-34.

Wiley, D.E. (1967). Latent partition analysis. *Psychometrika, 32,* 183-193.

Williams, R.F. (1986). Perceptions of mentally retarded persons. *Education and Training of the Mentally Retarded, 21,* 13-20.

Williamson, J.B., Karp, D.A., Dalphin, J.R., and Gray, P.S. (1982). *The research craft: An introduction to social research methods* (2nd ed.). Boston: Little-Brown.

Willis, J.B., Feldman, N.S., and Ruble, D.N. (1977). Children's generosity as influence by deservedness of reward and type of recipient. *Journal of Educational Psychology, 69,* 33-35.

Wilson, E.D. (1971). A comparison of the effects of deafness simulation and observation upon attitudes, anxiety, and behavior manifested toward the deaf. *Journal of Special Education, 5,* 343-349.

Wilson, G., and Paterson, J. (1968). A new measure of conservatism. *British Journal of Social and Clinical Psychology, 8,* 264-269.

Wish, M. (1975). Subjects' expectations about their own interpersonal communication: A multidimensional approach. *Personality and Social Psychology Bulletin, 1,* 501-504.

Wish, M. (1976). Comparisons among multidimensional structures of interpersonal relations. *Multivariate Behavioral Research, 11,* 297-324.

Wish, M., D'Andrade, R.G., and Goodnow, J.E., II. (1980). Dimensions of interpersonal communication: Correspondences between structures for speech acts and bipolar scales. *Journal of Personality and Social Psychology, 39,* 848-860.

Wood, F. (1972). *Pupil Observation Schedule.* Unpublished manuscript, University of Minnesota, Minneapolis.

Woodmansee, J.J., and Cook, S.W. (1967). Dimensions of verbal racial attitudes: Their identification and measurement. *Journal of Personality and Social Psychology, 7,* 240-250.

Wright, B.A. (1983). *Physical disability—A psychosocial approach* (2nd ed.). New York: Harper and Row.

Yamamoto, K., and Dizney, H.F. (1967). Rejection of the mentally ill: A study of attitudes of student teachers. *Journal of Counseling Psychology, 14,* 264-268.

Yamamoto, K., and Wiersma, J. (1967). Rejection of self and of deviant others among student teachers. *The Journal of Special Education, 1,* 401-408.

Yuker, H.E. (1965). Attitudes as determinants of behavior. *Journal of Rehabilitation, 31,* 15-16.

Yuker, H.E. (1986). The fakeability of the Attitudes Toward Disabled Persons Scale: Some comments. *Rehabilitation Counseling Bulletin, 29,* 200-204.

Yuker, H.E. (1987). (Ed.). *Attitudes toward persons with disabilities.* New York: Springer.

Yuker, H.E., and Block, J.R. (1986). *Research with the Attitude Toward Disabled Persons Scales (ATDP): 1960-1985.* Hempstead, NY: Center for the Study of Attitudes Toward Persons with Disabilities, Hofstra University.

Yuker, H.E., Block, J.R., and Campbell, W.J. (1960). *A scale to measure attitudes toward disabled persons* (Human Resources Study No. 5). Albertson, NY: Human Resources Center.

Yuker, H.E., Block, J.R., and Younng, J.H. (1966). *The measurement of attitudes toward disabled persons* (Human Resources Study No. 7). Albertson, NY: Human Resources Center.

Yuker, H.E., Block, J.R., and Younng, J.H. (1970). *The measurement of attitudes toward disabled persons* (Human Resources Study No. 3). Albertson, NY: Human Resources Center.

Zuckerman, M., Persky, H., Eckman, R.M., and Hopkins, T.R. (1967). A multitrait-multimethod measurement approach to the trait (or states) of anxiety, depression, and hostility. *Journal of Projective Techniques and Personality, 31,* 39-48.

Zych, K., and Bolton, B. (1972). Galvanic skin responses and cognitive attitudes toward disabled persons. *Rehabilitation Psychology, 19,* 172-173.

Appendix A

NAMES AND ADDRESSES OF PRIMARY AUTHORS OF THE 22 SCALES REVIEWED IN PART III

CHAPTER 9

Acceptance Scale (9-1, 9-2, 9-3)

Luanna H. (Voeltz) Meyer
Department of Special Education
Syracuse University
805 S. Crouse Ave.
Syracuse, New York 13244

Attitude Toward Disabled Persons Scale (9-4, 9-5, 9-6)

Harold E. Yuker
Center for the Study of Attitudes Toward Persons With Disabilities
Hofstra University
Hempstead, New York 11550

Disability Factor Scales (9-7)

Jerome Siller
Department of Educational Psychology
New York University
1032 Shimkin Hall, Washington Square
New York, New York 10003

Disability Social Distance Scale (9-8)

John L. Tringo
Address Unknown

Rucker-Gable Educational Programming Scale

Chauncy A. Rucker
Department of Educational Psychology
University of Connecticut
Storrs, Connecticut 06268

Scale of Attitudes Toward Disabled Persons (9-9)

Richard F. Antonak
Department of Education
Morrill Hall
University of New Hampshire
Durham, New Hampshire 03824

CHAPTER 10

Attitudes to Blindness Scale (10-1)

Emory L. Cowen
Department of Psychology
University of Rochester Medical Center
Rochester, New York 14627

Attitudes to Deafness Scale (10-2)

Emory L. Cowen
Department of Psychology
University of Rochester Medical Center
Rochester, New York 14627

Scale of Knowledge and Attitudes Toward Epilepsy and People With Epilepsy (10-3)

Richard F. Antonak
Department of Education
Morrill Hall
University of New Hampshire
Durham, New Hampshire 03824

Disability Social Relationship Scale (10-4)

Sheldon A. Grand
Department of Counseling Psychology
State University of New York at Albany
1400 Washington Ave.
Albany, New York 12222

CHAPTER 11

Custodial Mental Illness Scale (11-1)

Doris C. Gilbert
Department of Psychology
San Francisco State University
1600 Holloway Ave.
San Francisco, California 94132

Mental Health Information Questionnaire (11-2)

Jum C. Nunnally (Deceased)
Department of Psychology
Vanderbilt University
Nashville, Tennessee 37240

Opinions About Mental Illness Scale (11-3)

Jacob Cohen
Department of Psychology
New York University
New York, New York 10003

CHAPTER 12

Attitudes Toward the Retarded Scale

Rosalyn E. and Herman Y. Efron
Address Unknown

Attitudes Toward Mentally Retarded People Scale (12-1)

C. J. Bartlett
Address Unknown

Multidimensional Attitude Scale on Mental Retardation (12-2)

Robert Harth
Department of Special Education
National College of Education
2840 Sheridan Rd.
Evanston, Illinois 60201

Mental Retardation Questionnaire (12-3)

Jennifer Gan
450 N. Bedford Rd., Suite 205
Beverly Hills, California 90210

CHAPTER 13

Attitudes Toward Disablement Scale (13-1)

Richard F. Antonak
Department of Education
Morrill Hall
University of New Hampshire
Durham, New Hampshire 03824

Attitudes Toward Mainstreaming Scale (13-2)

Joan D. Berryman
Department of Speech Pathology and Audiology
556 Aderhold Hall
University of Georgia
Athens, Georgia 30602

Educational Attitude Survey (13-3)

William M. Reynolds
Department of Educational Psychology
Educational Sciences Building
1025 West Johnson St.
University of Wisconsin-Madison
Madison, Wisconsin 53706

Mainstreaming Opinionnaire (13-4)

Liora Pedhazur Schmelkin
Department of Counseling Psychology and Research in Education
Hofstra University
Hempstead, New York 11550

Opinions Relative to Mainstreaming (13-5)

Barbara Larrivee
Teaching Research Associates
25 Skycrest Ave.
East Providence, Rhode Island 02914

INDEX

Q

R

S

U

V